SUCCESS AND FAILURE OF MICROBUSINESS OWNERS IN AFRICA

A Psychological Approach

Edited by Michael Frese

Q

QUORUM BOOKS
Westport, Connecticut • London

Library of Congress Cataloging-in-Publication Data

Success and failure of microbusiness owners in Africa : a psychological approach /
edited by Michael Frese.

   p.   cm.

Includes bibliographical references and index.

ISBN 1-56720-296-9 (alk. paper)

1. Small business—Africa—Management—Psychological aspects—Case studies. 2.
Success in business—Africa—Case studies. 3. Business failures—Africa—Case studies. I.
Frese, Michael, 1949–
HD62.7.S895 2000
658.02'2'096—dc21   99–046059

British Library Cataloguing in Publication Data is available.

Library of Congress Catalog Card Number: 99–046059
ISBN: 1-56720-296-9

First published in 2000

Quorum Books, 88 Post Road West, Westport, CT 06881
An imprint of Greenwood Publishing Group, Inc.
www.quorumbooks.com

Printed in the United States of America

The paper used in this book complies with the
Permanent Paper Standard issued by the National
Information Standards Organization (Z39.48–1984).

10 9 8 7 6 5 4 3 2 1

Contents

Tables and Figures

TABLES

FIGURES

Preface

This book looks at psychological variables that affect success and failure in microbusiness in Africa. The book first gives an introduction to the literature (Chapter 1), then there are four chapters on five empirical studies in Zambia, Uganda, South Africa, and Zimbabwe (Chapters 2, 3, 4, and 5), followed by two chapters by people of our research group who have worked professionally with the informal sector in Africa (Chapters 6 and 7). Chapter 8 is directed to the expert who wants to know more about the underlying methods of our studies (all other chapters are nontechnical). Finally, Chapter 9 presents an executive summary, some generalizations across the studies, and policy implications. To our knowledge, this is one of the first studies that focusses on psychological factors of entrepreneurial success in developing countries in a detailed way (prior studies were done by McClelland & Winter, 1971; Gebert, 1992; and Spencer & Spencer, 1993).

This book is written for the following groups of people:

- People who are interested in entrepreneurship in difficult situations, such as the inner city, with immigrants, or in transitional economies (e.g., East Europe), or entrepreneurship in developing countries.
- Policy makers in developing countries.
- Developmental-aid professionals.
- Psychologists interested in high achievement.
- Management consultants.
- Management practitioners who want to increase intrapreneurship in companies.
- Industrial and organizational psychologists.
- Researchers in entrepreneurship.

Books about developing countries and particularly about Africa are often primarily conceptualized to show "something different" from

Western countries. An assumption is that one cannot learn anything from them for entrepreneurship in Western countries. We think that this attitude is wrong and that entrepreneurship in Africa can teach us a lot. We think that this book contributes to knowledge about entrepreneurship in general. At the same time, we want to look at the situation in Africa and contribute to the improvement of the success rate of microbusinesses there.

This book presents original data. Such books are often difficult to read. We have done everything to make it as user friendly as possible. This was done by presenting relationships as frequencies and percentages, by explaining all our empirical points to make them easy to understand, and discussing practical suggestions that follow from our results.

It is a unique book: The authors have worked together. We disagreed at times, and we do not want to gloss over those disagreements. At the same time, we have developed a common general concept which we used as a starting point for our studies (see Figure 1.1). We have taken a perspective from below. This means we are looking at the situation of entrepreneurship from the perspective of the microbusiness owners. This is in contrast to many other studies and books on entrepreneurship in Africa and in developing countries in general which look at microbusiness owners from the perspective of a policy maker. It is interesting that our perspective has persuaded us to be rather optimistic about microbusiness in developing countries, especially in Africa (although we see problems and we point them out). We also think that policy makers can learn a lot from our perspective. In the last analysis, one cannot achieve economic progress by working against those people who are most important in developing economic progress. Therefore, their perspective, their perceptions, and their conceptualizations are important. At the same time, our methodology is sophisticated and goes beyond a subjectivistic approach which allows us to arrive at firm results and to give clear suggestions. Our specific approach of doing interviews and using interviewers as an important source of data helps us move toward these goals (see Chapter 8).

The studies reported in this book were done within the period from 1997 to 1998. The study in Zambia was done first. After this, we improved our approach and did the studies in Uganda and South Africa. After another round of improvement of our measurement instruments, we did the studies in Zimbabwe. We are currently involved in further studies in Africa.

This book has been supported by many people and by many institutions. First, we want to thank the Department of Psychology, University of Amsterdam, which has supported travel in many cases. Furthermore, we want to thank the following institutions and individuals.

The study in Zambia (Chapter 2) was supported by the following institutions and individuals: MS (Danish Volunteer Organization); SNV

(Dutch Volunteer Organization); Amsterdamse Universiteitsfonds; AUV (Amsterdamse Universiteits Vereniging); Kamer van Koophandel, Amsterdam; Chamber of Commerce, Lusaka, Zambia; Zambia Ministry of Commerce, Trade and Industry; and, last but certainly not least, Mr. Pearson Kalungulungu.

The study in South Africa was supported by Stichting Katholieke Noden; University of the Western Cape; SBDC Cape Town; Institute of Small Business; Department of Management, University of the Western Cape; Clotex (Clothing and Textile Service Center), Western Cape.

The study in Uganda was supported by Centenary Rural Development Bank (Koen Wasmus); Uganda Coffee Development Authority (David Kiwanuka); Bancafé (Steven Banya); Pioneer Group, Agnes Byaruhanga; and Professor John Munene (Makerere University of Uganda).

The studies in Zimbabwe were supported by the Gesellschaft fuer Technische Zusammenarbeit; Deutsche Forschungsgemeinschaft (DFG, Fr 638/13-1); and Mrs. Josephine Jordan, who helped at several points before we started the research.

Among other people who have helped has been Heike Clasen, my secretary at the University of Giessen. Without her help, we would not have been able to create this book and publish it in time. Hubertus Trageser-Aichner, the technician in Giessen, produced the tables and figures. My wife Sharon Frese read and reread many pages and helped us to correct the English. Many people (particularly Mr. David Harrison and Mr. Theo Sparreboom) read and commented on Chapter 9. We are very grateful to these individuals.

We are most grateful to the microbusiness owners who gave us their time, their effort, and their stories of what it means to be a microbusiness owner. We owe them a great deal of shared enthusiasm and joy. Thanks to them for helping this research along, and we hope that they and their colleagues will eventually profit from this book and our approach: A perspective of the entrepreneur as an individual who admirably copes with a situation that is often difficult and often seems to be without hope. Among these business owners, we have met many people whom you would want to have as a friend because of their enthusiasm in difficult times and situations. The book is meant to show what they stand for.

REFERENCES

Gebert, D. (Ed.). (1992). *Traditionsorientierung und unternehmerischer Erfolg.* Saarbruecken: Breitenbach.

McClelland, D. C., & Winter, D. G. (1971). *Motivating economic achievement.* New York: Free Press.

Spencer, L. M., Jr., & Spencer, S. M. (1993). *Competence at work: Models for superior performance.* New York: John Wiley & Sons.

1

Psychological Success Factors of Entrepreneurship in Africa: A Selective Literature Review

Michael Frese and Mechlien de Kruif

This introductory chapter has the following purposes: First, we will summarize the relevant literature. This is not a complete overview of the literature, but rather a selective account. The literature is wide, multidisciplinary, and often hard to find because it is distributed widely across different journals and books in various languages (a more comprehensive literature review on the Western literature is provided in Rauch & Frese, 2000). Second, we want to present a theoretical framework that allows the study of psychological variables within the area of entrepreneurship. Third, we would like to convince the reader that psychological concepts are important for the study of entrepreneurial success (we take up this issue again in Chapter 9).

WHY STUDY PSYCHOLOGICAL FACTORS OF ENTREPRENEURIAL SUCCESS IN AFRICA?

Micro- and small-scale enterprise owners are important contributors to the economies of developing countries. While it has been shown in Western countries that small-scale entrepreneurs are an important force for economic development, innovation, and flexibility, they are even more important in developing countries. Without the contribution of micro- and small-scale business owners, there would be widespread starvation in many African countries (more on this later). Therefore, it makes sense to look at the small and microbusiness in the African context. As a matter of fact, there are good studies on microbusiness in Africa, particularly from an economic perspective.

However, there are only very few studies from a psychological perspective and a purely economic orientation falls short for theoretical and practical reasons. There are three theoretical reasons. First, the main actor is the business owner. The microfirms with at most ten employees are dependent upon the owner for survival and development. Without him (or her) nothing much happens in the firm. Usually the owner is present, makes important decisions on products and production process, motivates (or demotivates) the employees, talks to all important customers, attracts new customers, and keeps track of the cash flow. In big organizations, all of these functions are assumed by different people. However, in the small-business sector, the unifying force encompassing all these functions in his or her person is the owner/manager. Thus, all these tasks are related to decision making, motivation, communication, orientations, and personality, which are psychological concepts.

Second, there is no success without actions. It is not conceivable that entrepreneurial success should come about without appropriate actions by actors involved. Psychology has been concerned with the issue of what regulates and drives actions since its beginning. However, the theory we work from (action theory, cf. Frese & Zapf, 1994; Hacker, 1998; Miller, Galanter, & Pribram, 1960) has been particularly concerned with how thoughts, ideas, and attitudes regulate and control actions (more on this later). As argued, the main actor is the owner/manager in the small-business sector. Thus, we have to look at the determinants of actions of the owner/manager.

Third, a psychological point of view helps to identify the diversity of approaches with which organizations and owners can achieve their goals (Katz & Kahn, 1978). Some of the firms have been founded only because there was no other job available and their start-up was a simple matter of survival. Other microbusiness owners had employment, but were motivated to be independent and to do a certain kind of work. Moreover, we shall argue a little later that there are different strategies that can lead to success, given a certain personality and a certain environment. The psychological action strategy used by the business owner must be compatible with his or her personality characteristics and with environmental restrictions and resources. Thus, psychological research needs to be done in this area as well.

The World Bank has also recognized the problem of using only an economic model of development. Stiglitz (1998), the chief economist of the World Bank, described in a famous speech why a simple economic model of development has failed: Development implies not just a superficial transfer of capital, but a much deeper transformation of the culture and the society and there has to be a readiness on the part of the receivers of developmental aid to participate in this transformation process. The most important processes are learning, ownership, and participation. It is interesting that Stiglitz mentions these psychological terms but does not take the next step, namely, to use psychological knowledge. However, his speech reveals that the time is ripe for focussing on a psychological approach to development.

There are also practical reasons that speak for using a psychological approach next to other ones in developing countries. Economists have rightly argued that economic and legal frameworks determine to a large extent whether or not entrepreneurs can flourish. However, this point of view needs to be complemented by a psychological approach. There is a gap between a government attempting to stimulate the development of the private-enterprise sector and actual successes of the owners. This gap between general policy decisions and actual behavior by the actors in the market can only be addressed adequately with psychological knowledge. Issues to be addressed are, for example, training of entrepreneurs, stimulating would-be entrepreneurs to actually start their business, selecting the right people to receive credit, stimulating owners to overcome barriers to grow from the informal sector into the formal one, or helping to develop a school system in such a way as to provide skills and motivation to people to become business owners. Many owners do not have the skills and the knowledge available to succeed as business owners and make serious mistakes in approaching customers, suppliers, banks, and other agents related to their success. All these factors are psychological ones. One has to get to know them to be able to change and influence them. Thus, a psychological approach is an approach from below: It does not directly attempt to change the larger economic conditions, but it focusses on concrete actions of concrete individuals in the market and looks at resources and barriers for these actions and how to improve them. In the long run, a psychological approach also affects indirectly the larger economic conditions.

MICROBUSINESS AND THE ECONOMY OF DEVELOPING COUNTRIES

The International Labor Organization (ILO) was the first organization to recognize the existence of informal small-scale business in Africa in 1972. They identified the informal sector as "small-scale (size), labor intensive and low skill nature, low wage, producing goods and services for low income people and generally living off the crumbs of the large scale formal sector" (International Labor Organization, 1972, p. 223). Most of the microfirms are informal, although there are differences in the ratio of informal to formal businesses in the various African countries (related to tax laws and other economic and political conditions).

Micro- and small-scale business has a major influence on the economy of a country, be it for the mere reason that it creates jobs and provides income for the population (Parker, 1996). In addition, microbusiness is able to give a flexible answer to global competition and can service the small markets in Africa better (Pedersen, Sverrisson, & Van Dijk, 1994). Mead and Liedholm (1998) gave an overview of their studies in five African countries: About 17–27 percent of people of working age are involved in micro- and small-scale enterprises outside agriculture. In Africa, the number of people working in this sector is about double that of those employed in the official large-scale enterprises, including the public sector. Mead and Liedholm also showed that there are more micro- and small-scale enterprise start-ups than closures and that there is a high amount of expansion with new employees in those enterprises that survive. Thus, there is a net positive employment effect of the microbusiness sector. For example, in Kenya this effect constitutes about 100,000 additional jobs per year. Nevertheless, the growth of microenterprises is often limited by capital, managerial skills, and a hostile environment (Kiggundu, 1988).

These are all reasons why small-scale business is of particular interest for developing countries (Gray, Cooley, Lutabingwa, Mutai-Kaimenyi, & Oyugi, 1996). Gray and colleagues give three additional reasons for the need to support the development of this sector in Africa. First, during colonial times, governments dominated economic activities. In some countries, Africans were not allowed to become small-scale entrepreneurs (e.g., in South Africa and Rhodesia). After independence, there was no developed local private sector and, therefore, the government took over the role of an economic manager (Kiggundu, 1988) and fostered large-scale government-owned industries. Post-independence Africa continued with the tradition of strong government impact on the economy, often driven by socialist ideologies. Therefore, little was done to promote the informal sector. On the other hand, state-owned enterprises left major gaps in the output of goods, services, and jobs. Microenterprises can fill these gaps and react quickly to new demands. Small-scale entrepreneurs are also more flexible, can react more quickly to crises, and can reactivate themselves more quickly than state-owned enterprises (Gray et al., 1996). Thus, furthering the microenterprise sector can reduce government dependency and compensate for the colonial legacy. Second, instead of favoring capital-intensive technologies by multinational corporations, labor-intensive work is necessary in a continent with a shortage of capital and an abundance of labor (Gray et al., 1996). The informal sector can provide a large number of workplaces with small capital requirements (Parker, 1996). Third, developing entrepreneurship in a country helps to make economic activities more indigenous. A new middle class can develop with the development of micro- and small-scale enterprises. The microbusiness owners are inhabitants of Africa, depend largely on domestic sources of capital and savings, come mostly from the lower-income population, do not need sophisticated infrastructures, and use technology more appropriate to local conditions.

However, there are also clear limits of the contribution of microbusiness to the economy, as pointed out by Mead (1995). Only 20 percent of microenterprises grow, which means that 80 percent remain stagnant or die and do not add any new employees to their ranks. Only 1 percent of microenterprises that start out small (with less than five employees) gradually become small-scale businesses (with more than ten employees). Mead and Liedholm (1998) established that enterprises with ten to fifty employees (the small-scale enterprises) only constitute 2 percent of the enterprises in Africa.

The empirical studies to be reported in this book concentrated on micro- and small-scale businesses with at least one employee. We think that this group is the most important one, both from an economic and a psychological point of view. Business owners who work alone and therefore only sell their own labor power are different from business owners who have at least one employee. The step from zero employees to one employee implies a change in responsibility, in one's self-description and identity as a businessperson, in the psychological investment into one's career as a businessperson, in the necessity to produce a steady source of demand for one's products and services, in the need for managerial skills, and so on. Thus, business owners who run a business with at least one employee should show a different trajectory than business owners who do not have an employee. In Africa, this first employee is often a family member. We would assume that owners who employ just one family member should be in the middle between the entrepreneur with one employee outside the family and the microbusiness owner who works on his or her own. This is presumably so because payment for family members can be deferred. It is easier to explain to a family member that one wants or needs to stop one's business because one has found a job than to a nonfamily member. However, this hypothesis still needs to be established empirically.

Up to this point, we have worked with implicit definitions. Although we do not want to waste much space on discussing various definitions of entrepreneurs, a few words are necessary. The microenterprise sector consists of firms with zero to ten employees, the small-scale enterprise sector with firms of eleven to fifty employees. There are many difficulties in defining the informal and formal sectors (Peattie, 1987). Some definitions actually include the results in the definition by arguing that the informal sector is per se a poverty-driven sector. If one takes that definition, it is not surprising that one finds the informal sector to be characterized by poverty. We define firms to be informal when they do not pay taxes and/or are not registered. Another issue of high controversy is how to define entrepreneur, owner/manager, and so on (Rauch & Frese, 2000). Some authors distinguish between entrepreneurs, owner/managers, and other terms (e.g., Carland, Hoy, Boulton, & Carland, 1984). Entrepreneurs are seen to be more growth and profit oriented and innovative than small-scale business owners. In this book, we do not differentiate between them because we are interested in describing innovation, growth, and profit orientation as variables that vary between the different owners. Thus, we agree with Gartner (1989), who used a descriptive definition of entrepreneur. In this book, we look at people who have started their firm and who carry the load of daily and long-term management.

CULTURAL FACTORS

The general theory of entrepreneurship has to be placed in the context of African cultures (Kiggundu, 1988). Cultures have an influence on all processes that are related to entrepreneurship, such as personality, actions taken by the entrepreneurs, relations with employees, and what is regarded as success. One of the first successful attempts to understand culture was presented by Hofstede (1980, 1991), who distinguished five dimensions of culture: power distance, individualism, masculinity, uncertainty avoidance, and Confucian dynamism. His study was based on IBM employees between 1968 and 1972, and one can assume that these highly qualified employees are different from the entrepreneurs, whose qualification level is probably lower. Hofstede distinguished East, West, and South Africa in his study of IBM employees. East Africa consisted of Ethiopia, Kenya, Tanzania, and Zambia. Ghana, Nigeria, and Sierra Leone represented West Africa in his research. The IBM data gathered in South Africa included Whites only (Hofstede, 1991). This is only a rough division of countries into clusters. One has to be cautious exercising generalizations about Africa. Africa is not a unified region. Empirical findings developed for one setting do not necessarily generalize to others on the same continent (Kiggundu, 1988). Nevertheless, Hofstede's data give a first idea of the distribution of these dimensions.

Power distance refers to whether the culture accepts and expects people who are more powerful to behave differently from the ones lower in the hierarchy. African cultures rank high on power distance (East Africa ranks 21–23 and West Africa ranks in the highest 10–11 out of fifty-three countries). The less powerful members in a high power distance country may subscribe to the view that "the boss knows best." In these cultures, power is seen as a fundamental fact of life and the legitimacy of power is not questioned. The only way to change a social system is to dethrone those in power (Hofstede, 1991). Obvious hypotheses for our topic are that there is a high power distance between the boss and his or her employees and that this should be true even for small firms. A fit hypothesis would imply that given a high power distance culture, an autocratic approach leads to a higher success rate (a plausible counterhypothesis suggests that people across different cultures will work better if they are led by a participatory leadership style). Another hypothesis implies that people with a high need for independence find it impossible to work for another boss. This may be an added factor contributing to a high degree of entrepreneurship.

African cultures score high on *collectivism* (East Africa 33–35 and West Africa 39 out of fifty-three countries). In collectivist cultures, people form strong and close groups, often evolving around kinship. These groups provide lifelong protection in return of unconditional loyalty. Loyalty implies that the groups share their means of support (Hofstede, 1991, p. 71). Collectivism has several consequences for entrepreneurship. Positive influences of collectivism could be that we-group members help each other financially and we-group contacts are useful, both in penetrating a market and in providing support when things get tough. Negative influences could be that business owners have to support other members of the group at a point where they cannot actually afford it yet and the owners do not strive toward profit maximization, but just to provide security for their families (Gray, Cooley, & Lutabingwa, 1997; Javillonar & Peters, 1973). A consequence is that money earned with an enterprise is not reinvested in the business, but directly passed on to the family.

Masculinity refers to a strict separation of the genders, with men to be tough and assertive and focussed on material success and women to be modest and tender and focussed on the quality of existence. African cultures tend to be in the middle between femininity and masculinity (East Africa ranks 39 and West Africa 30–31 out of fifty-three countries). Many women work, often as (informal) small-scale entrepreneurs, to provide extra income.

Uncertainty avoidance implies that people feel threatened by unclear situations and that they make the situation predictable by clear rules (Hofstede, 1991, p. 144). African cultures generally score medium to low on uncertainty avoidance (East Africa ranks 36 and West Africa 34 out of fifty-three countries). Cultures with low uncertainty avoidance perceive risks as acceptable. Since the business environment for starting entrepreneurs is always uncertain, low uncertainty avoidance should help to develop an entrepreneurial culture. On the other hand, members of cultures with a high degree of uncertainty avoidance should be more prone to plan in detail because planning is a way to decrease uncertainty. In countries with low uncertainty avoidance, planning is probably less appreciated and planning should, therefore, not be very effective for entrepreneurs (Rauch, Frese, & Sonnentag, 1999). Entrepreneurs in countries with low uncertainty avoidance should be more innovative, because their culture is more tolerant of different or deviant ideas. However, the entrepreneurs in these countries may find it more difficult to practically execute their innovative plans because of their lack of planning (Hofstede, 1991).

Confucian dynamism was not studied on IBM managers (Chinese Culture Connection, 1987), but Hofstede (1991) integrated this dimension into his system. Confucian dynamism focuses on the long term and is connected to the following values: perseverance, sensitivity for status, thrift, and shame. A short-term focus is connected to the following values: equilibrium, fear for loss of face, tradition, and obligation. African cultures tend to be very low on the long-term focus (Zimbabwe ranks 19 and Nigeria 22 out of twenty-three countries). A long-term focus is stimulating for entrepreneurship because it reinforces the values of perseverance and thrift. Shame helps to stabilize relations because it makes people feel obliged to their promises. Status means that people get respect for what they stand for. There is a clear relationship between Confucian dynamism and economic growth of countries (Hofstede, 1991).

A more recent and updated study on cultures has been put forth by the GLOBE (Global Leadership and Organizational Behavior Effectiveness Research Program) project (Hanges, House, Dickson, Dorfman, & coauthors, 1998; House, 2000). It used the same dimensions as Hofstede (1991), but improved the measurement of these dimensions and included more dimensions. This study also collected data from four different countries of the southern region of Africa (three of which we report on in this book: Zambia, Zimbabwe, and Black South Africa). Finally, it asked participants not only what kinds of values they see their cultures espouse ("as is"), but also what values they should have ("should"). The data were collected from middle managers of different firms in three different industries.

Table 1.1 presents the results in a summary form (Hanges et al., 1998; House, 2000). A, B, C, and D are clusters: A is the highest cluster of countries; B, the second highest; C, the second lowest; and D, the lowest cluster (in a few cases, there is even an E, but this does not need to

Table 1.1
GLOBE Cultural Dimensions in Africa

		Zambia	Zimbabwe	South Africa (Blacks)	Namibia
Performance	-As is	B	B	A	B
	-Should	A	A	C	A
Future Orientation	-As is	C	C	A	C
	-Should	A	A	B	A
Assertiveness	-As is	A	B	B	B
	-Should	B	A	B	B
Collectivism Society	-As is	B	B	B	C
	-Should	B	B	B	B
Collectivism Family	-As is	A	A	B	B
	-Should	B	A	C	A
Gender Egalitarianism	-As is	C	C	A	A
	-Should	B	B	B	B
Humane	-As is	A	B	B	B
	-Should	A	B	B	B
Power Distance	-As is	A	A	C	A
	-Should	D	C	B	C
Uncertainty Avoidance	-As is	C	C	B	D
	-Should	B	B	B	A

Source: R. J. House, ed., (2000). *Cultural influences on leadership and organizations* (tentative title) (Manuscript in preparation).

Note: A means highest cluster, B second highest, C second lowest, D lowest.

concern us here). Performance orientation is high if the culture encourages people to improve their performance (this dimension is based on McClelland, 1961). Black South Africans belong to the highest cluster, while the other three African countries belong to the second-highest cluster. It is interesting that the cultures scoring in this middle category B think that performance orientation should be much higher in their country.

Future orientation (planning, investing in the future, and delaying gratification is seen as positive, similar to Confucian dynamism) is relatively low in Zambia, Zimbabwe, and Namibia. These three countries also think that future orientation should be much higher than it currently is. South African Blacks, on the other hand, show a high degree of future orientation.

Assertiveness orientation implies a certain aggressiveness in the pursuit of one's goals (originally, this construct was part of Hofstede's [1991] masculinity scale). Zambia is in the highest group, while Zimbabwe, South Africa, and Namibia are in the middle group. Competitive aggressiveness by entrepreneurs is likely to be related to this dimension.

Collectivism was split into a society concept, where being in groups is important, and into collectivism in the sense of family orientation. Zambia and Zimbabwe are in the second-highest cluster with regard to the society concept and in the highest cluster with regard to family orientation. One would assume that entrepreneurs of those cultures that have a high family orientation will be under more pressure to employ family members.

Gender egalitarianism is the other part of Hofstede's (1991) masculinity scale. Those countries scoring low on it, such as Zambia and Zimbabwe, assume that women do not have the same rights as men, while those scoring high, such as South Africa and Namibia, assume that males and females have the same rights. This variable should be related to the number of female entrepreneurs with high longevity of their firms. That is, in countries with egalitarian approaches, there should be a higher degree of longstanding female entrepreneurs, while in countries with low egalitarianism, ownership should only be a transitory condition for females.

Only Zambia is in the highest group in humane orientation (society wants its members to be fair, altruistic, generous, caring, and kind), while the other cultures are in the middle group.

Zambia, Zimbabwe, and Namibia turn out to be in the highest group for power distance. This would imply that there should be a high degree of distance between the boss and the employees. However, these cultures are not comfortable with the power distance and think that there should be less (this is particularly so in Zambia). Thus, a redirection might take place and a tendency toward a decrease in power distance between boss and employees might develop in comparison to what one would assume from the "as is" score. On this dimension, the exception among these four countries is South Africa.

Zambia, Zimbabwe, and Namibia are low on uncertainty avoidance. This means that entrepreneurship is encouraged in these cultures. This is less so in South Africa. However, all four countries are higher on the "should" scores; thus, they assume that it would be better to have more structure, more planning, and more rules to deal with the uncertainties of the future.

It is important to note that this book is not on cross-cultural differences in entrepreneurship. The GLOBE study on culture has only been presented to show the degree of difference among the African countries that we studied, because culture influences all the factors that affect entrepreneurial success.

A PSYCHOLOGICAL FRAMEWORK FOR ENTREPRENEURIAL SUCCESS

Figure 1.1 presents the Giessen–Amsterdam Model of Entrepreneurial Success. There are two important features of this model. First, it assumes that success is determined by the actions of the entrepreneurs. The concept that is nearest to actions—action strategies—is the one that determines success in this model. This implies that no other variable of the model has a direct influence on success. Thus, environment, human capital, and personality should not be directly related to success but should work via goals and strategies on success. Personality has an influence on success because it changes the goals and the strategies that entrepreneurs have. There is some evidence for this prediction (Goebel, 1998; Utsch & Rauch, in press). However, there are interactive effects; for example, certain strategies interact with the environment. A German study (Rauch & Frese, 1998) found that planning is more useful in a highly hostile environment. It is not the task of this book to check on whether the particular prediction of this model is correct. Rather, it follows from this model that strategies are of particular importance, because they should predict entrepreneurial success most directly. Therefore, we have concentrated on the issue of action strategies.

Figure 1.1
The Giessen–Amsterdam Model of Entrepreneurial Success

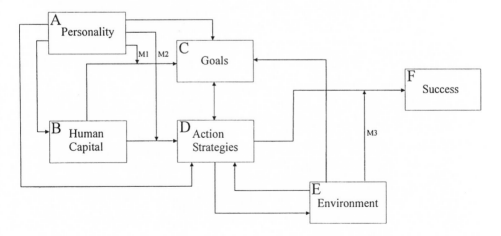

Second, one assumption of the model is that the individual entrepreneur needs to be studied in micro- and small-scale business research. This is controversial, because some authors have preferred to start out with the firm level of analysis (Covin & Slevin, 1989; Lumpkin & Dess, 1996). We argue that in micro- and small-scale firms the founder of the enterprise is the main decision maker of the enterprise. The founder influences how things are done in a firm, which people are selected, what priorities exist, and the general culture and strategic orientation of the firm. The pervasive influence of founders on their firms, and their dominance in the decisions made, makes it possible to assume a high degree of equivalence between the individual (the owner/manager) and organizational level of analysis (Frese, van Gelderen, & Ombach, in press; Rajagopalan, Rasheed, & Datta, 1993). This is, of course, true only of small units (e.g., one to twenty employees). We are open to the suggestion that, with the growth of the firm, the influence of the founder gets smaller.

Entrepreneurial Action Strategies
(Content, Process, Orientations)

Since action strategies are most important in our Giessen–Amsterdam Model of Entrepreneurial Success, we want to start with the discussion of constructs related to strategy. Strategy is often conceptualized as related to environmental analysis, assessment of internal strengths and weaknesses, goal planning, evaluation of alternative courses of action, and the development of a comprehensive plan to achieve goals (Hart, 1992, p. 328). However, unlike the usage of strategy as a "positive" term in management sciences, we use the concept in a value-free sense. For example, not having a plan of action is also an action strategy. From a psychological view, strategy is defined as a sequence of actions to achieve a goal (Miller et al., 1960, p. 16). The concept of strategy relates to the way to get to a goal, whatever that goal may be. Strategy is used to deal with uncertain situations, because strategy presents a guideline that can be applied in various situations (Frese, van Gelderen, & Ombach, in press). Hence, it helps to deal with the limited processing capacity of the human mind (Frese & Zapf, 1994).

Strategies can be described on three dimensions, as Figure 1.2 suggests. Every action strategy is focussed on some *content*: What is it that an entrepreneur does? Business studies have been concerned with the question of the right strategy (e.g., the pros and cons occupying a low-entry market). *Process* characteristics of strategies refer to how something is put into action (e.g., is there a lot of planning). Finally, there is a third dimension, entrepreneurial *orientations*, which are related to values and attitudes that lie behind the strategies (e.g., com-

Figure 1.2
Three Dimensions of Entrepreneurial Action Strategies

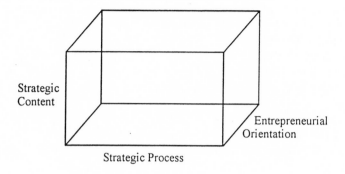

petitive aggressiveness). We think of these three dimensions as being, in principle, independent of each other. For example, a niche strategy may be planned in detail or it may be derived from keen observations of opportunities in the market. The niche strategy may be performed with the attitude of competitive aggressiveness (to drive competitors who occupy the same niche out of the market), or with a more "live and let live" attitude.

Content of Strategies

Strategic content concerns itself with the following issues: customers, suppliers, employees, products, production factors (e.g., machinery), marketing, capitalization, competitors, and dealing with state regulations. Porter (1980) distinguished focus, differentiation, and cost leadership. In other words, an entrepreneur has to decide to pay attention to a particular product or market segment (focus), to develop a product or service that is unique (differentiation), and to become cost effective, quality oriented, or both (cost leadership).

Wilfert (1992) has looked at the strategy content of Nigerian middle-range firms and found the following strategies to be important: cost minimization, increase of sales, influencing state agencies, change of line of business, and reduction of production, including stopping production. While the first two strategies are in line with Western strategies, the last three are specific to the situation in Nigeria. Influencing government agencies helped to get import licenses which allowed quick profit, change of line of business was also in reaction to government actions, and production was stopped when it was easier and quicker to achieve profit through trading as a result of getting import licenses (or foreign currency licenses). In some cases, the majority of the entrepreneurs attempted to make the "fast buck" with trading on import licenses. These strategies do not work any longer in Africa, because the Structural Adjustment Programs have done away with many of the government interventions. Interestingly, Wilfert found those entrepreneurs who had responded opportunistically to government interventions and who had maximized their returns with the aid of this strategy to have more difficulties adjusting to the economic requirements after the Structural Adjustment Programs went into effect.

A new development in some African countries has been the introduction of networks of small entrepreneurs (or informal sector associations). Obviously, there is an old tradition of cooperatives, but modern networks are driven by a stronger commercial and developmental orientation, which is supposed to lead to better quality and improved competitiveness in comparison to the larger companies (Rabellotti, 1998; Schmitz, 1998). One program financed by the GTZ (Gesellschaft fuer Technische Zusammenarbeit, Germany) has introduced networks which work together with marketing intermediaries (Nell, Kohlheyer, Muza, & Masaka, 1998) who work on a commercial basis to help with supplies, tool hiring, and selling/marketing the products of microenterprises (Carlton & Hancock, 1998). Another function of the market intermediaries is quality assurance. An example of a particularly successful marketing approach through intermediaries has been the horticultural consortium marketing in Zimbabwe (Muzamani, 1995). Networks have been shown to be effective in Western countries as well (see, e.g., Bruederl & Preisdendoerfer, 1998).

There is no doubt that most microbusinesses are seriously under-capitalized (see, e.g., Gray et al., 1997; Van Dijk, 1995). Usually they have to "make do" with whatever they have saved, because owners very rarely receive credit: Most of the prerequisites of getting a commercial loan are not met; among others, collateral and a good business plan (Gray et al., 1997; Kiggundu, 1988). Moreover, small loans usually carry such high transaction costs that banks do not usually find them worth the effort. Given that in most African countries inflation is high and commercial loans carry high interest rates, it is a mixed blessing to receive a loan. It is hard, for example, to pay an interest rate of 80 percent, as is true in some countries we studied. Nevertheless, there is an active and growing interest in the issue of microcredits (Friedrich Ebert Foundation, 1998; Harper, 1998; Yunus, 1989). This literature is so well-documented that it is not necessary to repeat it here (for some of the differences among entrepreneurs for the types of credit they need, see Daniels, Mead, & Musinga, 1995). It is a paradoxical result that in some African countries the entrepreneurs do not get any credits but give credits. Parker (1996, p. 37) points out for Zambia, "In general, micro and small-scale enterprise owners are credit providers rather than credit users. Although the amount of credit extended to customers is typically small, poor repayment is pervasive."

The entrepreneur has to make a decision to become formal or stay informal. Most microbusiness owners are not that worried about this issue (Mead, 1995). Most companies that eventually become formal start out as informal businesses (Neshamba, 1997). Obviously, the vast majority of the enterprises stay informal. There are various interactions with the formal business sector; for example, buying raw material (frequently), selling to the formal sector (infrequently), subcontracting with the formal business (very infrequently), and learning the skills from the formal sector by having been employed there first (very frequently) (Van Dijk, 1995).

Dealing with tax structure and government interference is of little concern for most entrepreneurs (Mead, 1995), although there are fluctuations from country to country. By and large, government effects on microbusinesses are relatively small, since most African governments have done away with complicated application procedures for start-ups or do not enforce the procedures any longer. This does not mean that government does not have indirect effects on the functioning of microbusiness—it obviously does (Van Dijk, 1995). Some not so obvious effects can be the following: Microfirm owners attempt to stay outside the tax system and one way to do this is to not keep books that could potentially be checked. While this motive is understandable, there is the long-term side effect that the owners themselves do not know exactly how much money they are making with which products. Bookkeeping would help them to be more innovative and to stick to those products that are sold profitably.

One of the content issues of strategy is whom to employ: family members or no family members. Wild (1994) argues that members from extended families are not only unqualified to do the job but also steal from company owners. In contrast, Gebert (1992) finds that Nigerian entrepreneurs employ family members precisely because of their higher loyalty. In the Asian context, families are also seen as a support system for the successful owner/manager (Javillonar & Peters, 1973).

The final issue that we think is important for our studies is the issue of marketing. By and large, entrepreneurs in Africa do not bother about marketing. "The most noteworthy factor in the area of business management was the absence of an aggressive marketing strategy. . . . Promotion was the least used component of the marketing mix. Most businesses relied on 'word of mouth' to disseminate information to their target markets. No case of a systematic promotion process was discovered" (Gray et al., 1996, pp. 128, 129).

Obviously, there are other issues that could be discussed here; for example, getting too high a credit if one is available, storing too many supplies and products because of fear that it would be difficult to get them again later on, too little reinvestments, and too much diversification (Dieter Fricke, personal communication, 15 September 1998). This discussion should suffice, because the issues of process characteristics and entrepreneurial orientation discussed next are more important for our purpose.

Process Characteristics of Action Strategies

Strategic process is concerned with the formulation and implementation of strategic decisions (Olson & Bokor, 1995). Cognitive and action theories have differentiated the following process characteristics of action strategies (Frese, van Gelderen, & Ombach, in press; Hacker, 1998; Hayes-Roth & Hayes-Roth, 1979; Zempel, 1994): Complete planning, critical point, opportunistic, and reactive strategies. Figure 1.3 presents the conceptual distinctions between these process characteristics. The first level that differentiates process characteristics is whether or not people are planning.

A person using a *complete planning strategy* plans ahead and actively structures the situation. This strategy implies a comprehensive representation of the work process, a long time frame to plan ahead, a large inventory of signals, a good knowledge and anticipation of error situations, and a proactive orientation (Frese & Zapf, 1994; Hacker, 1998). The advantages of complete planning are that one is actively structuring one's situation, one develops a better knowledge of important environmental cues and feedback, and one is able to better interpret them. Moreover, top-down planning also implies some back-up plans for situations in which something goes wrong. But it also entails costs in terms of time and money. An alternative to complete planning which reduces the costs of planning is to concentrate on the most important point and to just plan for this particular point. This is called the *critical point strategy*, which is a form of localized planning (Sonnentag, 1997; Zempel, 1994). Only after solving the first critical point are further steps planned. It constitutes an iterative problem-solving strategy. The advantage is that it does not need a lot of planning and is, therefore, more economic to use. On the other hand, there are few back-up plans available if something goes wrong. Moreover, critical point planning does not invest as much time and effort into developing active forms of understanding the environment (e.g., producing feedback cues that signal which problems are developing in the environment).

The nonplanning side consists of a proactive and a reactive strategy. The proactive form is the *opportunistic strategy*. An opportunistic strategy is characterized by a high degree of scanning of environmental opportunities. Opportunities are recognized more frequently and

Figure 1.3
The Psychological Process Characteristics of Strategies

the entrepreneur can capitalize on them. The advantage is that one does not "lose out" on opportunities and one actively searches and structures one's situation. One does not need to plan for these opportunities. In comparison to the planning strategies, there are few "sunk costs" in planning processes. Small to medium-size American companies whose chief executives scanned the environment proactively are more successful (Daft, Sormunen, & Parks, 1988). The disadvantage is that an opportunistic strategy deviates quickly from goal pursuit if other opportunities arise. The entrepreneur may lose sight of his or her goals and this may mean that he or she does not put enough effort into the long-range development of the firm. As a matter of fact, Nigerian businesspeople who were too opportunistic (and used influence with the government and opportunities to make money) were shown to be less successful in the long run (Wilfert, 1992).

In contrast to the opportunistic strategy, the *reactive strategy* does not take a proactive stance. This strategy is driven by the situation. A reactive strategy implies that one reacts to the situation: One does not plan, is not goal oriented, and is driven by the immediate situational demands without influencing them. An example of a reactive orientation is when a firm owner copies the products of other firm owners around him and then waits for the distributors to tell him what to do. A reactive orientation should be negatively related to success. This is, indeed, the case in studies in the United States (Doty, Glick, & Huber, 1993) and The Netherlands (Frese et al., in press).

It is much more difficult to predict relationships between the other three strategy characteristics—complete planning, critical point, and opportunistic—because whether they are effective probably depends on the situation. The general rule should be that complete planning has a positive effect on success if the situation is very complex and hostile (and the entrepreneur thus needs a good idea of what cues in the environment presignal coming difficulties and have back-up plans available if things go wrong). Additional issues should be knowledge of the entrepreneur, because with little knowledge one cannot plan very well. Critical point planning should be useful in moderately regular, complex, and hostile situations in which no problems appear if one does not have a ready-made answer available when things go wrong. An opportunistic strategy should be useful in those situations in which there are many opportunities; for example, in countries that have been socialist or which are dominated by sclerotic monopolies, or which are economically in a boom period. In the Netherlands, the critical point strategy showed the highest relationship with success (Frese et al., in press).

Entrepreneurial Orientation

Entrepreneurial orientation looks at the process behind why an entrepreneur takes certain actions. Values, beliefs, and general orientations are important here. We think that the following eight orientations are of major importance: autonomy, innovativeness, risk orientation, competitive agressiveness, emotional stability and learning orientation, achievement orientation, integrity, and traditionalism versus modernism. The first four of these have been taken from Lumpkin and Dess (1996). (They also had a fifth orientation, proactiveness; however, proactiveness is in our view a process characteristic and not an orientation and was, therefore, discussed as a part of process characteristics.) In contrast to Lumpkin and Dess, we talk about the orientations of the entrepreneurs, while they prefer to talk about enterprises' orientations.

Lumpkin and Dess (1996, p. 140) describe *autonomy* as "the ability and the will to be self-directed in the pursuit of opportunities." An autonomous person acts independently and makes decisions in spite of constraints; for example, resource limitations. The autonomous person also defends his or her autonomy against suppliers or larger companies. The second component, *innovativeness*, implies "to have ideas about new products, services, and technological processes." Lumpkin and Dess distinguish between product-market and technological innovation, the first emphasizing product design, market research, and promotion, and the second competencies in the latest technologies and production methods. Many studies have commented on the fact that innovativeness is not high in African companies (e.g., Gray et al., 1996, p. 128, "In most cases, the businesses produced products which were carbon copies of others in the industry"). *Risk taking* is often divided into three types (Baird & Thomas, 1985): venturing into the unknown, committing a large portion of one's assets to starting up a business, and borrowing heavily. Risk taking is probably related to uncertainty avoidance, which is comparatively low in Africa (except in South Africa, where it is medium). Rauch and Frese (2000), in their overview of the Western literature, find a small negative linear correlation of risk taking with success, suggesting that risk taking may not be a positive factor. However, theoretically, one should probably not assume a linear relationship with success. Rather, we assume that there is a curvilinear relationship in such a way that a moderate amount of risk taking is successful, while both lack of risk taking and a very high level of it leads to nonsuccess. On the other hand, there is no doubt that all entrepreneurs have taken the risk to be independent and to commit some of their own capital to this—and thus there is always a certain amount of risk taking. The fourth component is *competitive aggressiveness*, which makes it difficult for competitors to enter the same market. Aggressive entrepreneurs attempt to outperform and ultimately to undo their competitors in the marketplace. Lumpkin and Dess argue that this has a positive relationship with success. However, it may be useful to check how networking and competitive aggressiveness are related and whether these are two complementary strategies which can both lead to success. According to Gray and colleagues, African owners rarely use an aggressive marketing approach.

Stability and learning orientation means that the entrepreneur does not become emotional and despondent when things go wrong, but learns from such experiences. Since entrepreneurs have to act quickly in situations of high uncertainty, they are bound to make mistakes. Learning from these mistakes and errors is particularly important for success in business (Hartley, 1997; Van Dyck, Frese, & Sonnentag, 1998). *Achievement orientation* has been introduced by McClelland (1987) and has been shown to be related both to economic development of nations (McClelland & Winter, 1971) and to small-scale entrepreneurs' success (Rauch & Frese, 2000). People with high achievement orientation are attracted to challenging tasks, are motivated to do better at such tasks, take personal responsibility, and seek feedback on the quality of their work (McClelland, 1987). *Personal integrity* was emphasized by Locke (1997), who used the term "honesty." It means that the entrepreneur instills a sense of reliability and trust in his or her customers and suppliers, which should, therefore, lead to higher success. *Traditionalism versus modernism* implies attitudes toward the marketplace and technology, and the orientation toward old customs, and usually couples with paternalism toward employees and some religiosity. This is an important concept in Africa. Gebert (1992) showed that nontraditional orientations with regard to employees were related to success for Nigerian small and medium-size entrepreneurs.

Goals

Another concept that is near to action is the goal that guides the action. Researchers agree that there needs to be some kind of an idea of what one wants to achieve to be able to act effectively. Goals challenge, motivate, and lead to good performance (Baum, 1994; Lee, Locke, & Latham, 1989). Lee and colleagues called it goal setting; Baum called it vision and defined vision as the cognitive structure or image of a desired business state and found a positive effect on performance.

One may, of course, differentiate two types of goals: start-up goals and operative goals. Start-up goals are developed from motives for why one wants to be an entrepreneur (Galais, 1998; Rauch & Frese, 1998). In principle, one can differentiate subsistence, lifestyle (making one's hobby one's business), and growth goals (and, of course, any combination of them). One assumption is that most entrepreneurs in Africa are starting their own firms because they cannot find jobs otherwise and are, therefore, subsistence oriented. Thus they are poverty and subsistence driven and mainly motivated to just earn enough to live (Wild, 1994; Van Dijk & Alberts, 1994). It sounds plausible that this type of survival motivation actually prevents further success, because there is little motivation to grow and to be innovative. Whenever the owner finds a job, he or she will gladly give up the firm. Friedrich (1992) reported cases where firm owners had abandoned their firm for a while after they had made enough money. If this is so, then there should be more entrepreneurs in the Third World who are hindered in their growth by their subsistence motive than in Western countries, where to be independent is the most important motive to start a company (Hisrich, 1990). Lately we have become more critical of the idea of a start-up goal to influence later success. This concept is too static and we think that people can and actually do change their goals. People who have started because of a subsistence motive may fiercely defend their independence and autonomy or become growth oriented sometime later. From informal observations, we found that surprisingly many entrepreneurs would not want to give up their businesses even if they could make more money as employees. For policies directed toward the development of small enterprise in the developing countries, this is an important issue. We do not think there are good data on the influence of starting motives on success in developing countries so far and we shall, therefore, test this assumption in this book.

Operative goals refer to those goals that are operative in the day-to-day dealings with the firm. The postulates of goal-setting theory (Latham & Locke, 1991; Lee et al., 1989) probably also apply for African entrepreneurs. Hard and specific goals should lead to higher job performance than a general "do your best" approach or no goals at all. One prerequisite of setting high goals for oneself is high self-efficacy. Self-efficacy implies that people believe that they have the capabilities to achieve their goals. Thus, self-efficacy implies that one is in control of one's life (Bandura, 1997). It makes sense that high self-efficacy is one of the determinants of success in Africa.

Goals are surprisingly rarely studied in entrepreneurship research, although success can only be determined if one takes goals into account. The goal is the most important reference point to call somebody or oneself successful. Without knowing what the goal of a person is, it is hard to say whether or not he or she has been successful.

Environment

Entrepreneurial acts are done within and with regard to a certain environment. The environment of an organization contains technology, customers, competition, location, economic situation, politics, and climate (Mintzberg, 1983, p. 143). The environment can be conceptualized rather broadly (e.g., culture is an environment) or rather specifically (e.g., the environment in which a specific entrepreneur works). It is the latter concept that stands in the foreground of entrepreneurship research.

Different theorists have different concepts of environmental factors. There is some agreement that three aspects of the environment can be differentiated: munificence versus hostility, dynamism versus static nature, and complexity versus simplicity (Rauch & Frese, 2000; Mintzberg, 1983). Covin and Slevin (1989) defined a hostile environment as characterized by intense competition, complex business climate, and the lack of exploitable opportunities. Dynamism is interpreted as unpredictability in the rate of change and innovation in an industry (Mintzberg, 1983), as well as the uncertainty or unpredictability of actions by competitors and customers (Miller & Friesen, 1983). Complexity is defined by the degree of sophisticated knowledge necessary to operate in a given environment (Wood, 1986). It is probably a fair description to say that African microbusiness environments are typically hostile, of low complexity, and of moderate and even low dynamism. Hostility is high due to a high degree of competition (Parker, 1996; McPherson, 1991). Competition is high because microentrepreneurs generally enter low-barrier, saturated markets rather than searching out unmet demands in difficult-to-enter markets (Parker, 1996). Trade firms most frequently cite problems due to excessive competition, while those in manufacturing or service activities more frequently cite low levels of consumer demand as the critical market constraint (Parker, 1996).

The environment is important for three reasons. First, it influences goals and strategies. For example, a munificent environment leads to more opportunistic strategies. Second, the environment is not something immutable but is changed by the strategies taken by the entrepreneurs. As a matter of fact, only the reactive strategy does not attempt to change the environment: Other strategies actually influence the environment in which the entrepreneur works. The clearest example is the market niche. A market niche is by definition a more business-friendly environment than the general environment. Third, the extent to which strategies predict entrepreneurial success should be contingent on the business environment. This is, for example, suggested by Lumpkin and Dess (1996). Entrepreneurs have to be more entrepreneurially oriented in a complex, dynamic, and hostile environment to be successful. In contrast, it is not necessary to show a high degree of entrepreneurial orientation in a simple, stable, and friendly environment. A similar interaction effect was shown by Rauch and Frese (1998); high quality and detailed planning was more successful in hostile or uncertain environments. Hostile markets are not necessarily negative for the long-term performance of firms. For example, Shane and Kolvereid (1995) found the most hostile country to have a higher performance rate in a three-country comparison in Europe.

There is one theoretical perspective that has mainly looked at the influence of the environment on firm start-up and survival rates: the ecological perspective (e.g., Aldrich & Widenmayer, 1993; Preisendoerfer, 1998). We do not want to describe it in detail here, beyond pointing out two findings: the liability of newness and the liability of smallness. This means that new start-ups have a lower survival rate than older ones. In addition, the smaller the firm, the higher its likelihood to go under or to be dissolved. Death rates of 50 percent and above within a five-year period have often been reported in the literature (Bruederl, Preisendoerfer, & Ziegler, 1992). Note that the theory of population ecology is contrary to our model in Figure 1.1, because it assumes that the entrepreneurs' actions are not of primary importance. We think that this theory is highly implausible, but the two findings just discussed may still be valid but need a psychological explanation. For example, in the beginning, entrepreneurs may have less knowledge and, therefore, their strategies may be out of tune with the requirements of the environment.

Liability of newness has been shown to appear in Africa as well (Mead & Liedholm, 1998). Additional determinants of survival in Africa are growth in the past, initial smaller size (in contrast to the West), not operating in trade (but in manufacturing and service), being located in urban areas, and being male owned (Mead & Liedholm, 1998).

Personality

The influence of personality on entrepreneurship is twofold: First, certain personality characteristics may contribute to starting a firm (firm emergence). Second, personality characteristics may influence the strategies, and thus influence success (firm success). It is a plausible hypothesis that personality characteristics may be more important for becoming a starter than to succeed (Utsch, Rauch, Rothfuss, & Frese, 1999). Most frequently, need for achievement, risk taking, and locus of control have been hypothesized to be related both to success and to starting a firm. Indeed, Rauch and Frese (2000) showed in their meta-analysis of the literature that need for achievement and locus of control have been found to be related both to becoming a starter (emergence) and to being successful as an owner/manager in Western countries.

Of particular influence was McClelland's (1987) need for an achievement concept which implies a desire to do well, not so much for the sake of social recognition or prestige, but to attain a feeling of personal accomplishment. McClelland and Winter (1971) developed a training program for Indian entrepreneurs which essentially emphasized goal setting, paying attention to other entrepreneurs and learning from them, goal commitment, increasing self-confidence and self-efficacy, and convincing the businessmen of the importance of what they were doing. The trained entrepreneurs were more successful than those who were not trained, and the city in which training took place was also more economically successful than a comparison city where no training had taken place (by the way, McClelland and Winter's study is also an example of a good evaluation design that is methodologically more sophisticated than most others in the area of training interventions in developing countries). The training effects were later replicated in a study on minority entrepreneurs in the United States (Miron & McClelland, 1979).

McClelland's (1987) ideas have been controversial. While there are a few studies that contradict the notion that achievement motive is important for entrepreneurs (e.g., Javillonar & Peters, 1973, who have a very small sample, however), the critique has been mainly ideological and was not based on empirical data. As mentioned, Rauch and Frese (2000) show in a meta-analysis that there is a clear-cut, albeit small, relationship of the achievement motive both with emergence of entrepreneurship and with entrepreneurial success.

Another approach, also based on McClelland's (1987) work, is the one by Spencer and Spencer (1993). They distinguished eight competency variables that differentiated successful from unsuccessful entrepreneurs: seeing and acting on opportunities, persistence, information seeking, concern for high quality of work, commitment to work contract, systematic planning, self-confidence, and use of influence strategies. Successful entrepreneurs also scored higher on power and achievement motives. They found that the competencies of successful entrepreneurs were essentially the same in three different countries: Malawi (Africa), Ecuador (Latin America), and India (Asia).

Miner (1997) has suggested a typology of four different avenues to success for small-scale entrepreneurs: the personal achiever, the supersalesperson, the real manager, and the expert idea generator. Thus, different people may have different ways of achieving success. Such a typology is promising, although the empirical basis is weak at the moment and to our knowledge this typology has not been used in developing countries at all.

The issue of personality has been very controversial in entrepreneurship and some scientists have argued that using personality as a predictor was misleading right from the start and should not be pursued any further (Gartner, 1989). We think, however, that what is really needed is a more sophisticated approach to personality. Our arguments for this are in brief (for more, see Rauch & Frese, 2000):

1. As our model (Figure 1.1) suggests, personality should not be simply related to success, but the mediating mechanisms (in our model, goals and strategies) need to be spelled out. Thus, an achievement-motivated person may plan more, and better plans lead to more success.

2. The content of personality variables should be tightly coupled with entrepreneurial tasks. A general personality test is unlikely to be related to entrepreneurial tasks. However, issues related to entrepreneurship, such as achievement motive and locus of control (and possibly risk taking) are related to success.

3. Personality factors interact with the environment and this interaction determines how one behaves.

4. A situation can be very forceful and highly determine the behavior of people (strong situation), or it can be a weak situation in which there is enough leeway to let personality factors have an influence. For example, franchisers determine how one has to run a franchise business to a large degree. In such a situation, personality factors should not have a strong effect on strategies and success.

5. Any one personality factor cannot, and should not, have a strong influence on success, because entrepreneurial success is multifactorially determined. This is particularly true of personality, which is always a step removed from the real actions taken.

6. Personality can be managed. Thus, an entrepreneur who knows that he or she has difficulties leading and dealing with employees may rely heavily on his or her manager to work closely with the employees. In such a situ-

ation, there should be no relationship between the leadership problems of the entrepreneur with entrepreneurial success.

The reader may have wondered about the conceptual relationship between entrepreneurial orientations and personality variables. As we conceptualize orientations to be attitudes, beliefs, and values of individuals, there is some overlap with personality constructs. We think of personality variables to be more general, to be distal causes, and to be on a higher level of abstraction. Orientations are more specific, more proximal causes of behavior, and more concrete. For example, the achievement motive as a trait implies that one tends to interpret situations to be achievement situations. The specific achievement orientation implies that one wants to achieve high goals in one's business.

Human Capital

Human capital is the accumulation of knowledge and skills with which the entrepreneur attempts to deal with his or her tasks. Various indicators of human capital have been developed, many of them indirect ones. Traditional measures of human capital are years of schooling, work experience, and industry-specific and leadership experiences (Bruederl et al., 1992; Hisrich, 1990; Preisendoerfer & Voss, 1990). In addition, prior self-employment and the presence of models (such as parents and other relatives being entrepreneurs) have also been used as indirect measures of human capital. In Western countries, human capital has been shown to be related to entrepreneurial success, although this relationship is small (Rauch & Frese, 1998). Similar findings appeared in Africa; for example, in Zimbabwe (Daniels et al., 1995), and in Zambia (Parker, 1996). Parker found a relationship between enterprise profit and education, work experience, and industry experience of the entrepreneur. Training was also related to business success.

An interesting human-capital factor is parental and other family members' self-employment. Children of entrepreneurs get positive role models of entrepreneurship starting at an early age. This may lead to a higher degree of motivation to become self-employed and to a higher knowledge of what entrepreneurship means. Moreover, the owners will probably get help from their families after having started their firm. These factors may explain why certain minority members (e.g., Indians or Coloreds in South Africa) have a headstart when they become self-employed.

In Africa, the lack of general formal education and business experience works to the disadvantage of the entrepreneurs (Gray et al., 1996). Especially, the lack of accounting and financial-management skills and practice affects success negatively (Kiggundu, 1988; see also Chapter

7). It is not unheard of that some owners (and some of their employees) confuse sales with profits and are, therefore, astonished if there is no more money for supplies after they have used up their profits of the day.

SOCIODEMOGRAPHIC VERSUS PSYCHOLOGICAL PREDICTORS OF SUCCESS

Different disciplines focus upon different predictors of entrepreneurial success. With regard to person variables, sociologists and economists have been interested in sociodemographic concepts, such as human capital (education). Our psychological prediction model (see Figure 1.1) integrates these variables into a larger framework, but is particularly interested in those variables that are more closely related to behavior—particularly goals and strategies. Practically and theoretically, it is important to know which type of variables will lead to better prediction of entrepreneurial success. This is one of the main issues of this book. A major theme is that psychological variables should be considered more frequently and in more depth than has hitherto been done in research on entrepreneurship in general, and in developing countries in particular. In the last analysis, it will be an empirical question to find out which variables and which variable complexes lead to success in microbusiness in Africa. The following chapters will attempt to answer this question.

REFERENCES

Aldrich, H. E., & Widenmayer, G. (1993). From traits to rates: An ecological perspective on organizational foundings. In J. A. Katz & R. H. Brockhaus (Eds.), *Advances in entrepreneurship, firm emergence, and growth* (Vol. 1, pp. 145–195). Greenwich, CT: JAI Press.

Baird, I. S., & Thomas, H. (1985). Towards a contingency model of strategic risk-taking. *Academy of Management Review, 10*, 230–243.

Bandura, A. (1997). *Self-efficacy: The exercise of control*. New York: Freeman.

Baum, J. R. (1994). *The relation of traits, competencies, vision, motivation, and strategy to venture growth*. Unpublished doctoral dissertation, University of Maryland.

Bruederl, J., & Preisendoerfer, P. (1998). Network support and the success of newly founded businesses. *Small Business Economics, 10*, 213–225.

Bruederl, J., Preisendoerfer, P., & Ziegler, R. (1992). Survival chances of newly founded business organizations. *American Sociological Review, 57*, 227–242.

Carland, J. W., Hoy, F., Boulton, W. R., & Carland, J. C. (1984). Differentiating entrepreneurs from small business owners: A conceptualization. *Academy of Management Review, 9*, 354–359.

Carlton, A., & Hancock, D. (1998). ISTARN—An approach to informal sector business support in Zimbabwe. *Small Enterprise Development, 9* (2), 41–49.

Chinese Culture Connection. (1987). Chinese values and the search for culture-free dimensions of culture. *Journal of Cross-Cultural Psychology, 18*, 143–164.

Covin, J. G., & Slevin, D. P. (1989). Strategic management of small firms in hostile and benign environments. *Strategic Management Journal, 10*, 75–87.

Daft, R. L., Sormunen, J., & Parks, D. (1988). Chief executive scanning, environmental characteristics, and company performance: An empirical study. *Strategic Management Journal, 9*, 123–139.

Daniels, L., Mead, D. C., & Musinga, M. (1995). *Employment and income in micro and small enterprises in Kenya: Results of a 1995 survey* (GEMINI Technical Report No. 92). Bethesda, MD: Growth and Equity through Microenterprise Investments and Institutions.

Doty, D. H., Glick, W. H., & Huber, G. P. (1993). Fit, equifinality, and organizational effectiveness: A test of two configurational theories. *Academy of Management Journal, 36*, 1196–1250.

Frese, M., van Gelderen, M., & Ombach, M. (in press). How to plan as a small scale business owner: Psychological process characteristics of action strategies and success. *Journal of Small Business Management.*

Frese, M., & Zapf, D. (1994). Action as the core of work psychology: A German approach. In H. C. Triandis, M. D. Dunnette, & L. M. Hough (Eds.), *Handbook of industrial and organizational psychology* (2d ed., Vol. 4, pp. 271–340). Palo Alto: Consulting Psychologists Press.

Friedrich, C. (1992). *Promotion of SSE.* Talk at a congress of the Zimbabwe chamber of commerce, Victoria Falls, 28 May 1992.

Friedrich Ebert Foundation. (1998). *Conditions for access to financial services for micro and small-scale entrepreneurs* (discussion paper). Harare: Friedrich Ebert Stiftung.

Galais, N. (1998). Motive und Beweggruende fuer die Selbstaendigkeit und ihre Bedeutung fuer den Erfolg. In M. Frese (Ed.), *Erfolgreiche Unternehmensgruender: Psychologische Analysen und praktische Anleitung fuer Unternehmer in Ost- und Westdeutschland* (pp. 83–98). Goettingen: Hogrefe.

Gartner, W. B. (1989). "Who is an entrepreneur?" is the wrong question. *Entrepreneurship Theory and Practice, 13* (4), 47–68.

Gebert, D. (Ed.). (1992). *Traditionsorientierung und unternehmerischer Erfolg.* Saarbruecken: Breitenbach.

Goebel, S. (1998). Persoenlichkeit, Handlungsstrategien und Erfolg. In M. Frese (Ed.), *Erfolgreiche Unternehmensgruender: Psychologische Analysen und praktische Anleitungen fuer Unternehmer in Ost- und Westdeutschland* (pp. 99–122). Goettingen: Hogrefe.

Gray, K. R., Cooley, W., & Lutabingwa, J. (1997). Small-scale manufacturing in Kenya. *Journal of Small Business Management, 1*, 66–72.

Gray, K. R., Cooley, W., Lutabingwa, J., Mutai-Kaimenyi, B., & Oyugi, L. A. (1996). *Entrepreneurship in micro-enterprises: A strategic analysis of manufacturing industries in Kenya.* Lanham: University Press of America.

Hacker, W. (1998). *Allgemeine Arbeitspsychologie. Psychische Regulation von Arbeitstaetigkeiten.* Bern: Hans Huber Publ.

Hanges, P. J., House, R. J., Dickson, M. W., Dorfman, P. W., & coauthors (1998). *The development and validation of scales measuring societal culture and culturally shared implicit theories of leadership.* Manuscript submitted for publication.

Harper, M. (1998). *Profit for the poor.* London: Intermediate Technology Publications.

Hart, S. L. (1992). An integrative framework for strategy-making processes. *Academy of Management Review, 17* (2), 327–351.

Hartley, R. F. (1997). *Management mistakes and successes* (5th ed.). New York: Wiley.

Hayes-Roth, B., & Hayes-Roth, F. (1979). A cognitive model of planning. *Cognitive Science, 3,* 275–310.

Hisrich, R. D. (1990). Entrepreneurship/intrapreneurship. *American Psychologist, 45* (2), 209–222.

Hofstede, G. (1980). *Culture's consequence: International differences in work-related values.* Newbury Park, CA: Sage.

Hofstede, G. (1991). *Allemaal andersdenkenden: Omgaan met cultuurverschillen.* Amsterdam: Contact.

House, R. J. (Ed.). (2000). *Cultural influences on leadership and organizations* (tentative title). Manuscript in preparation.

International Labor Organization. (1972). *Employment, incomes and equality: A strategy for increasing productive employment in Kenya.* Geneva: Author.

Javillonar, G. V., & Peters, G. R. (1973). Sociological and social psychological aspects of Indian entrepreneurship. *British Journal of Sociology, 24,* 314–328.

Katz, D., & Kahn, R. L. (1978). *Social psychology of organizations* (2d ed.). New York: Wiley.

Kiggundu, M. N. (1988). Africa. In R. Nath (Ed.), *Comparative management* (pp. 169–243). Cambridge: Balliger.

Latham, G. P., & Locke, E. A. (1991). Goal setting—A motivational theory that works. In R. M. Porter & L. W. Steers (Eds.), *Motivation and work behavior* (pp. 357–370). New York: McGraw-Hill.

Lee, T. W., Locke, E. A., & Latham, G. P. (1989). Goal setting theory and job performance. In L. A. Pervin (Ed.), *Goal concepts in personality and social psychology* (pp. 291–326). Hillsdale, NJ: Lawrence Erlbaum.

Locke, E. A. (1997). Prime movers: The traits of great business leaders. In C. L. Cooper & S. E. Jackson (Eds.), *Creating tomorrow's organizations: A handbook for future research in organizational behavior* (pp. 75–96). New York: Wiley.

Lumpkin, G. T., & Dess, G. G. (1996). Clarifying the entrepreneurial orientation construct and linking it to performance. *Academy of Management Review, 21,* 135–172.

McClelland, D. C. (1961). *The achieving society.* New York: Free Press.

McClelland, D. C. (1987). *Human motivation.* Cambridge, England: Cambridge University Press.

McClelland, D. C., & Winter, D. G. (1971). *Motivating economic achievement.* New York: Free Press.

McPherson, M. A. (1991, December). *Micro and small-scale enterprises in Zimbabwe: Results of a country-wide survey* (GEMINI Working Paper No. 25). Bethesda, MD: Growth and Equity through Microenterprise Investments and Institutions.

Mead, D. C. (1995). How the legal, regulatory, and tax framework affects the dynamics of enterprise growth. In E. P. English & G. Hénault (Eds.), *Agents of change* (pp. 75–86). London: Intermediate Technology.

Mead, D. C., & Liedholm, C. (1998). The dynamics of micro and small enterprises in developing countries. *World Development, 26,* 61–74.

Miller, D., & Friesen, P. H. (1983). Strategy-making and environment: The third link. *Strategic Management Journal, 4,* 221–235.

Miller, G. A., Galanter, E., & Pribram, K. H. (1960). *Plans and the structure of behavior.* London: Holt.

Miner, J. B. (1997). *A psychological typology of successful entrepreneurs.* Westport, CT: Quorum Books.

Mintzberg, H. T. (1983). *Structure in fives: Designing effective organizations.* Englewood Cliffs, NJ: Prentice Hall.

Miron, D., & McClelland, D. C. (1979). The impact of achievement motivation training on small businesses. *California Management Review, 21* (4), 13–28.

Muzamani, J. T. (1995). Increasing small-enterprise competitiveness in export markets through consortium marketing: An exploratory study. In E. P. English & G. Hénault (Eds.), *Agents of change* (pp. 261–274). London: Intermediate Technology.

Nell, M., Kohlheyer, G., Muza, A., & Masaka, M. (1998). *Informal sector training and resources network (ISTARN)* (project progress review). Frankfurt: Gesellschaft fuer Technische Zusammenarbeit (GTZ).

Neshamba, F. (1997). The transition of enterprises from informality to formality: Some evidence from Zimbabwe. *Small Enterprise Development, 8* (4), 48–53.

Olson, P. D., & Bokor, D. W. (1995). Strategy process–content interaction: Effects on growth performance in small, start-up firms. *Journal of Small Business Management, 33,* 34–44.

Parker, J. C. (1996). *Micro and small-scale enterprises in Zambia: Results of the 1996 nationwide survey.* Report submitted to Overseas Development Administration (ODA) by Graham Bannock and Partners, Ltd., London.

Peattie, L. (1987). An idea in good currency and how it grew: The informal sector. *World Development, 15,* 851–860.

Pedersen, P. O., Sverrisson, A., & Van Dijk, M. P. (Eds.). (1994). *Flexible specialization.* London: Intermediate Technology.

Porter, M. (1980). *Competitive strategy.* New York: Free Press.

Preisendoerfer, P. (1998). *Bausteine fuer eine Theorie der Unternehmensfuehrung.* Rostock: Wirtschafts- und Sozialwissenschaftliche Fakultaet Manuscript.

Preisendoerfer, P., & Voss, T. (1990). Organizational mortality of small firms: The effects of entrepreneurial age and human capital. *Organization Studies, 11* (1), 107–129.

Rabellotti, R. (1998). Helping small firms to network: The experience of UNIDO. *Small Enterprise Development, 9* (1), 25–34.

Rajagopolan, N., Rasheed, A.M.A., & Datta, D. K. (1993). Strategic decision processes: Critical review and future directions. *Journal of Management, 19,* 349–384.

Rauch, A., & Frese, M. (1998). A contingency approach to small scale business success: A longitudinal study on the effects of environmental hostility and uncertainty on the relationship of planning and success. In P. D.

Reynolds, W. D. Bygrave, N. M. Carter, S. Manigart, C. M. Mason, G. D. Meyer, & K. G. Shaver (Eds.), *Frontiers of entrepreneurship research* (pp. 190–200). Babson Park, MS: Babson College.

Rauch, A., & Frese, M. (2000). Psychological approaches to entrepreneurial success: A general model and an overview of findings. *International Review of Industrial and Organizational Psychology, 15*.

Rauch, A., Frese, M., & Sonnentag, S. (1999). Cultural differences in planning - success relationships: A comparison of small enterprises in Ireland, West Germany, and East Germany. Manuscript submitted for publication.

Schmitz, H. (1998). Fostering collective efficiency. *Small Enterprise Development, 9* (1), 4–11.

Shane, S., & Kolvereid, L. (1995). National environment, strategy, and new venture performance: A three country study. *Journal of Small Business Management, 33*, 37–50.

Sonnentag, S. (1997). Expertise in professional software design: A process study. *Journal of Applied Psychology, 83*, 703–715.

Spencer, L. M., Jr., & Spencer, S. M. (1993). *Competence at work: Models for superior performance*. New York: John Wiley & Sons.

Stiglitz, J. (1998). *Towards a new paradigm for development: Strategies, policies, and processes*. (www.worldbank.org/html/extdr/extme/jssp101998.htm). Washington, DC: World Bank.

Utsch, A., & Rauch, A. (1999). Innovativeness as a mediator between achievement orientation and venture performance. *European Journal of Work and Organizational Psychology*.

Utsch, A., Rauch, A., Rothfuss, R., & Frese, M. (1999). Who becomes a small scale entrepreneur in a post-socialist environment: On the differences between entrepreneurs and managers in East Germany. *Journal of Small Business Management 37* (3), 31–42.

Van Dijk, M. P. (1995). Regulatory restrictions and competition in formal and informal urban manufacturing in Burkina Faso. In P. English & G. Hénault (Eds.), *Agents of change* (pp. 106–125). London: Intermediate Technology.

Van Dijk, M. P., & Alberts, W. (1994). *Economic activities of the poor in Accra, the capital of Ghana*. Workshop on De-Agrarianzation and Rural Employment, Leiden, 4 May 1994.

Van Dyck, C., Frese, M., & Sonnentag, S. (1998). *Organizational error management climate: On enhanced error handling and organizational performance*. Manuscript submitted for publication.

Wild, V. (1994). *Versorgungskapitalisten*. Muenchen: Weltforum.

Wilfert, A. (1992). *Die Strategien nigerianischer Unternehmer bei wechselnden ökonomischen Rahmenbedingungen*. Fuchsstadt: Wilfer.

Wood, R. E. (1986). Task complexity: Definition of the construct. *Organization Behaviour and Human Decision Processes, 37*, 60–82.

Yunus, M. (1989). Grameen Bank: Organization and operation. In J. Levitsky (Ed.), *Microenterprises in developing countries*. London: Intermediate Technology.

Zempel, J. (1994). *Psychologische Strategien der Handlungsplanung*. Unpublished diploma thesis, Department of Psychology, Giessen.

2

The Psychological Strategy Process and Sociodemographic Variables as Predictors of Success for Micro- and Small-Scale Business Owners in Zambia

Madelief Keyser, Mechlien de Kruif, and Michael Frese

This chapter first looks at psychological success factors in microenterprise owners; second, it describes the situation in Zambia and how microenterprise owners use psychological strategies to manage their firms; and third, it presents case descriptions to give a qualitative feel for what we discuss and elaborate.

ENTREPRENEURSHIP IN ZAMBIA: AN OVERVIEW

Before 1991, small-scale business owners were actively discouraged. When Zambia became independent from Great Britain in 1964 and President Kaunda and his United National Independence Party ruled the country, its economic orientation was socialist or state capitalist; the government played the leading role in stimulating economic activities. A number of factors persuaded the political body in Zambia to change to a more active encouragement of small-scale entrepreneurs. The price of copper, the most important export product of Zambia, dropped dramatically in 1974, while the costs of imports rose (McIntyre, 1996; De Temmerman, 1997; Posthumus, 1997). This made Zambia one of the poorest countries in the world (World Bank, 1997; United Nations Development Program [UNDP], 1998; McIntyre, 1996).

The gross national product per capita (GNP) decreased from $440 in 1970 to $275 in 1995 (UNDP, 1998). The economic growth (Gross Domestic Product [GDP]) between 1990 and 1995 was –0.2 percent (World Bank, 1997; UNDP, 1998). The inflation rate was very high, it was about 90 percent per year in the decade between 1985 and 1995. In July 1998, the inflation rate was 26.3 percent.

After Frederic Chiluba and his Movement for Multi-Party Democracy was elected in 1991, a new policy of liberalizing and privatizing the economy and a free-floating kwacha (the local currency) were introduced (Structural Adjustment Program). Small firms were actively encouraged for the first time in Zambia. This was also done to reduce the dependency on exporting copper. This worked well; while, in 1991, 91 percent of all exports were copper, this percentage was reduced to 72 percent by 1995. Another issue was the need to increase employment in the country. Between 1991 and 1995, 70,000 jobs disappeared in the government and private companies (Posthumus, 1997). The government hoped that by improving the situation of small-scale entrepreneurs, more jobs would be created.

In terms of education, the government had long offered free primary and secondary education and vocational training after independence. After the fall of the price of copper, the government was not able to support this educational system any longer. Spending on education declined from 4.7 percent in 1985 to 1.8 percent in 1995 (UNDP, 1998). Still, in 1995, 89 percent of the population were enrolled in primary school and 28 percent attended secondary school; the adult literacy rate was 78.2 percent (UNDP, 1998; Kiggundu, 1988, p. 228).

We would like to describe the situation in 1995, which was about the same situation as in 1997 when we did our study there. Forty-one percent of the population were employed by or owned a company in 1995. Three-quarters of the total labor force worked in agriculture (which produced 22% of GNP), 8 percent were employed in industry (40% of GNP), and 17 percent had service jobs (37% of GNP) (UNDP, 1998). There were only a few large companies, very few medium-size firms, and a large number of very small microbusiness firms in Zambia. Almost 18 percent of the labor force was employed in the small- and microscale sector in 1995 (Parker, 1996). The micro- and small-scale sector in Zambia can be roughly divided into four sectors: trading, manufacturing, service, and craft (Parker, 1996). Nearly half of the small and microbusiness owners in Zambia in 1995 were involved in trading, 41 percent in manufacturing, and 10 percent in service (Parker, 1996). The small firms were usually family owned.

There were a number of problems that the microbusiness sector had to deal with. Their growth was restricted by lack of managerial skills of the entrepreneurs (Kiggundu, 1988). In the urban areas, the trade sector experienced a high degree of competition, while the manufacturing and service sectors reported low levels of consumer demand as their critical market constraint (Parker, 1996; McPherson, 1991). Competition resulted from low entry barriers for other micro- and small-scale entrepreneurs. Unfortunately, most Zambian business owners did not search for unmet demands when they wanted to enter a market, but often only emulated the existing firms, which led to increased competition (Parker, 1996). (This is true for business owners in other African countries, as well.) The average annual business profit for the small-scale sector was $170.69 in 1995. Although a majority of the entrepreneurs had the goal to expand their enterprise, only 19 percent showed any growth since start-up. On average, Zambian enterprises closed after a period of 4.4 years, mainly because of financial or market constraints (Parker, 1996). Lack of capital was a problem most Zambian entrepreneurs faced at start-up and during development and growth. High interest rates make it very difficult and risky to borrow money from a bank (the average interest rate was 80% in 1997). Serious undercapitalization is a problem throughout Africa, because small-scale business owners do not have enough collateral to secure a bank loan (Gray, Cooley, & Lutabingwa, 1997). Moreover, bank officers view small-scale borrowers as being risky with high credit-delivery costs (Gray, Cooley, Lutabingwa, Mutai-Kaimenyi, & Oyugi, 1996).

It is a paradoxical fact that the small-business owners in Zambia were actually the largest creditors rather than borrowers in 1995. Forty-nine percent of the entrepreneurs in the trade and manufacturing sector sold their products on credit to their customers (Parker, 1996; Gray et al., 1997). Credit was given because the business owners feared losing their customers to competitors. This often led to problems, because the owners had difficulties retrieving their credits from customers during hard times (Parker, 1996). This resulted in reduced cash flow, which meant that the business owners were not able to replenish their stocks or buy new raw materials.

These country-specific conditions mean the following for small-scale owners:

- There is a high degree of competition, particularly in low-entry-barrier fields.
- Money and capital are tight, therefore most businesses are undercapitalized.
- Human capital is relatively low, particularly in the very small businesses.
- Bookkeeping skills are probably low.
- Small-scale business owners are often motivated to just keep up subsistence.
- Environmental economic conditions are changing very quickly because of continuing liberalization and privatization.
- There is a high degree of competition from abroad.

THE STUDY SAMPLE

Our sample consists of fifty-nine microbusiness owners located in complexes in and around Lusaka, the capital of Zambia. All entrepreneurs were approached with the help of a Zambian expert on entrepreneurship, Mr. Kalungulungu. All those approached participated in the interview. Thus, there was no rejection rate. The most important descriptive results on the sample are given in Table 2.1. The sample comprised thirty-four men and twenty-five women. Many of the enterprises were relatively old; the median years of existence was five years; 10 percent of the sample started business in the year prior to our study. For more than half the entrepreneurs, the reason given for starting a business was a pull factor like developing own ideas, being independent, gaining influence, creating something lasting, or having contact with interesting people. This means that there was a large percentage that did not become entrepreneurs in order to survive. On the other hand, 44 percent of the microbusiness owners entered self-employment to be able to survive and because they were unemployed. The enterprises were in diverse lines of business, like manufacturing, service, trade, and craft. Most people were involved in trade or manufacturing. Many entrepreneurs traded in spare car parts or electrical machines. The manufacturing businesses consisted mainly of tailor shops.

The main legal form of the companies was limited (48%). The distinction between the formal and the informal sector is hard to make. The International Labor Organization (1972, p. 223) defined the informal sector as "small-scale (size), labor intensive and low skill nature, low wage, producing goods and services for low income people and generally living of the crumbs of the large scale formal sector." A formal business is registered at the Ministry of Commerce, Trade and Industry or at the Chamber of Commerce and pays taxes. When we asked the entrepreneurs whether they paid taxes, we often received confusing results because they had very different views on whether or not they were paying taxes. Therefore, we based the decision on whether they were in the formal or informal sector on whether they were a limited company or not. This resulted in 51 percent of the companies being counted as informal.

One-quarter of the sample had no employees at all, which means that these entrepreneurs probably ran their business in a different way than those who had employees: They had no responsibilities toward other people within the company (Zambia was the first study in the series of studies reported in this book, and afterward we made the decision to sample only from entrepreneurs with at least one employee). About one-half of the entrepreneurs had one to five employees, and the remaining 22 percent had more than five employees.

Table 2.1
Sample Descriptions, Zambia

Characteristic	Percentage
Gender	
- Male	58
- Female	42
Age of Business	
- Older than 10 years	12
- 6-10 years	32
- 2-5 years	46
- 1 year	10
Push/pull factors	
- Push (survival, unemployed)	44
- Pull (independence, money)	56
Line of Business	
- Manufacturing	37
- Craft	2
- Trade	39
- Service	22
Legal form	
- Formal sector	48
- Informal sector	51
Number of employees	
- 0	25
- 1	14
- 2-5	39
- 6-10	19
- 10-50	3
Hours of work	
- 44 hours or less	36
- More than 44 hours	65
Loan	
- Loan	24
- No loan	76
Market niche	
- Niche	27
- No niche	73

	Low	Middle	High
Human capital			
- experience	81	15	4
- training	91	5	4
- Organization of knowledge	55	25	20

In Zambia, the standard working hours are from eight in the morning until five in the evening and on Saturdays in the morning. A relatively large percentage (36%) of the entrepreneurs worked less than the standard forty-four hours a week. However, a large number of entrepreneurs also worked many more hours. Thus, the median for working hours was forty-eight hours per week.

A common problem in starting a business was lack of capital. Only 24 percent of the interviewees received a loan for the start of their business. These loans were provided by nongovernmental organizations (NGOs) or the government (43%, data not shown in Table 2.1), friends (15%), banks (15%), or family members (7%).

It is often argued that occupying a niche is a good strategy for small-scale business. Only 27 percent of the enterprises in our sample served a niche. This is a small number and is in line with other African countries (Gray et al., 1997). Most people entered noninnovative, saturated markets with low entry barriers, such as sewing overalls.

Human capital and strategies toward employees and business are the primary issues we are concerned with here. Bruederl, Preisendoerfer, and Ziegler (1992) argued that two important human-capital factors, level of education and amount of work experience, determine business success. We defined human capital, similarly to Bruederl and colleagues, as the amount of experience and training in different areas relevant for running a business; for example, accountancy, marketing, and management. Our results show that most entrepreneurs had little experience (81%) or training in entrepreneurially relevant skills (91%). One result of education is that people have ready-made descriptors of the reality and can present their ideas in a logical and concise way. We called this variable *organization of knowledge*. Only a minority of entrepreneurs explained their ideas in a highly logical and precise way (20%), most others were not able to do so (55%).

RELATIONSHIP OF SOCIODEMOGRAPHIC
CHARACTERISTICS WITH SUCCESS

The sociodemographic descriptors just discussed can be related to success. Figure 2.1 shows the important relationships of firm and entrepreneur characteristics with success. This figure only reports significant relationships and compares the number of highly successful entrepreneurs for the appropriate subgroups; whenever it was not significant, "n.s." signifies this fact (statistical significance was calculated on the basis of correlations and analyses of variance; see Chapter 8). For example, the first entry means that among those firms that have more than five employees, 29 percent were highly successful, while among the firms that have less than five employees, only 10 percent

Figure 2.1
Sociodemographic Factors and Success, Zambia

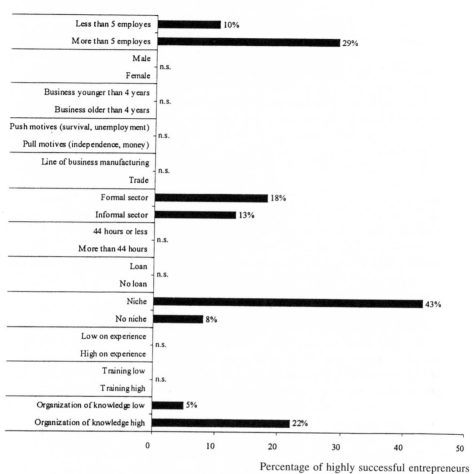

Percentage of highly successful entrepreneurs

were highly successful. This is not surprising, of course, because our success measure implied that the enterprise grew. The interviewers who made the success judgment used the size of the enterprise as one important indicator for their judgments (see Chapter 8).

Many of the results in Figure 2.1 are interesting, precisely because we did not find significant differences between groups which are often thought to differ. An example is that male and female entrepreneurs did not differ in their success (the difference was not significant). This means that gender was not an important variable in our study. This is in contrast to Mead and Liedholm (1998), who showed that women tended to be in those industries that were least successful.

However, they also showed that women were usually working alone without any employees. Since our sample consisted mainly of micro-business owners who had at least one employee, it is not surprising that we did not find a relationship with success.

Another example where we did not find differences is the age of the firm. There was no "liability of newness" (Bruederl et al., 1992) in our study. Those who started their enterprise more than four years ago were as successful as those who started afterward.

Push and pull factors did not make a difference for success. At first it is plausible that those who start a firm just because they have to will behave differently than those who wanted to be independent for a long time before they actually became a small-business owner. How-ever, this is apparently not an important factor for success. On the other hand, this is good news, because in developing countries there is a large percentage (as we have seen) who become small-business owners for reasons of survival and unemployment. If this does not have far-reaching consequences on success, it means that policy mak-ers do not have to be concerned about the motives for starting a busi-ness. While it is plausible that the original motivation to start a company leads to different strategies at first (e.g., people with a push motivation shying away from additional investments to grow), this turns out not be important for the business at a later stage.

No difference is found for the different lines of business (in this case, only the two large groups, manufacturing and service/trade were com-pared). Thus, there is no reason to think that success is dependent upon the line of business in our sample.

Formal companies were more successful than firms in the informal sector. A likely explanation is that entrepreneurs enter the formal sec-tor when they have grown to a certain size. Thus, they already have shown a certain degree of success. Therefore, this is not surprising.

It is a common assumption that one indicator of how hard people work is how many hours they work. However, in our sample, there were no significant differences between owners who worked more than forty-four hours in comparison to owners who worked fewer hours. At first sight, this is surprising. However, on closer examination, we had the impression that people in badly run businesses were frequently sitting around idly. So both the employees and the employer were at work in terms of work time but were not really busy to make money.

It is a common assumption that one of the problems of microbusiness in Africa is lack of capital. From this perspective, it is a surprising result that whether a firm received a loan made no significant differ-ence on how successful it was. Both those who received a loan and those who did not had the same rate of highly successful entrepre-neurs. On the other hand, our data on working in a niche shows that economic data found in the West can be reproduced in Africa: Business owners who worked in a niche were more successful than those who did not work in a niche.

Our results also stand in contrast to predictions from human-capital theory (Bruederl et al., 1992). We found no significant differences between those entrepreneurs who had business-specific experiences—for example, in marketing, accountancy, management, and other skills—and those who had no experiences of this kind. Similarly, there were no significant differences between those who had some training for working as a business owner and those who did not. Possibly, those who did not receive training did not need the training so much. Similarly, the leadership-experience variable also did not show a significant difference on success. People who used to be a manager or director in a previous occupation were not more successful than people who had no experience as manager or director. However, there was at least one aspect of human capital that showed significant findings: the variable of organization of knowledge. People who had a good organization of knowledge (they were able to explain their ideas in a sensible, logical way), were more likely to be successful than owners who had difficulties presenting their knowledge in an organized fashion.

It should be noted that some of our results differ from the Zambian study by Parker (1996), which supports human-capital theory. In that study, those Zambian entrepreneurs who brought business experience to their current activity, either as farmers or civil servants, showed higher business profits than those with no prior experience. Entrepreneurs who finished the upper secondary school or attended the university had higher hourly business profits than entrepreneurs who had less years of education. One obvious explanation is that the study by Parker had more participants than our study and, therefore, small relationships with success became statistically significant in comparison to our study, which showed significant differences only when there were large (and practically important) relationships.

DESCRIPTIVE RESULTS ON PSYCHOLOGICAL STRATEGIES

The Zambian study was particularly concerned with psychological characteristics of strategy use, development, and leadership (for its theoretical base, see Chapter 1). In the area of leadership, we expected, along with Hofstede (1980), a large power distance between bosses and their employees. However, our results on the entrepreneurs gave no evidence for a large power difference. The results are presented in Table 2.2. The interviewers coded each answer of the business owners into a 5-point answer scale; thus, the interviewers used their knowledge and training and the detailed interviews with the entrepreneurs

Table 2.2
Descriptive Results of Psychological Factors, Zambia (Percentages)

Strategy variables	Low	Middle	High
Toward employees			
- Employee discipline	39	23	38
- Employees encouraged to take initiative	39	12	49
- Systematic approach to motivating employees	20	34	46
- Extent of training for employees	35	30	35
Checking			
- Business	5	-	95
- Employees	42	20	38
- Customers	31	16	53
- Finance	20	15	65
- Products	18	26	56
Marketing			
- Extent of analysis of demand for product	39	26	35
- Advertising	68	-	32
Goals and strategies			
- Business plan	67	-	33
- Operational targets	22	-	78
- Concreteness of goals and description	53	37	10
- Realistic goals	47	45	8
- Action towards the goal in the past	77	2	21
- Complete planning	86	12	2
- Critical point	96	4	0
- Reactive	73	25	2
- Opportunism	54	35	11
Entrepreneurial orientation			
- General	75	23	2
- Autonomy	8	20	72
- Competitive agressiveness	50	30	20
- Risk taking	78	14	8
- Innovation	88	12	0
Success	39	24	36

to make, for example, a judgment on how strong the owners emphasized employee discipline. We combined the 5-point answer scale into
three categories. The first entry in Table 2.2 shows that 39 percent were
not concerned with enforcing discipline among the employees; thus,
they were not frequently watching the employees, did not set specific
rules, or did not develop control systems. Nearly one-half the sample
of entrepreneurs with one or more employees encouraged the employees to take initiative. One would have expected both of these percentages to be lower in a high power distance culture. In addition, most
employers had a systematic approach to motivate employees. They
organized meetings on a regular basis and let their employees partici-

pate in decision making. Approximately one-third of the sample offered their employees on-the-job or even external training.

In order to lead a company, the owner needs to know what is happening on a day-to-day basis. He or she can do this by asking for the opinion of customers, by checking what the employees do, and by bookkeeping (all these are summarized under the rubric "checking"). To get information about the extent of checking, we asked the respondents to indicate the level of checking in general, on employees, customers, finance, and products. Five percent of the entrepreneurs did not check anything. Thirty-eight percent did a lot of checking on their employees. Checking on customers, finance, and products was carried out by the majority of our sample. Thirty-five percent had intensively analyzed the demand for the product before starting the enterprise. Most of them knew the demand situation quite well, because they had been working in the same line of business before; others observed and asked people and other entrepreneurs to find out whether there was adequate demand for their products.

Marketing issues are important and often difficult for entrepreneurs in Zambia. However, a relatively high percentage of the entrepreneurs (32%) used advertising. Advertising was mainly done via newspapers or signs outside the shop. Before starting the business, only a third of the entrepreneurs wrote up a business plan. Once started, most people (78%) developed concrete goals (operational targets) for the coming period. Among the operational targets often mentioned were to get more customers or to increase stock so that one could immediately satisfy customers' demands. While these were clear goals, the ways toward these goals were not usually so well-developed. Most entrepreneurs had difficulties indicating specifically how to reach their goals. Psychological characteristics of goals and strategies were ascertained by asking open questions. After these open questions, we would prompt, "Tell us more about it," "how did you go about it?" and so on. The answers were judged on how much planning the strategy entailed, how concretely the goals were described, and how realistic they were. It is important to differentiate goals from wishes and dreams. One way to do that is to ask whether people actually had done something to reach their goal in the past.

Unfortunately, only 10 percent were very concrete in defining their goals. Only 8 percent presented highly realistic goals to the interviewers. Obviously, a difficult judgment had to be made by the interviewers to determine whether something was realistic or not. Nevertheless, one can often recognize quite well whether people are talking about goals that are achievable or not (e.g., somebody who just has one table on the street presents the goal that he will move into the city and open up a big posh shop there). To find out whether people were pursuing goals actively, we asked what they had done to reach similar goals in the past. Twenty-one percent were able to give a good description of such steps taken, 77 percent had difficulty explaining actions toward their goals in the past.

The use of prompts also gave us some knowledge of the plans and strategies used by the entrepreneurs to achieve their goals. As described in Chapter 1, planning implies that one has a set of rules for how to get to the goal; it leads to a clear intention to actually implement one's goals. Psychological characteristics of the strategies were divided into four categories. Complete planning indicates a full and detailed plan; critical point planning means that planning is restricted to one important or critical area only. Complete and critical point planning both imply a certain amount of planning. There are also two strategies that do not require planning in detail: reactive and opportunistic strategies. These two strategies are differentiated by the level of proactivity. A reactive strategy implies no planning and no proactivity. Thus, a reactive strategy is characterized by people reacting to environmental demands rather than being able to influence the environment. The opportunistic strategy is proactive; an opportunist is constantly actively searching to take advantage of chances that present themselves. However, it is not a planning strategy because opportunities are exploited whenever they arise. The percentages in Table 2.2 indicate that Zambian entrepreneurs were not planning a lot. Eighty-six percent scored low on complete planning and only 4 percent were using a high degree of critical point strategy. The reactive strategy was used by more than one-quarter of the entrepreneurs, either to a very high or middle degree (the reactive strategy turned out to lead to failure; more on this later). Eleven percent were highly opportunistic.

Another aspect of strategy is the orientation of the owner (see Chapter 1). Entrepreneurial orientations are related to success. We followed Lumpkin and Dess (1996), who defined entrepreneurial orientation to contain autonomy, competitive aggressiveness, innovation, and risk taking (as described in Chapter 1, we did not include proactivity because we assume that it belongs to psychological process characteristics and not to orientation). The urge to work independently from others and without someone who sets the rules implies autonomy. Despite the relatively high number of people who were forced to start to earn a living as owner of a microbusiness, most Zambian entrepreneurs were highly autonomous (72%) and would not sell their company even if they could continue to work in their firm as a well-paid manager.

Competitive aggressiveness is moderately present in the sample of Zambian entrepreneurs: Half the entrepreneurs were not competitive at all and half of the sample was moderately to highly competitive. Since entrepreneurship does not have a long tradition in Zambia, this is not surprising. An example is one of the complexes for small-scale entrepreneurs: Many spare-part dealers were gathered in the same alley and each dealer had a small collection of spare parts. If a customer asked for a certain part that one businessperson did not have, he or she would usually direct the customer to another dealer in the alley. In a highly competitive society, this businessperson would probably have suggested to the customer that he or she would get it and would have then sold it to the customer at a higher price than he or she would have had to pay. Africa, in general, and Zambia show a high level of collectivism (Hofstede, 1980), which indicates that individuals form strong and close groups who provide lifelong protection in return for loyalty. This dimension works very well for a state-run economy, but leads to difficulties when a certain level of competitive aggressiveness is necessary to build up a business.

Risk taking was defined as borrowing money and venturing into the unknown. To borrow money as a small-scale entrepreneur is almost impossible because of lack of collateral and high interest rates. Risks are taken only by a very small minority among the Zambian entrepreneurs: Only 8 percent take high risks and only 14 percent take moderate risks. This is not surprising given the extremely negative consequences if risk taking does not work out.

Another aspect of entrepreneurial orientation is innovation, measured by whether people offer something new to customers (both in terms of a new product and the way of selling the product). Again, it was a difficult judgment for the interviewers to make and they may have been too conservative on some accounts. Nevertheless, none of the entrepreneurs was judged to be highly innovative, and only a minority of 12 percent were judged to be moderately innovative. The lack of innovation within the small-scale sector may be attributable to the fact that many entrepreneurs see a certain kind of business as profitable and try to emulate this. An example of a highly innovative entrepreneur (interviewed during the pilot study and therefore not included in the results presented here) is a man who made simple ovens with high heat efficiency from burning wood suitable in rural areas without electricity. An entrepreneur who was judged to be moderately innovative in marketing made leather shoes and sold them not only in shops but also at the street markets to gain more customers (to increase sales). He argued that many Zambians like to shop in the markets because they perceive them as cheaper and can bargain for a lower price there.

RELATIONSHIPS BETWEEN PSYCHOLOGICAL STRATEGY AND BUSINESS SUCCESS

Three aspects of strategy stand in the foreground: How one behaves toward employees, how one plans or is proactive toward one's business, and entrepreneurial orientation (see Chapter 1). These issues are presented in Figure 2.2, which is organized in the same way as Figure

Figure 2.2
Strategy Variables in Relation to Success, Zambia

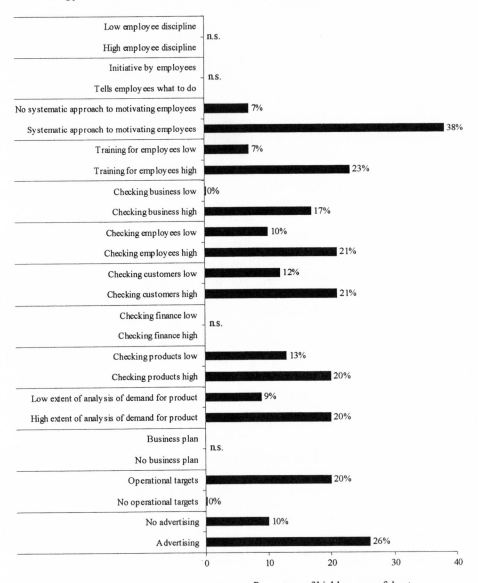

Low employee discipline
High employee discipline — n.s.

Initiative by employees
Tells employees what to do — n.s.

No systematic approach to motivating employees — 7%
Systematic approach to motivating employees — 38%

Training for employees low — 7%
Training for employees high — 23%

Checking business low — 0%
Checking business high — 17%

Checking employees low — 10%
Checking employees high — 21%

Checking customers low — 12%
Checking customers high — 21%

Checking finance low
Checking finance high — n.s.

Checking products low — 13%
Checking products high — 20%

Low extent of analysis of demand for product — 9%
High extent of analysis of demand for product — 20%

Business plan
No business plan — n.s.

Operational targets — 20%
No operational targets — 0%

No advertising — 10%
Advertising — 26%

Percentage of highly successful entrepreneurs

2.1. It is obvious from a first glance at this table that there are many more significant findings than in Figure 2.1, which leads us to the first tentative conclusion that psychological factors may be more important than sociodemographic ones.

Figure 2.2 (*continued*)

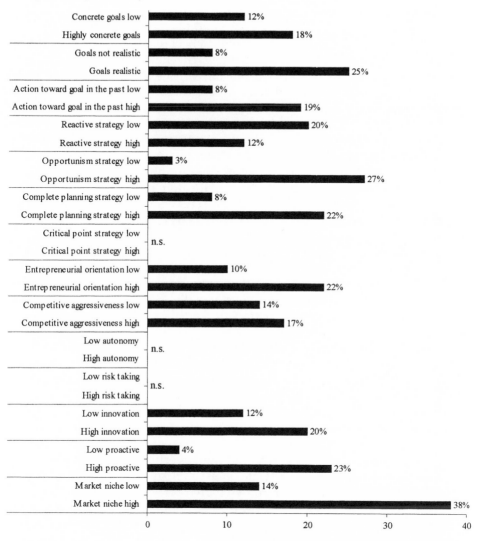

Percentage of highly successful entrepreneurs

The way the entrepreneurs managed their employees was partly related to success. While disciplining employees and encouraging initiative in the employees produced no differences in success, the systematic approach to motivation did. Those who had a systematic approach to motivating their employees and those who offered training facilities were more often highly successful than entrepreneurs who did not have a systematic approach to motivation and did not train their employees.

Checking was by and large positive. Of those entrepreneurs who checked their business (we used an overall checking index for this), 17 percent were highly successful compared to 0 percent in the group of entrepreneurs who were not thoroughly checking their business. Similarly, the subunits of checking, namely, checking products, employees, and customers, also produced differences in success. The only checking item that did not make a difference for success was, surprisingly, checking finance. Checking means that people pay close attention to the business processes and are, therefore, "on top" of things. They know their problems well and are, therefore, able to deal with problems more quickly than firm owners who are often absent and who do not attempt to get to know everything about the business. Another form of checking is to analyze the demand for the product or service before one starts one's business. This again produced relationships with success. Entrepreneurs who analyzed the demand for the product or service before they started their business were more likely to be highly successful (20%) than entrepreneurs who did not do this analysis before their start-up (9%).

Whether such an analysis is then translated into a business plan does not matter much. Success was equally high in those who had developed a business plan at start-up and those who did not (there was not a significant relationship here). This does not mean that planning is useless, because developing a clear idea of one's business targets for the next year was related to success. Of the entrepreneurs who had operational targets for the coming year, 20 percent were highly successful in contrast to those who had no operational target: None of these were in the group of highly successful entrepreneurs.

Business owners who were actively advertising for their company with billboards or advertisements in the newspaper, for example, were more successful than those who did not advertise for the company.

In the following we concentrate on psychological process characteristics of strategies. As described, we scored how entrepreneurs developed and used strategies and how they developed goals. We start with the goals in Figure 2.2. All three relevant variables—concreteness, reality orientation, and action toward the goal in the past—had a positive relationship with success. People who explained their goals in a concrete and realistic way were more successful than people who were vague and unclear about their goals and how to reach them. When people had already done things to reach their goals, they were more frequently in the group of highly successful entrepreneurs than those who had not yet done anything to reach their goals.

As expected, we found that a high reactive strategy was related to failure. Business owners who mainly reacted to what other people told them to do or what became obvious in a certain environment were clearly less successful (12%) than people who did not use such a reactive strategy (20%). Problems of the reactive approach are that one does not clearly define a goal, one is not proactive and does not check for problems far in advance, and one does not scan the environment for opportunities or develop plans for how to accomplish one's goals. One is simply reacting to environmental demands. For example, a reactive tailor in our study who made skirts and suits was not aware of the competition of the second-hand market (called *Salaula*, where second-hand clothes donated from rich countries are sold) until he was directly confronted with the problem. He then suddenly felt threatened by the *Salaula* market; by then it was too late to develop an effective counterstrategy (e.g., to work a niche market). Others who had prepared for the problems had already developed knowledge and skills in alternative markets when the problem became acute. Case 1 gives a detailed description of an entrepreneur who used a reactive strategy in running a business.

Twenty-seven percent of Zambian entrepreneurs who used an opportunistic strategy were highly successful, compared to only 3 percent of the people who did not use an opportunistic strategy. An opportunistic tailor, for example, constantly changed his products in accordance with events in his surroundings, like changing weather or a football match. At the time Zambia participated in the Soccer World Championships, he made garments in the colors of the national soccer team. One summer he noticed a lot of people wearing imported T-shirts from South Africa and he decided to manufacture these types of T-shirts and sell them at a lower price. An opportunistic strategy is stated to be advantageous in a highly uncertain environment; a potentially negative effect is that one may lose sight of what is really important if one constantly searches for opportunities (Frese, van Gelderen, & Ombach, in press). A description of an opportunistic entrepreneur is given in Case 2.

Owners who used the critical point strategy were not more likely to be highly successful than people who did not use this strategy. In critical point planning, one focuses on one important factor which is planned in detail.

Using a planning strategy had a positive effect on the level of success. Twenty-two percent of the owners who used this strategy were highly successful, compared to 8 percent of those who did not use this strategy. While this strategy was clearly successful, it was not frequently used, perhaps because it requires a comprehensive and good intellectual representation of the work process, and a longer time frame to plan ahead (Frese & Zapf, 1994). An example is a tailor who visited factories and schools as part of her marketing strategy to attain orders for uniforms. She took examples to show her work and changed her style of uniforms every year. An entrepreneur who had a business in repairing radios and selling radio spare parts told us about a well-developed and detailed plan to start a school that teaches how to repair electrical machines. Case 3 gives a description of an entrepreneur who used the planning strategy in running his business.

Another aspect of strategy is entrepreneurial orientation. As expected, people who scored high on the orientation strategy were more frequently highly successful (22%) than people who did not use entrepreneurial orientation (10%). Three of the five traditional aspects of entrepreneurial orientation were significantly related to success: competitive aggressiveness, innovation, and proactivity (remember, however, that we think proactivity to be conceptually distinct from entrepreneurial orientation).

CASE DESCRIPTIONS

Case 1: A Reactive Entrepreneur

Mary Mbele (name changed by the authors) started a tailoring business with her husband in 1994. The enterprise was situated in a big complex near the main market of Lusaka. In this complex, around seventy tailoring enterprises were situated. Mary's business fabricated clothes for women, men, and children on customer order. Before starting her business, Mary had worked for somebody else's tailor shop for eight years, where she learned her tailoring skills. Otherwise she did not know a lot about entrepreneurship (particularly not about marketing or accounting). Her reason to start the firm was to become her own boss and to be independent. She liked the idea that customers would come straight to her instead of to another shop.

The business location was out of the way in a little dark corner of the complex. There were three people present in the business, including Mary. During the interview, her husband was busy sewing a suit, while their only employee was gazing into the room. There were three sewing machines, each on a little table with piles of cloth on the floor next to it. Mary explained that business was not doing well. Her profit, the number of customers, and the turnover had decreased by 80 percent during the last year. She did not get enough orders from customers to keep all three of them working. The employee was waiting for a customer to pass by and give her work. Mary did not produce any clothes without an order, because otherwise she could not be sure to get her investment back. The reason for the current situation was the development of a second-hand clothes market supported by Western donor organizations. The number of customers declined continuously.

It was much cheaper to buy Western clothes at the *Salaula* market than to buy cloth and give an order to a tailor to make a dress, for example.

The main problems for Mary were the competition through the *Salaula* market and the lack of capital. "The only way to survive is to give the product to the customers on credit." Besides giving her product on credit, she did not have any other strategies to keep her customers or to obtain new customers. She was not interested in advertising. "Customers come through friends or pass by," she commented. According to her opinion, she performed moderately well compared to other tailors in the complex. The difference between them and her was that she was able to provide better-quality products. "It is just the way we make them." The interviewer was much more skeptical about her success and judged her not to be successful.

Mary may have an escape route when her tailor business fails. She has plans to start a bottle store in one of the compounds of Lusaka. A friend of hers has such an enterprise and suggested Mary try a bottle shop as well.

Case 2: Using Opportunistic Strategy

Knerung Building Ltd., a construction business, was established in February 1992 as a limited company. Ben Rucha was the owner of the enterprise with two other active partners. The three had been managers in the manufacturing industry before. Ben, who was the one we interviewed, had been employed in the mining sector as stock controller for three years and had been Chief Buyer Deposits, handling purchases from 1986 until 1992. He had become unemployed in 1992, and decided to start a business. The first two years of entrepreneurship their main task was simply to survive; they were trading from their homes and the car was their office. For this kind of business they did not need a high amount of starting capital. After two years of trading they were able to rent a place in a complex and to start their construction business. The main reason for starting an enterprise in this line of business was their mutual experience in this field of work. "We just felt we could make it." They recruited customers by walking around and offering their services at whatever building site they saw. They checked the newspapers for assignments, visited customers from their previous jobs, and placed advertisements. At the time of the interview, one partner was in Livingstone to sign a roadwork contract. Though this client had responded to an advertisement, he had to be personally convinced. Besides recruiting new contracts, they maintained strong relations with existing customers. They made sure that quality was good by using good materials and by constantly checking on their work for mistakes. One specific problem they faced was that many assignments came from the government, for example, roadwork. The government did not pay on time; payments were sometimes withheld for over six months. They think that service is very important in their business: "You are better off serving five customers who are extremely happy and give you follow-up orders than serving ten customers whom you cannot give the attention they need."

Their workforce included at the time of the interview thirty-five full-time and sixty part-time employees. The sixty part-timers were not continuously employed, but were called in when, for example, roadwork required a lot of manual work. According to Ben there was a lot of competition in the manufacturing sector in Zambia and, therefore, it was wise to specialize, though he acknowledged the fact that it was risky business to specialize. During the last three years, the number of customers had increased by 60 percent, the turnover tripled, and their profit increased by 275 percent.

The most important business goal of Ben was to exist beyond the year 2000 and be seen as an example of good quality and service (he was talking about being a "trademark"). While he had long-term goals, he did not plan a lot on how they would get there. For the near future they were planning to expand by using new methods and modern technologies they had encountered in brochures from South Africa; for example, innovative roof-protection methods that required highly specialized technical skills to make the roof waterproof, or up-to-date air conditioning.

Case 3: A Planner

Venus Ungetsinge started a catering service in 1994 after various jobs in formal employment, including working as a food parasite controller for the health care section of the government. Because the job as parasite controller depended on crops that are season-bound, he decided to diversify into another line of business. Right after his secondary school, before he started working, he had enjoyed a two-year education in catering, which had been his hobby before.

Before starting the catering enterprise, he had made a plan in which he determined several goals for the business. He wanted to start a restaurant with a cooking area and he wanted to cater lunches and dinners for companies in town. He wanted the restaurant to offer a wide range of food which he had learned to prepare at school. He also wanted to offer a good service, and a nice environment for having dinner. To be able to reach these goals he provided on-the-job training twice a week for his employees, in which he taught them how to prepare the dishes and how to interact with the customers. He also used these meetings to discuss criticism and remarks from customers. "My employees have the most contact with the customers, they give me feedback." He offered his employees breakfast and lunch on their workdays. To keep control over the business, he had appointed a chief cook who also kept an eye on the business when Venus was out.

His marketing strategy at start-up made use of all the people he had gotten to know in his previous jobs and friends. He made personal contacts with them or sent them letters to introduce his new business. A few weeks later he tried to contact the people who had not reacted on his first contact. This procedure was repeated once every six months.

His long-term goal was to have a chic restaurant in the center of Lusaka with a wide variety of dishes on the menu. Venus's knowledge and specific goals were used to develop a detailed strategy which included marketing aspects, leadership, his skills, and issues related to accounting (planning strategy). He made a detailed plan of his expected costs and benefits and was aware of the risks he was taking. His success was high. The number of customers increased by 50 percent during the last three years, especially people who work in the city and order lunch. With the increase in customers, sales and profit also increased.

Case 4: An Entrepreneurially Oriented Entrepreneur

Steve Kuban started his steel fabrication business in 1990. Prior to 1990, he had served for twelve years as a general manager of construction. His reasons given for starting a company were to have more job satisfaction and to be able to execute his own ideas. The first half year he combined his business with his regular employment. His knowledge for this line of business came from education in engineering and the practical experience he had gained in his former job.

In 1990, business in steel fabrication was booming. There were many orders in his former job and he did not want to miss this chance for his own business. He wanted to use his knowledge in the engineering field in an innovative way. He wanted to make new designs and look for new and unmet markets instead of making the same machines every day.

To investigate unmet markets within the steel industry, he looked at all newspapers and other useful sources. With this information he made a draft of his new idea and produced a sample. He visited fairs and advertised in media to present his new products. His newest inventions were an oil machine and a water pump. Both products were made to suit the needs of customers in rural areas. The oil machine offered an easy way to separate oil from seeds. The water pump had a simple design and could easily be placed and fixed by the users themselves. In addition, he had new ideas in mind but had not yet worked them out in detail.

He had six full-time employees, four part-time employees, and two apprentices working in his company. The employees attended short training courses from a special institute, one at a time. To let them participate in business he "kept the challenge on them." He did not give them all details of the business but told them the big lines of his vision once in a while. His vision was to expose people to steel-fabrication technology. Besides working for his company, he also wanted to start a school on steel-fabrication technology. Steve's role as entrepreneur in the business was to "scoop up" new assignments and customers for his innovations.

Steve knew he still had a lot of catching up to do in comparison to his competitors, who had larger companies and were able to get cheaper and better materials from traders. His sales and profit had increased, although the number of customers had stayed the same during the last three years: He had sold more products to the same number of customers.

SUMMARY

In this chapter, we looked primarily at the function of orientation toward employees and psychological strategy process characteristics for success. Entrepreneurs who have a systematic approach toward motivating their employees were more successful. The systematic approach is also shown in the amount of checking. Those who kept a tight check on their business and who attempted to know in detail what was done in their business were by and large more successful. It helps to have operational targets and concrete and realistic goals. Whenever entrepreneurs had already done something in the past to achieve their goals, they showed a higher degree of success.

Strategy process characteristics were found to be highly related to success; this is true of complete planning, opportunistic, and low reactive strategies. Thus, people can either succeed by being very precise in their long-term planning or by looking out for opportunities (with little planning involved). These two positive strategies are different in Zambia than in the other countries studied in this book. Zambia has probably the toughest environment of the countries studied, as a sort of Manchester capitalism reigns with little effective business regulation. In this environment, it pays to either plan everything in great detail (and, thus, to think about back-up plans when things go wrong) or not to plan at all, but to scan the environment for opportunities. A medium form of planning—as in the case of critical point planning—was not related to success. Not planning and not being proactive, as in the case of a reactive strategy, led to business failures. Entrepreneurial orientation, particularly competitiveness and innovativeness, were positively related to success.

REFERENCES

Bruederl, J., Preisendoerfer, P., & Ziegler R. (1992). Survival chances of newly founded business organizations. *American Sociological Review, 57*, 227–242.

De Temmerman, E. (1997). *Afrika: Continent in beweging*. Antwerpen: Icarus.

Frese, M., van Gelderen, M., & Ombach, M. (in press). How to plan as a small-scale business owner: Psychological process characteristics of action strategies and success. *Journal of Small Business Management*.

Frese, M., & Zapf, D. (1994). Action as the core of work psychology: A German approach. In H. C. Triandis, M. D. Dunnette, & L. M. Hough (Eds.), *Handbook of industrial and organizational psychology* (2d ed., Vol. 4, pp. 271–340). Palo Alto: Consulting Psychologists Press.

Gray, K. R., Cooley, W., & Lutabingwa, J. (1997). Small-scale manufacturing in Kenya. *Journal of Small Business Management, 1*, 66–72.

Gray, K. R., Cooley, W., Lutabingwa, J., Mutai-Kaimenyi, B., & Oyugi, L. A. (1996). *Entrepreneurship in micro-enterprises: A strategic analysis of manufacturing industries in Kenya*. Lanham, MD: University Press of America.

Hofstede, G. (1980). *Culture's consequence: International differences in work-related values*. Newbury Park, CA: Sage.

International Labor Organization. (1972). *Employment, incomes and equality: A strategy for increasing productive employment in Kenya*. Geneva: Author.

Kiggundu, M. N. (1988). Africa. In R. Nath (Ed.), *Comparative management* (pp. 169–243). Cambridge: Balliger.

Lumpkin, G. T., & Dess, G. G. (1996). Clarifying the entrepreneurial orientation construct and linking it to performance. *Academy of Management Review, 21*, 135–172.

McIntyre, C. (1996). *Guide to Zambia*. London: Bradt.

McPherson, M. A. (1991, December). *Micro and small-scale enterprises in Zimbabwe: Results of a country-wide survey* (GEMINI Working Paper No. 25). Bethesda, MD: Growth and Equity through Microenterprise Investments and Institutions.

Mead, D. C., & Liedholm, C. (1998). The dynamics of micro and small enterprises in developing countries. *World Development, 26*, 61–74.

Parker, J. C. (1996). *Micro and small-scale enterprises in Zambia: Results of the 1996 nationwide survey*. Report submitted to Overseas Development Administration (ODA) by Graham Bannock and Partners, Ltd., London.

Posthumus, B. (1997). *Zambia; mensen, politiek, economie, cultuur*. Nijmegen: SSN.

United Nations Development Program. (1998). *Human development report 1998*. New York: Oxford University Press.

World Bank. (1997). *World development report 1997: The states in a changing world*. New York: Oxford University Press.

3

Sociodemographic Factors, Entrepreneurial Orientation, Personal Initiative, and Environmental Problems in Uganda

Sabine Koop, Tamara de Reu, and Michael Frese

This chapter will cover sociodemographic factors, entrepreneurial orientation, initiative, and other psychological factors that are supposed to contribute to entrepreneurial success. The study was carried out in Kampala, the major urban center and capital of Uganda. We shall first cover the theoretical concepts and then discuss the economic situation in Uganda. Then we shall present descriptive and analytical results.

ENTREPRENEURIAL ORIENTATION AND PERSONAL INITIATIVE

There are important practical implications if we find that there are relationships between entrepreneurial orientation and personal initiative (PI) and success. First, one can select those entrepreneurs who are most entrepreneurially oriented and show a high degree of initiative and support them with capital and advice. This is particularly useful if there is a high scarcity of capital in a country, as is true of most African countries. Second, one can train people to be more strongly entrepreneurially oriented and show more initiative. Third, one can critically examine school curricula, cultural stereotypes, and government policies and ascertain whether they support the development of entrepreneurial orientation and personal initiative.

Entrepreneurial Orientation

Entrepreneurship is the ability to seek opportunities and turn them to profitable businesses. A central predictor for becoming an entrepreneur and for being successful in it is entrepreneurial orientation (Lumpkin & Dess, 1996, p. 136). Lumpkin and Dess argue that entrepreneurial orientation consists of five dimensions: autonomy, innovativeness, risk taking, competitive aggressiveness, and proactiveness. Lumpkin and Dess (p. 140) describe autonomy as "the ability and the will to be self-directed in the pursuit of opportunities." An autonomous person acts independently and makes decisions in spite of constraints, for example, organizational rules or resource limitations. The second component, innovativeness, implies "to have ideas about new products, services, and technological processes." Lumpkin and Dess make a distinction between the concepts of product-market innovation and technological innovation, the first emphasizing product design, market research, and promotion and the second achieving competencies in the latest technologies and production methods. Risk taking is often divided into three types (Baird & Thomas, 1985): "venturing into the unknown," which means acting while being aware of uncertainties; "committing a relatively large portion of one's assets to the business"; and "borrowing heavily." The last two types of risks are related to finance. The fourth component of Lumpkin and Dess's concept of entrepreneurial orientation is competitive aggressiveness, which implies that one makes it difficult for competitors to enter the same market and attempts to outperform one's competitors in the marketplace.

A proactive person takes the initiative to actively exploit market opportunities. Thus, proactiveness and initiative are closely related. Our project has differentiated process characteristics of strategies from entrepreneurial orientation (see Chapter 1). Thus, we have a more differentiated picture of entrepreneurial strategies than the one used by Lumpkin and Dess (1996). One of our three dimensions is largely equivalent to Lumpkin and Dess's concept of entrepreneurial orientation. However, in our view, proactiveness does not belong to the orientations but is a process characteristic. Since proactiveness and initiative are conceptually the same, we operationalized proactiveness with a measure of personal initiative developed before (see the next section). In addition, we assume that there is a substantial correlation between proactiveness/initiative and entrepreneurial orientation.

In addition to these components of entrepreneurial orientation described by Lumpkin and Dess (1996) we added three aspects: Stability and learning orientation, achievement orientation, and personal integrity. Stability and learning orientation means that the entrepreneur does not become emotional and despondent when things go wrong, but rather develops an orientation to learn from such experiences. Since entrepreneurs have to act quickly in situations of high uncertainty, there is by definition a good chance to make mistakes. Learning from these mistakes and errors is particularly important to succeed in business (Hartley, 1997; Van Dyck, Frese, & Sonnentag, 1998). Achievement orientation was introduced by McClelland (1987; see also McClelland & Winter, 1971) and has been shown to be related both to economic development of nations as well as to small-scale entrepreneurs' success (Rauch & Frese, in press). People with high achievement orientation are attracted to challenging tasks, are motivated to do better at such tasks, take personal responsibility, and seek feedback on the quality of their work (McClelland, 1987). They attempt to do better every time. The last aspect, personal integrity, was emphasized by Locke (1997), who used the term "honesty." It means that the entrepreneur instills a sense of reliability and trust in his or her customers and suppliers which should, therefore, lead to higher success.

Personal Initiative

Personal initiative means that one is self-starting, active, and overcoming barriers; it is an important characteristic for successful entrepreneurs (Frese, Fay, Hilburger, Leng, & Tag, 1997). Personal initiative should help an entrepreneur to be ahead of his or her competitors. Further, the high-initiative entrepreneur acts as a role model for his or her employees. Personal initiative contributes to organizational effectiveness (Borman & Motowidlo, 1993). Initiative is goal directed and action oriented (Frese et al., 1997), and, therefore, closely linked to an active strategy. Initiative can be considered as a psychological variable behind entrepreneurial orientation. Whenever people decide to become entrepreneurs, they need to show the behavior described in the entrepreneurial orientation construct. However, behind this lies the concept of initiative. So, for example, autonomy is consistent with entrepreneurial orientation; personal initiative is needed to show autonomy because personal initiative assumes that one has to act oneself and cannot wait for others to do it. When people are innovative, they need to overcome many problems, which is a component of initiative. Innovation does not take the routine ways and, therefore, barriers will appear that need to be overcome. Risk taking does not imply that one frivolously risks losing money but that one takes the risk associated with a (new) course of action (this is also true of personal initiative). Similarly, a certain amount of stability is shown when one is active and changes the environment. Finally, achievement orientation is related to personal initiative, because achieving is the goal of personal initiative. Only competitive aggressiveness and personal integrity—both oriented toward the social environment—are not clearly related to personal initiative. Initiative can be the intervening mechanism (mediator) between entrepreneurial orientation and success. This implies that entrepreurial orientation leads to personal initiative—which, in turn, leads to success.

Personal initiative was measured in two ways. The first scale was operationalized by asking questions on putting new ideas into practice (e.g., with regard to customers or products). An overall judgement by the interviewers was based on the answers to these questions (Frese et al., 1997). The second scale used the measure of overcoming barriers reported in the literature (Frese et al., 1997), and asked the entrepreneurs to solve difficult problems. For each problem-solving response given, the interviewer presented a barrier (by saying that this solution does not work in this particular case). The score of an entrepreneur on this scale was a combination of the amount of barriers overcome and the activity in finding solutions. The two measures of personal initiative were significantly related with each other.

Environmental Factors

The environment of an organization contains technology, customers, competition, location, economic situation, politics, and climate (Mintzberg, 1983, p. 143). Mintzberg (p. 143) distinguished four environmental dimensions: stability versus dynamism, simplicity versus complexity, friendliness versus hostility, and integrated versus diversified markets. Dynamism is interpreted as unpredictability (Mintzberg, 1983); that is, the rate of change and innovation in an industry as well as the uncertainty or unpredictability of actions by competitors and customers (Miller & Friesen, 1983). Complexity is defined by the degree of sophisticated knowledge necessary to operate in a given environment. Covin and Slevin (1989) define a hostile environment as characterized by intense competition, complex business climate, and the lack of exploitable opportunities. The last of Mintzberg's dimensions—integrated versus diversified markets—was not used in this study because we assumed that the environment of microbusinesses in Africa did not vary on this dimension.

The environment is important for two reasons. First, it should have an influence on the strategies that entrepreneurs use (see the Giessen–Amsterdam Model of Entrepreneurial Success in Chapter 1). Second, the extent to which entrepreneurial orientation and personal initiative predict entrepreneurial success should be contingent on the business environment. This is also suggested by Lumpkin and Dess (1996). Entrepreneurs have to be more entrepreneurially oriented in a complex, dynamic, and hostile environment to be successful. In contrast, a simple, stable, and friendly environment does not make it necessary to show a high degree of entrepreneurial orientation. In our view, the environment should not have a direct influence on success because success is determined by the actions of the entrepreneur. Since actions are intimately related to strategies, the environmental influence on success should run via strategies (see Chapter 1 for more extensive reasoning).

THE SITUATION IN UGANDA

The population of Uganda consists of 21 million people and is growing with a rate of 3.1 percent per year. The average life expectancy is forty-three years for men and forty-four for women. The capital, Kampala, where we did our study, has 650,000 inhabitants. The GDP (Gross Domestic Product adjusted for purchasing power in U.S. dollars) was $1,483 per person in 1995 (United Nations Development Program, 1998). Uganda has one of the highest economic growth rates in Africa, with a growth rate of 7.1 percent in 1995 (Comesa, 1999). The inflation rate between 1993 and 1997 was 5.2 percent per year. The agricultural sector is the most important one for the Ugandan economy; almost 86 percent of the population is working in this sector (Broere, 1994). This sector produces coffee, tea, cotton, poultry, and so on, and provides more than 60 percent of GDP.

The micro- and small-scale enterprise sector in Uganda is characterized by a wide-ranging number of relatively small manufacturing and service-oriented enterprises, employing about 70 percent of the nonfarming labor force. It produces 80 percent of the manufactured output and contributes 20 percent to the total GDP of Uganda (Kula, Robinson, Ritchie, & Ondeng, 1995).

SAMPLE

We concentrated on those entrepreneurs who had at least one and at most fifty employees, regardless of whether the employees came from inside or outside the family. The business had to exist for at least a year. The sample was drawn with a "random walk procedure," in which we asked the owners of small shops, found all over Kampala, to participate. Almost half of our sample was selected in this way. In certain areas of Kampala, certain industries could be found. The interviewers tried to get a cross section, including entrepreneurs from different industries; for example, manufacturing and services. Approximately two out of three entrepreneurs declined to participate in the study. We did not keep precise data on rejections because a large group did not say directly that they were not willing to participate, but made one or several appointments that were later not kept (about half of the people given appointments honored them). In other cases, we could not be sure whether or not an owner was present or whether in fact the owner was there but did not want to cooperate (and just said that the owner was absent). However, a participation rate of approximately 33 percent is not bad for this kind of study.

The second part of the sample (forty-two entrepreneurs) was selected in conjunction with the Centenary Rural Development Bank. This bank supported small-scale entrepreneurs financially. Two account managers introduced their customers to us, and we made an appointment with them after explaining that the research was not related to the bank. Of these, only three declined to participate. We checked whether the two samples came from the same population and found that they were similar enough to be combined into one sample.

The combined sample comprised one-hundred people, with sixty males and forty females. Table 3.1 describes the sample. It shows that most of the firms in the sample were quite young. The part of the sample that was only one year in business was as big as 23 percent, and only 36 percent of the sample had been in business more than five years. The trading sector was the largest sector. Other businesses consisted of tailors, manufacturers, and craftspeople. In terms of size, most firms can be categorized as belonging to the microbusiness sector, with less than ten employees; 16 percent of the entrepreneurs had one employee, 41 percent had between two and five employees, 24 percent between six and ten, and 19 percent of the sample had between eleven and fifty employees. Only 35 percent had family members employed in their business; thus, most firms had no family-member employees. Before they started their business, most people worked as normal employees. However, there was a large percentage of former managers in this sample. The group who started firms because of being unemployed was very small (1%). The biggest group (43%) started businesses because they wanted to earn money. However, a second important reason mentioned was that they wanted to be their own bosses. In keeping with most other microbusinesses, most firms began with very little starting capital. The majority had less than $1,000 when they started the company. Only 2 percent were above $5,000. Most firms did not get a loan. This sample, however, was different from other samples in this book, as 16 percent of them received a loan from a bank.

We asked about their biggest problems, and the most important one was that there was not enough capital at their disposal (finance, 44%); another much less important problem was location. Their most important goal was to make a profit (42%); however only 31 percent of the entrepreneurs focussed only on business. The human capital of

Table 3.1
Sample Descriptions, Uganda

Characteristic	Percentage	Characteristic	Percentage
Sex		- Bank loan	16
- Male	60	- Loan from other	27
- Female	40	- No loan	57
Age of business		**Problems**	
- 1 year	23	- Finance	44
- 2-5 years	41	- Equipment	4
- 6-10 years	31	- Location	10
- Older than 10 Years	5	- Competition	5
Line of business		- Other	34
- Trade	65	**Goals**	
- Service	21	- Make profit	42
- Other	14	- Other	58
Number of employees		**Focus**	
- 1	16	- On business	31
- 2-5	41	- On other activities	69
- 6-10	24	**Leadership experience**	
- 11-50	19	- Yes	49
Family members as employees		- No	51
- Yes	35	**Years of education of the owner**	
- No	65	- 1-6	1
Activities before start-up		- 7-10	5
- Unemployed	1	- 11-13	27
- Worker	42	- Above 13	67
- Manager	36	**Entrepreneurs in family**	
- Housewife	5	- Yes	38
- Other	16	- No	62
Reason for entrepreneurship			
- Money	43		
- Being own boss	27		
- Family pressure	4		
- Prestige	2		
- Other	23		
Starting capital in US $			
- Below 1000	57		
- 1001-5000	19		
- Above 5000	2		

entrepreneurs is often measured in the time that people had to gain experience in the line of business and in management. A large percentage (nearly half of the sample, 49%) had some kind of leadership experience before they started the company. Education was high in this group, with most of them going beyond high school education. A large percentage also received some rudimentary training from role models in their families who had their own firm (38%). In contrast to the other studies in this book, only two of the entrepreneurs were informal (i.e., they did not pay taxes). This was the case because people who just had a stall to sell things on the street were excluded. However, Uganda may also have a lower rate of informal-sector participants than the other African countries studied in this book.

The interview took approximately one and a half hours and consisted of general questions about the entrepreneur, entrepreneurial orientation, and the environment in which the entrepreneur was doing business. The interviewers scored the psychological variables from 1 to 5 on the basis of answers by the entrepreneurs. To determine whether an entrepreneur was successful in doing business, the interviewers asked the entrepreneurs about the increase or decrease in the number of customers, in the sales, and in profits during the last year. A score of 4 or 5 indicated a successful business.

DESCRIPTIVE RESULTS OF THE PSYCHOLOGICAL FACTORS IN THIS STUDY

Table 3.2 describes the major psychological variables in this study. The entrepreneurial orientation variables were measured by first finding out which business areas were most important for our interviewees (e.g., suppliers, customers, products, competitors). Then we asked separate questions on each entrepreneurial orientation which we had developed for all important business issues. For example, a question about innovativeness in the area of competitors was asked in this way: "Did you ever do something special about your competitiors, for example a special way to be a step ahead of them?" Another question—on competitive aggressiveness—was, "Do you give your competitors hints about a good product [reversed scoring]?" After the interview, the interviewers rated every aspect of entrepreneurial orientation (e.g., innovativeness or competitive aggressiveness) of an individual. The second rater worked from the written protocols of the interviews. These interviewer judgments were not always easy to make. The reader can easily imagine that there is a certain error in rating people's answers to a question on innovativeness (e.g., "Do you sometimes do something special for your customers?"). However, in each case, there were two independent raters of the material and they usually agreed quite well.

We used a statistical technique (factor analysis) to find out whether all these orientations were part of a general approach, called "entrepreneurial orientation." This was the case, except for autonomy and stability, which produced a separate factor. The scores ranged from 1 to 5. Table 3.2 shows the low (adding the scores of 1 and 2), the middle (3) and the high scores (4 and 5) of all the entrepreneurial orientation

Table 3.2
Descriptive Results of Psychological Factors, Uganda (Percentages)

	Low	Middle	High
Strategy			
- Entrepreneurial orientation (summary score)	16	47	36
- Autonomy	10	40	49
- Innovativeness	39	31	29
- Risk taking	38	51	10
- Competitive aggressiveness	35	34	30
- Stability	16	39	44
- Learning orientation	14	29	56
- Achievement orientation	14	36	49
- Personal integrity	6	29	65
Personal initiative			
- Initiative	41	37	21
- Overcoming barriers	42	40	7
- Encouraging employees to take initiative	43	-	51
Environment			
- Complexity	26	31	42
- Hostility	39	14	46
- Dynamism	21	29	49
Success	15	26	58

factors. The first entry in Table 3.2 is the entrepreneurial orientation summary scale of innovativeness, risk taking, competitive aggressiveness, learning orientation, achievement orientation, and personal integrity. It shows that most of the people were in the middle category. Thus, there is room for improvement for the Ugandan entrepreneurs: It would be good if the majority of them had a high entrepreneurial orientation. A look at each of the orientations separately reinforces this impression. Only in two aspects of entrepreneurial orientation (learning orientation and personal integrity) was the absolute majority in the high category. In all other aspects the majority was in the low or middle range in entrepreneurial orientation. Most prominently, risk taking, competitive aggressiveness, and innovativeness were low in Ugandan business owners. It would help to increase these orientations through training, because, as we will show later, they contribute to success.

Personal initiative was measured in three ways: The first two measures referred to the personal initiative shown by the entrepreneur him- or herself. The third measure referred to whether the entrepreneur encouraged and fostered his or her employees to take personal initiative. The first measure—initiative—was measured in the same way as the orientations. For this reason, there was also a high relationship between orientations and personal initiative. Most owners showed a low or medium degree of personal initiative on this measure.

The same was also true of overcoming barriers, the second measure of entrepreneurs' personal initiative. It was ascertained by presenting problems to be solved by the entrepreneurs. Every time a solution was given, the interviewer presented a barrier by telling the interviewee that their solution did not work in this given case and asked the entrepreneur to find another solution. The score was a combination of the number of barriers overcome and the degree to which these solutions implied an active orientation. This measures a phenomenon that happens quite frequently in practice: One attempts to do something and gives up when problems appear. Many participants in Uganda had difficulties finding ideas to overcome barriers—only 7 percent were in the highest category. The results on both measures of personal initiative strongly suggest that it would pay to produce training courses in which personal initiative is developed in Uganda (again, we shall show a bit later that personal initiative is related to success).

Encouraging employee's initiative was a dichotomous yes/no item and shows that about half of the entrepreneurs helped their employees to increase their personal initiative and about half did not.

The business environment in Uganda is tough, and that is also shown by the data in Table 3.2: Most owners perceived the business environment to be complex (not easy to understand what is going on), hostile (difficult to get resources and to sell), and dynamic (unpredictable and changeable). Despite these limitations, which stem from low initiative and a harsh business environment and an only medium entrepreneurial orientation, the Ugandan firm owners were quite successful. More than half of them were judged to be successful by the interviewers. The success measure was a careful summary of consideration of all the factors that makes an entrepreneur successful; for example, high sales, increase of customers and profits, increase of number of employees, good workplace, and achieving one's goals with one's business (see Chapter 8).

SOCIODEMOGRAPHIC FACTORS AND ENTREPRENEURIAL SUCCESS

The following discussion is based on the results presented in Figure 3.1, which has to be read as follows. We always looked at those owners who were particularly successful (see Chapter 8). There are only two cases in which there are significant relationships with success and we only present the bar graphs for the significant relationships in the table (remember, the calculations on the significance were done with a different statistical procedure; see Chapter 8). The first significant entry is the relationship of the numbers of employees with success. Thus, among the employers with only one employee, 19 percent were highly successful. This percentage was much higher for those entrepreneurs who had six to ten or eleven to fifty employees.

There is no relationship of gender with success. Surprisingly, the age of the company makes no difference in whether the firm is successful. This speaks against the "liability of newness" discussed in Chapter 1. Apparently, the liability of newness problem does not exist in a new market such as Uganda, which opened up for business relatively recently. Another surprising result is the fact that different lines of business did not influence success. Trade, service, and other showed about the same percentage of highly successful entrepreneurs. This is in contrast to some of the results reported by Mead and Liedholm (1998), who argued that there are certain lines of business that are inherently less successful than others (e.g., garment industry being less successful than building industry). However, note that our sample was much smaller than theirs and, therefore, our study does not focus on small differences but only on large ones. The latter are, however, practically more important.

An obvious result appears for large versus small firms. Those firms with only one employee have a low percentage (19%) of successful entrepreneurs. In contrast, those with a high number of employees show a larger percentage of highly successful entrepreneurs. This confirms that our measure of success is meaningful. The interviewers judged the successfulness of a firm partly on the basis of whether it employed many people and whether there was an increase in employment. The difference of the second category (two to five employees) and the other categories should not be taken too seriously, because there is in principle a linear increase of success with the number of employees.

There are many within the developing-aid community who argue that tradition forces African entrepreneurs to employ family members who are not well qualified, reducing the chances to be successful. The results of this study show that this belief may be based on a myth. There are no differences in successfulness of those who employed family members and those who did not. Another issue frequently discussed by those who work with microenterprises is whether people become microbusiness owners only because there are no other jobs available and that, therefore, subsistence motives prevail. This is not correct, as we have already seen in Table 3.1, which showed that there was a large group of people who started their business for other reasons than subsistence (remember, however, that we only took owners into our sample

Figure 3.1
Sociodemographic Factors and Success, Uganda

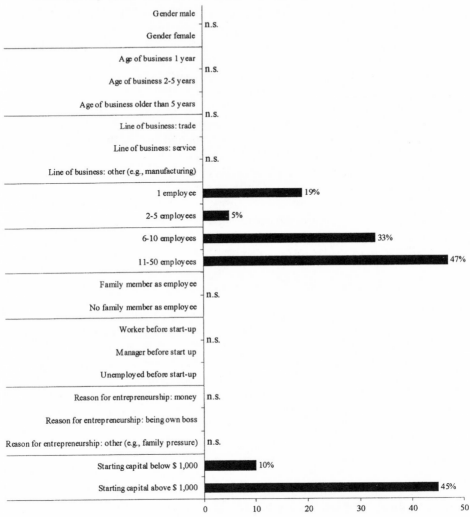

Percentage of highly successful entrepreneurs

who have at least one employee). Figure 3.1 shows, in addition, that it does not matter where people came from, whether they had worked as blue or white collar workers, as managers, or started their business because they would have been unemployed otherwise. Similarly, it did not matter whether money, being own boss, or other motives (e.g., family pressure) led to the start-up decision. These two findings are encouraging, because they mean that one is not forever restricted by

Figure 3.1 (*continued*)

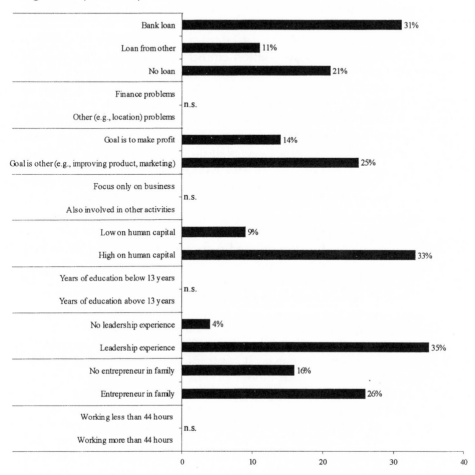

Percentage of highly successful entrepreneurs

one's motives and reasons at the start of one's entrepreneurial career, but that it is much more important to look at the concrete behavior that people show.

The amount of starting capital made a difference in success. Bigger firms in the beginning of their career are more successful later. Since one part of our sample had bank loans (sixteen people), we could examine the relationship to success. Indeed, those who received a bank loan were successful (44%). This contrasts clearly with those who did not get a bank loan or received it from other sources. A bank loan is granted only on the basis of a good business plan and the conviction by experts that this is a viable business. Apparently, this bank made good decisions (the Centenary Rural Development Bank, which finances microenterprises). On the other hand, securing starting capital from a bank also gives people a certain head start, so securing a loan may be one cause for the success later on. A loan, however, can be a mixed blessing in a high-inflation country (the interest rate was almost 80% at the time of our research); a loan may help to expand the business on the one hand, but will lead to an enormous amount of expenditures on the other hand.

Almost half of the sample told us that they had financial problems; other problems were most frequently related to finding a good business location and being able to get well-qualified employees (see Table 3.1). However, it did not matter for success which problems were perceived to be in the foreground. An additional issue that is related to finances is that in some African countries (e.g., Zambia; see Chapter 2) entrepreneurs are forced to give credit to their customers. In contrast to these countries, the Ugandan entrepreneurs did not give credit. The financial problems they mentioned focussed on the difficulty of getting a loan and on high tax rates.

While making profit is important for most entrepreneurs, only 14 percent of those who were oriented to making profit were highly successful. This stands in high contrast to a rate of 25 percent of those who had other goals, like improving their products or their marketing, or expanding their business. This difference was significant, but it was not really large; however, it contradicts some popular opinions that only those with a clear money orientation can be successful.

A large number of the entrepreneurs mentioned that they did not want to be dependent on only one source of income and, therefore, they cultivated other side jobs to earn some money (they were involved in other activities). These other activities were, for example, growing crops or keeping cattle. However, there was no relationship between this variable and being successful.

Human capital is a summary index of kind and years of education and leadership experience. Those high on human capital were successful much more frequently (33% were highly successful) than those low on human capital (9% were highly successful). This replicates other findings from other countries (see Chapter 1). However, education is not the most important factor as it is not significantly related to success. Another human-capital factor, leadership experience, is more relevant. Of those who had no leadership experience at all, 4 percent were very successful, in contrast to 35 percent in the group of entrepreneurs with leadership experience. Some entrepreneurship researchers suggested that an indirect way in which experiences get transmitted is by family education on entrepreneurship. This happens only when there are other entrepreneurs in the family. They often function as a good model of entrepreneurship and can help the future entrepreneur to develop skills and knowledge to be successful. This expectation proved to be right. Those with a entrepreneur as a family member were more successful than those without such a family member.

It is also interesting to look at differences in the number of working hours of entrepreneurs and their success. In this study, no significant relationship between success and the number of work hours was found.

PSYCHOLOGICAL FACTORS AND
ENTREPRENEURIAL SUCCESS

The relationship between entrepreneurial orientation and success was high and positive, as shown in Figure 3.2. In this overall measure, all aspects of entrepreneurial orientation were summed. Of those owners who had a low entrepreneurial orientation, only 12 percent were very successful, as compared to 28 percent in the group of entrepreneurs with a high degree of entrepreneurial orientation. All of this strengthens the suggestion that entrepreneurial orientation is of paramount importance for entrepreneurial success.

Most of the aspects of entrepreneurial orientation—innovativeness, risk taking, competitive aggressiveness, learning orientation, achievement orientation, and personal integrity—were positively related to the success of an entrepreneur. The two most important factors were achievement orientation (10% were very successful entrepreneurs in the low achievement-oriented group and 30% in the high achievement-oriented group) and competitive aggressiveness (9% versus 29%). When one takes these two variables together and looks at those entrepreneurs who are high on achievement orientation and on competitive aggressiveness, the overall rate of very successful entrepreneurs is 38 percent. Compare this to the group of owners who are low on both achievement orientation and competitive aggressivessness, and who only show a high success rate of 9 percent. This suggests that these two variables are important for success and that it is useful to pay attention to these psychological variables.

As discussed before, we think that personal initiative is a concept that lies behind the relationship between entrepreneurial orientation and success. Indeed, initiative is highly related both to entrepreneurial orientation and to success. Of those who show a high degree of initiative, 29 percent were very successful, in contrast to only 13 percent of those owners who were not taking initiative. Initiative and entrepreneurial success were also positively related. Moreover, the relationship between entrepreneurial orientation and success was mediated by initiative. This means that the relationship between orientation and success was reduced when controlling for the level of

Figure 3.2
Psychological Factors of Success, Uganda

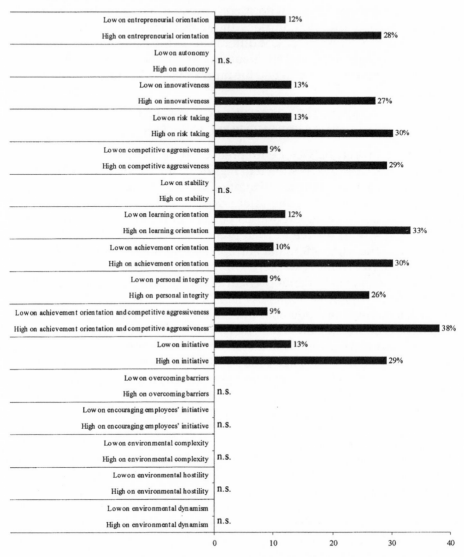

Percentage of highly successful entrepreneurs

initiative. Thus, the data suggest that initiative may be the concept that lies behind this interesting relationship. Another interesting point of initiative and its influence on success is the way entrepreneurs treat their employees. These differences were not significant, however. The environment in which an entrepreneur is doing business might also be important for success. However, empirically, this did not play a big role. As one can see from Figure 3.2, the direct relationships between the environment and success were not significant. This implies that at least the perception of the environment by the entrepreneurs did not matter much as far as whether the entrepreneurs were successful.

CASE STUDIES

A Successful Entrepreneur

The following case study presents an example of a successful entrepreneur who shows a high degree of proactivity and personal initiative. The entrepreneur is a forty-year-old man, born in Uganda. He is the oldest child in a family of three children. After primary and secondary school, he graduated from the Faculty of Commerce of the Makerere University in Kampala at the age of twenty-three. He started working in a bookstore as a salesman. During that time, he saved enough money to buy a ticket to the United Kingdom; this took him five years. In London, he first started working in a bookstore as storehouse clerk and was promoted to salesman after one year. He worked for six years in the store and during that time he tried to learn as much as possible about running a bookstore.

In 1991, he decided to return to Uganda. He had saved enough money to be able to start his own business in Kampala. The intention was to start a bookstore, but after he looked at the market carefully, it was clear that there were already two stores that would compete with his. So he decided to look for a job while looking for other business opportunities. He got a job in a bookstore and started his own market research. Intuition and information were important for him to find a gap in the market. He started gathering information about the needs of businesspeople. By looking around, by talking to a lot of different people, and due to his experiences in London, he detected that there was a need for creative and effective ways to present businesses. The business image is important, because it distinguishes one business from the others. A good image leaves a good impression, and people remember the business.

He decided to produce rubber stamps. He started with eight different models from which his customers could choose. He was able to run his business from home, because producing stamps did not need much space. Once he was better known by the businesspeople in Kampala, and after the number of customers increased, he produced more models. Since these stamps were cheap, many businesspeople could afford one and they found this to be a good way of making themselves recognizable. He made enough money to expand his business.

His idea of being responsible for developing a good business image was well-received in the market. Thus, he searched for other opportunities in this area. One idea was to produce business cards. Again, he did some market research by asking his customers first. In general, the reactions to his idea were positive. Producing business cards appeared to be a good idea. There was a potentially big market if the price of the cards was low.

Therefore, he expanded to produce business cards. He started looking for a printing machine. In Uganda or surrounding countries, it was difficult to buy a printing machine. For this reason, he contacted his former employer in the United Kingdom to ask him to find a printing machine at a reasonable price. After several months, the machine was found and shipped to Kampala via Nairobi. In the meantime, he needed to find an office. Although the rent of newly built offices in Kampala was quite expensive, he took the risk of renting an office in a new building. Since he used a secondhand print machine, nearly every businessperson in Kampala was able to afford to buy his business cards. At this time, he used sixty different designs for business cards.

This businessman is constantly on the lookout for new business opportunities. He asks the customers what else they would want. There were some people who asked him to print pictures on shirts and mugs so they could be used as presents. Because his business-card business was doing well, he could afford to buy the machines he needed. And again people were enthusiastic about these products and bought the products as gifts for Christmas, birthdays, and weddings. He argues that it also is important to treat one's customers well. This is a prerequisite for getting other customers by word of mouth. You also have to ask them if they want something that you do not yet offer. If that is the case, you have to try to find or produce it. This is an extra service for your customers.

This entrepreneur shows several important features. First, he is active in developing his own environment (he does not do the first thing that comes to mind and open up another bookshop). Second, he is innovative, as shown by expanding his business to products unfamiliar in Uganda. He searches actively for opportunities. When he sees a gap in the market, he does some research, and when the possibility of success is high, he develops a detailed plan. Thus, he uses a combination of opportunistic and planning strategy. He takes personal initiative. He puts ideas into action and is very determined, even if difficulties arrive. He takes risks, but these risks do not constitute a betting into the unknown; he takes risks based on careful deliberation and research.

This entrepreneur attempts to be autonomous in doing business. He wants to be as independent as possible from others. He tries to be ahead of competitors by offering special products to his customers. He consciously attempts to understand what mistakes other entrepreneurs make and he attempts to learn from them. He is constantly changing and "on the move." He is highly achievement motivated. When he describes doing business, he compares it with the flow of water. This is fresh as long as it flows. In business, you also have to be fresh. You have to find new things your customers are willing to buy and that your competitors do not have yet. You have to continuously think of new ideas. If you think you have made it and you stop looking around for other things, competitors follow you and can be ahead of you. You have to follow the direction you decided to go, but you have to be flexible to see and pick up opportunities.

Doing business means facing ups and downs. You have to be prepared for that. If you are prepared for that, you can handle every situation. It is important to have the goal to keep growing. That is better than to have the goal to reach a certain amount of profit. The vision for the business of this entrepreneur is clear.

At the time of the interview, he had nine employees. He likes it when they take initiative, although they have to discuss new ideas with him and have to get his permission before executing them. He argues that it is good to stimulate one's employees to develop new ideas. He also wants them to respect him.

Uganda is not the best country in which to do business, he mentions. For example, its infrastructure and communications facilities are not good. It is also hard to get consistent information about business issues. Because of these difficulties, it constitutes a complex environment. On the other hand, Uganda presents many opportunities, as long as one perceives them and takes advantage of them. Uganda is not as competitive as the United Kingdom.

In the future, he wants to improve his marketing strategies. He also wants to expand beyond Kampala and do business in the whole of Uganda. He uses newspaper and even radio advertisements. His general motto is to do things well or not to do them at all. He knows that he is very successful and he likes to be successful, but the satisfaction of doing good work is also very important for him. He insists that one should never stand still and always develop new ideas.

A Less Successful Entrepreneur

The following case study is an example of an entrepreneur who is not very successful in doing business. The entrepreneur is a twenty-six-year-old woman who sells shoes. She comes from a family with two children, both girls, of which she was the oldest. Her father left her mother when the children were very young. After primary school, she went to secondary school. When she was fourteen years old her mother died. She had to stop school to look for a job to earn a living for her sister and herself. She found a job in a shop from a lady who sold clothes for newborns. She earned hardly enough money to buy food and her sister could not go to school.

She observed the lady's way of operating. She noticed that her employer made a lot of money compared to her meager income. She needed some capital to start her own business. Because her total salary was spent on living costs for herself and her sister, she could not save money. She decided to find a second job. This was difficult to find, but an opportunity opened up when her employer needed some extra personnel. She suggested hiring her sister. With the two incomes, they could save enough money to get a loan. The bank gave them the same amount that they had saved.

She had always liked shoes, so she decided to sell shoes. Finding a location was not easy, because rent in Kampala is very high and, therefore, she could not afford to rent her own shop. In Uganda, people have solved the problem of high rents by dividing a store into several parts. Businesspeople can hire these for a lower price. She found a place in a store with two other shoe sellers and three clothes sellers.

She bought forty pairs of new shoes from a salesman from Dar es Salaam and started her own store with them. She does not sell many shoes, but if she sells one pair a day she earns more money than what she earned in her former job. With the money she earns now, she can afford to send her sister to school. She does not have a steady group of customers. There are only a few who come to her every time they need new shoes. Sometimes they bring new customers with them. She follows a reactive strategy in doing business, which means she reacts to what comes her way. She does not plan the way she does business. She does not attempt to advertise for her store, because she thinks it is money not well spent because customers come anyhow. She has enough customers to earn a living and she finds this enough.

She does not buy her shoes from the same supplier all the time. She tries to find the cheapest supplies by looking around and talking with other shoe-shop owners. When she has found a supplier that has cheap shoes, she is willing to tell other shoe sellers about it. Being different from others is not important for her, because this would require higher investments. She is willing to do something special for her customers; for example, looking for a special pair of shoes if her customers ask her. But this must not cost too much effort or money, because then it is not worth it. She argues that finding a pair of shoes for a customer costs time and during this time she could have sold her shoes in the store. She does not have a marketing strategy. She is not active in doing business. She thinks it is useless to spend time and money to develop new ideas. The initiative of starting a business of her own is the only initiative she has taken. However, she is satisfied with her situation.

She has two employees, one works two days and one works four days a week. She pays them in cash, but whenever she does not make enough money, she pays them by giving them shoes. She does not stimulate them to take initiative and does not do anything special to motivate them.

She makes a little profit, but unfortunately the number of customers is decreasing. From the perspective of growth, innovation, and entrepreneurship, her business is not successful. However, she finds herself successful because she earns enough for her sister and herself to live on. She has a positive view of the future, but she does not have a vision. When her sister has finished school, she can also start a business of her own. They can support each other when needed.

SUMMARY

There is a clear relationship between entrepreneurial orientation and success. This is exemplified in both the case studies and the quantitative study. In principle, the causal relationship can go both ways: Entrepreneurial orientation may have an influence on success, but successful businesspeople may also develop a higher entrepreneurial orientation. Our study (as it is a cross-sectional study) is not able to decide which of these two alternative interpretations is correct. From our other studies (done as longitudinal studies in Europe; see van Gelderen & Frese, 1998; Frese, Garst, & Fay, 1998), we know that typically both processes happened at the same time. Thus, we assume that entrepreneurial orientation causes success, but that success also makes microbusiness owners more prone to show a higher degree of entrepreneurial orientation and personal initiative. It is important to also take initiative into consideration, because it is closely linked with entrepreneurial orientation and success and it mediates the relationship of entrepreneurial orientation and success. One problem in Uganda is, however, that most people do not show a high degree of initiative and innovation. Training should concentrate on the four issues of innovativeness, competitive aggressiveness, achievement orientation, and initiative to increase the success rate of microbusiness owners.

REFERENCES

Baird, I. S., & Thomas, H. (1985). Towards a contingency model of strategic risk-taking. *Academy of Management Review, 10*, 230–243.

Borman, W. C., & Motowidlo, S. J. (1993). Expanding the criterion domain to include elements of contextual performance. In N. Schmitt & W. C. Borman (Eds.), *Personnel Selection in Organizations* (pp. 71–98). San Francisco: Jossey-Bass.

Broere, M. (1994). *Uganda: Mensen, politiek, economie & cultuur*. Amsterdam: Koninklijk Instituut voor de Tropen.

Comesa. (1999). *Country Information*. Available: http://www.comesa.int/states/uganda/qugabame.htm (last visited June 1999).

Covin, J. G., & Slevin, D. P. (1989). Strategic management of small firms in hostile and benign environments. *Strategic Management Journal, 10*, 75–87.

Frese, M., Fay, D., Hilburger, T., Leng, K., & Tag, A. (1997). The concept of personal initiative: Operationalization, reliability and validity in two German samples. *Journal of Occupational and Organizational Psychology, 70*, 139–161.

Frese, M., Garst, H., & Fay, D. (1998). *Control and complexity in work and the development of personal initiative (PI): A 5-wave longitudinal structural equation model of occupational socialization*. Manuscript submitted for publication.

Hartley, R. F. (1997). *Management mistakes and successes* (5th ed.). New York: Wiley.

Kula, O., Robinson, P., Ritchie, A., & Ondeng, B. (1995). *Uganda private enterprise support, training, and organizational development (PRESTO) project*. Bethesda, MD: Pact Publications.

Locke, E. A. (1997). Prime movers: The traits of great business leaders. In C. L. Cooper & S. E. Jackson (Eds.), *Creating tomorrow's organizations: A handbook for future research in organizational behavior* (pp. 75–96). New York: Wiley.

Lumpkin, G. T., & Dess, G. G. (1996). Clarifying the entrepreneurial orientation construct and linking it to performance. *Academy of Management Review, 21*, 135–172.

McClelland, D. C. (1987). *Human motivation*. Cambridge: Cambridge University Press.

McClelland, D. C., & Winter, D. G. (1971). *Motivating economic achievement*. New York: Free Press.

Mead, D. C., & Liedholm, C. (1998). The dynamics of micro and small enterprises in developing countries. *World Development, 26*, 61–74.

Miller, D., & Friesen, P. H. (1983). Strategy-making and environment: The third link. *Strategic Management Journal, 4*, 221–235.

Mintzberg, H. T. (1983). *Structure in fives: Designing effective organizations*. Englewood Cliffs, NJ: Prentice Hall.

Rauch, A., & Frese, M. (in press). Psychological approaches to entrepreneurial success: A general model and an overview of findings. In C. C. Cooper & L. T. Robertson (Eds.), *International review of industrial and organizational psychology*. Chichester: Wiley.

United Nations Development Program. (1998). *Human development report 1998*. New York: Oxford University Press.

Van Dyck, C., Frese, M., & Sonnentag, S. (1998). *Organizational error management climate: On enhanced error handling and organizational performance*. Manuscript submitted for publication.

Van Gelderen, M., & Frese, M. (1998). Strategy process as a characteristic of small scale business owners: Relationships with success in a longitudinal study. In P. D. Reynolds, W. D. Bygrave, N. M. Carter, S. Manigart, C. M. Mason, G. D. Meyer, & K. G. Shaver (Eds.), *Frontiers of entrepreurship research* (pp. 234–248). Babson Park, MS: Babson College.

4

Problems and Coping, Strategies and Initiative in Microbusiness Owners in South Africa

Gwenda van Steekelenburg, Anne Maartje Lauw, Michael Frese, and Kobus Visser

OVERVIEW

This chapter discusses business problems of small-scale business owners in South Africa and how they are managed. Dealing with problems and stress situations has been described in the coping theory by Lazarus and Folkman (1984), and we have, therefore, used this theory as a starting point for our research. Lazarus and Folkman define the coping process as the "constantly changing cognitive and behavioral efforts to manage specific external and/or internal demands that are appraised as taxing or exceeding the resources of the person" (p. 141). Coping should not be confused with outcome. The term includes thoughts and behaviors regardless of how well or badly they work. Commonly, emotional coping and active problem solving are distinguished. Emotional coping implies distancing and escape avoidance; both mean that one deals only with the emotions that appear because of a problem but not with the problem itself. Distancing and escape avoidance make it possible to keep up a positive emotion even if a person is confronted with difficult problems (example of questionnaire items were, "I went on as if nothing had happened," "I tried to forget the whole thing," "I wished the situation would go away or somehow be over with," "I hoped a miracle would happen"). Entrepreneurs who deal with the frequent absenteeism of their employees by hoping for miracles or trying not to think about the problem do not take steps to end the problem. On the other hand, the active problem-solving approach tackles the problem itself in the sense of solving the problem or seeking social support that helps to deal with the problem (examples of items were, "I talked to someone to find out more about the situation," or "I made a plan of action and followed it"). By discussing the problem with another entrepreneur or by coming up with a plan of action to end absenteeism, one is actually doing something to change the situation.

Additional issues of this study were the level of proactivity with which small-scale business owners dealt with problems. Two concepts are important here: initiative as a self-starting process (Frese, Fay, Hilburger, Leng, & Tag, 1997), and proactive strategies (Frese, van Gelderen, & Ombach, 1998). In addition, we looked at many other issues that produce problems for microbusinesses, such as employees, marketing, finance, giving credit, production factors, transport, and so on. The firms in the sample were located in the townships around Cape Town, South Africa.

South Africa: Past and Present Situation

The Republic of South Africa (with a population of 40.7 million, with 75% Black, 13% White, 8% Colored, and 3% Asian; Paton, 1990) has suffered from the apartheid system, which strictly segregated the races and discriminated against Blacks, Coloreds, and Indians/Asians. This system has divided South Africa into First and Third World parts, with Whites belonging to the privileged First World and Blacks to the nonprivileged Third World part of the country. Blacks and Coloreds had no right to proper schooling, health care, or social welfare. They were not allowed to vote or to choose where to live, or where and what sort of business to start.

The new government which was voted into power in 1994 based on a general election by all South Africans ended the era of apartheid. However, the circumstances under which Whites and non-Whites live today are by no means the same (Mazwai, 1994). Vast racial inequalities still exist (South African Central Statistical Services, 1995); the real Gross Domestic Product per capita is $516 for the poorest 20 percent and $9,897 for the richest 20 percent. Availability of electricity, tap water, flush toilets, and telephones differs strongly between the groups (South African Central Statistical Services, 1995). In 1993, 97.5 percent of the richest 20 percent (mostly Whites) had electricity available. In 1995, electricity was available to just 51 percent of the poorest households (United Nations Development Program, 1998).

Blacks, Coloreds, and Whites had different rights during apartheid. The Coloreds represent a blend of all the racial groups, and had more rights than the Blacks. They were not placed in "homelands," but inhabited special districts in the regions reserved for Whites (Buckley, 1995). Therefore, their living conditions were better than those for Blacks. Furthermore, it was easier for Coloreds to reach the city than it was for Blacks. Blacks had inferior schooling and, therefore, they had a lower literacy rate (32%) than Whites (93%) and Coloreds (69%). Infant mortality rates were nearly five times higher for Blacks than for Whites (Canesso, 1989).

Entrepreneurship in South Africa

During apartheid, Blacks were not allowed to become entrepreneurs outside their homelands. This made it exceedingly difficult to thrive as business owners, because the homeland markets were too small and poor (Mazwai, 1994). All other business alternatives outside of the homeland were essentially illegal, although from the late 1970s onward they were increasingly tolerated.

Additional problems appeared during the time of the liberation struggle. Black activists were socialist and, therefore, they were often opposed to capitalists, such as entrepreneurs. Being a businessperson was not encouraged (Mazwai, 1994). Black business had to contribute to Black activism and support various boycotts and strikes, all of which were not good for business. In addition, this led to being blacklisted by the White government, which made it impossible to get loans. Microbusiness owners have told us that these blacklists still exist and are still sometimes used against them when they apply for a loan. Against this background, it is understandable that the share of Black and Colored businesses in the national economy of South Africa is small (Motsuenyane, 1989). At the time of the study, there were approximately 500,000 Black-owned businesses in the country. Because of the Group Areas Act during the apartheid regime, many of the Coloreds and Blacks still live concentrated in specific areas. Nowadays, Coloreds and Blacks can start businesses where they want to. However, they usually start them either from home or near their homes. This often makes it difficult for Black entrepreneurs to reach the more affluent parts of society—White society.

Most of the entrepreneurs are operating in trade and hawking, services, crafts, transport, and accommodation (Mazwai, 1994). Income for Black entrepreneurs is low: 70 percent have an income of 1,000 rand per month or below (Mazwai, 1994) (approximately $200). People often have other jobs beside their business to support themselves and their families. Firms in the informal sector of Khayelitsha, the biggest of Cape Town's townships, had on average 0.6 employees per business.

Small-scale entrepreneurship is important for South Africa; the GDP was estimated to be raised by 16 to 40 percent because of the small-scale business sector (Berthon, Morris, & Pitt, 1994). The new South African government has a policy of stimulating entrepreneurship, because it expects small enterprises to create jobs (Morris & Hooper, 1996). Small-scale business owners are supported not only because it makes economic sense but also for political reasons. Institutions such as the Urban Foundation and the Small Business Development Corporation (SBDC) provide capital, expertise, and rental facilities to small businesses of all racial groups.

SAMPLE AND DESCRIPTION OF THE SAMPLE

Our sample of business owners was drawn from townships near Cape Town between September 1997 and March 1998. The participants in the survey were chosen using four criteria. First, business age was at least one year. Second, at least one and at most fifty employees had to be employed by the business (employees could either be from the extended family or outside of it). Third, we only interviewed the owners of the business and not the managers. Fourth, we restricted our sample to Colored and Black business owners.

Participants were recruited from five SBDCs situated in the townships of Blackheath, Philippi, Mitchell's Plain, Athlone, and Strand. In addition, we also cooperated with Clotex, a service and support service for small clothing businesses, and with Wesgro, an agency promoting economic development and job creation in the Western Cape Province, to recruit participants for the study. The last source of participants was the Market Square at the central train station and the Town Hall in Cape Town. Here, many businessmen and women sell all sorts of goods in their market stalls. The SBDCs are set up by the authorities in order to provide entrepreneurs with affordable business sites. They also provide loans and advice. The SBDC hives are mostly located in abandoned factories, where small units are created for each business. Since people search for an SBDC that is nearest to their home, some SBDCs were mainly Black while others were mainly Colored. Clotex gave us the opportunity to visit home-based businesses in the townships and Wesgro provided us with addresses of small businesses.

Approximately 200 entrepreneurs were approached. The final sample consisted of 101 entrepreneurs, the main reasons given for not participating being lack of time and interest. In our sample, 72 percent were men and 28 percent women; 55 percent of the entrepreneurs were Colored and 45 percent were Black. A complete sample description is given in Table 4.1.

Table 4.1
Sample Descriptions, South Africa

Characteristic	Percentage
Gender:	
- Male	72
- Female	28
Ethnicity:	
- "Colored"	55
- "Black"	45
Type of Industry:	
- Manufacturing	30
- Craft	1
- Trade	25
- Service	18
- Tailoring	27
Age of Business:	
- 1 year	16
- 1-5 years	45
- 6-10 years	32
- Over 11 years	8
Formality:	
- Formal	38
- Informal	62
Links to formal sector:	
- Low	39
- High	60
Number of employees:	
- 1	32
- 2-5	47
- 6-10	10
- 11-50	12
Starting capital:	
- Below 1000 US $	66
- 1000-5000 US $	25
- Above 5000 US $	8
Activities before start-up:	
- Wage earner	76
- Other enterprise	15
- Unemployed	9
Years of schooling:	
- 1-6	23
- 7-10	39
- 11-13	25
- Above 13	14
Number of working hours:	
- Less than 44h	40
- More than 44h	60

The firms were active in manufacturing (30%), tailoring (27%), trade (25%), and service (18%), as well as in craft (1%). Over half of the businesses were not in existence longer than five years; the average age of the businesses was six years. Only 8 percent were older than eleven years. The average age of the entrepreneurs was forty-two years (not shown in Table 4.1). The interviewers classified 62 percent of the entrepreneurs as informal and 38 percent as formal, the criterion being whether they paid tax or not. The entrepreneurs who were paying taxes were categorized as formal, the rest of the entrepreneurs as informal (even if they were registered with the Department of Commerce). The entrepreneurs in the market stalls and in the townships were all informal. The entrepreneurs situated in the SBDCs were formal.

The average number of employees of the enterprises was five. One-third of the businesses employed just one person other than the owner. The vast majority of the businesses in the sample (90%) were microbusinesses with less than ten employees. However, the biggest firm studied had thirty employees.

THE PROBLEMS OF MICROBUSINESS
OWNERS IN SOUTH AFRICA

There are a number of problems that micro- and small-scale enterprises have to deal with: lack of capital, lack of technical and management skills, legal barriers and bureaucratic licensing procedures, and marketing and transport problems (Van Dijk, 1992; Erasmus, 1989). The category most frequently mentioned was finance. Much less frequently mentioned were equipment, location, competitors, and customers.

Finance

Most of the entrepreneurs (74%) mentioned finance as their most important problem. Another indicator for this is the amount of starting capital. Sixteen percent of the entrepreneurs started without any money and 30 percent with less than 400 rand. Two-thirds of the firms started with a capital of less than $1,000 (see Table 4.1). Often, firm owners have to ask for a deposit in order to be able to buy the necessary supplies and then produce products. External supply of loans is infrequent. Only 14 percent of the entrepreneurs received a loan, mostly from the SBDC. Banks are still hesitant to give loans, because owners cannot provide collateral for security and do not develop a formal business plan (only 40% developed a business plan). Another 14 percent were able to secure loans from their families. Entrepreneurs who made use of loan opportunities showed a higher growth rate. Sixty-two percent of the entrepreneurs who received loans reported that their profit increased in the last year. Among the entrepreneurs without loans, this was only 30 percent.

Giving Credit

Sixty-three percent of the entrepreneurs indicated that giving credit to customers was a problem, because they experienced difficulties getting their money back. To accomplish the return of their money, 32 percent asked for a deposit and 24 percent set a time limit. Most entrepreneurs were eager to get back their money and made frequent contacts with the debtor. However, in other cases they accepted the nonpayment, told themselves to accept the situation, and simply reacted, "If there is no money, he or she cannot pay me and I will have to suffer the costs myself."

Marketing

Marketing tools were not commonly used and the microbusiness owners were not worried about that: 67 percent did not advertise and 74 percent never made use of special offers. Most entrepreneurs indicated that it was not necessary to use marketing tools such as advertising or special offers. According to these entrepreneurs, word-of-mouth advertisement was the only and best strategy. It became clear in the interviews that they sometimes were not aware of all the potential marketing tools available. An indicator of this is that they sometimes asked the interviewers to explain marketing strategies to them. After potential marketing strategies were outlined, most of them showed some interest; however, they would often say that in their particular case marketing tools would not be effective. Marketing was a topic of major concern to only 18 percent of the entrepreneurs in our sample. Among this small group of entrepreneurs, ads in local papers or house-to-house advertising was used.

Production Factors

Fourteen percent of the entrepreneurs indicated production factors as a major point of concern. Machine problems were common; for example, the tailor shops (clothing production) were not able to purchase new sewing machines and maintain them. Most of them had bought secondhand machines and tried to repair the machines themselves. This problem was much more important in the start-up phase than later, because there was little starting capital to invest in expensive machines. A good way to solve this problem was to share communal facilities in special centers like the SBDCs. Here, entrepreneurs could make use of machines they could not otherwise afford.

Transport

Supplies and transport were mentioned by 10 percent of the entrepreneurs as a problem. Owning a truck was too expensive for most entrepreneurs. They borrowed each other's trucks or hired them. If they did not have transport, they were more or less tied to one area and were not able to enter the more affluent markets; for example, in the city.

Employees

Issues relating to employees caused problems for 70 percent of the entrepreneurs. Absenteeism was frequently mentioned (in 42% of the cases). Strategies used by some entrepreneurs to reduce absenteeism were financial punishments (25%), warnings (12%), or trying to establish a trustworthy relationship (31%). Theft was another problem (mentioned by 16%), particularly in businesses with expensive tools and in the larger firms. For example, in firms with more than four employees, 70 percent of the entrepreneurs reported theft. In businesses with less than four employees, the percentage was only 3 percent. Theft also occurred more frequently in those firms in which the relationships between boss and employees was more authoritarian than in those where relationships were based on mutual trust.

Competition

Pressure from competition was a problem not frequently mentioned in South Africa. The general attitude of entrepreneurs was to "live and let live." The economic environment was perceived as hard and uncertain. Entrepreneurs in the sample were proud of being independent and most of them also had some idealistic motive behind their business. They were hoping to make the country a better place to live for non-Whites than it used to be during apartheid. These values might be an additional reason why the attitude was less competitive and more one of stimulating each other.

Activities Before Start-Up

We asked the owners in our sample what they had done before they started their business. Most of them had been wage earners (76%), only a minority had been unemployed (9%), and a few had previously owned another business (15%). Most of the entrepreneurs who had previously been employed in other companies had a few things in common. They continued to work in the same line of industry in which they had been a wage earner. In this way, they started their business with a higher degree of experience and skills. Often, their motives were to be independent and to be their own bosses.

Family

Traditionally, Coloreds and Blacks in South Africa have a strong sense of community and strong ties to their families. For this reason, it is common to employ family members, even if they do not have the essential qualifications. More than 10 percent of the sample worked solely with members of the family; 24 percent worked with both family members and others. Over half of the sample supported not only their direct family (children, parents, siblings) but also their extended family (e.g., uncles, aunts, in-laws, "family-of-family"). It was, therefore, remarkable that only 30 percent of the entrepreneurs were in turn supported by their families; the other 70 percent did not receive financial support from their families (e.g., loans in the start-up phase).

DESCRIPTIVE RESULTS ON THE PSYCHOLOGICAL VARIABLES: GOALS, STRATEGIES, INITIATIVE, AND COPING

Entrepreneurs follow a set of steps (a psychological strategy) to achieve their goals. Psychological process characteristics of strategies can be differentiated according to proactivity and planning. Proactivity refers to an active influence on the environment. One way is to actively seek out opportunities. Chapter 1 differentiated the following four process characteristics of strategies: complete and critical point planning strategies, opportunistic strategy, and reactive strategy. Strategy use was measured by asking the entrepreneurs to choose a business goal from several goals important for businesses in Africa. This was stimulus material from which they described their own goals. After they had described their goals in details, we asked them to describe in detail how they would reach their goals. From this, we could judge whether they had developed a thought-out plan, whether they just had a few general ideas, or whether they actively sought opportunities. The questions were designed to understand the real behavior used to reach their goals. As can be seen in Table 4.2, only 18 percent of the entrepreneurs were rated as complete planners, and the strategy of critical point planning was used in 18 percent of the cases and an opportunistic strategy was used in 28 percent of the cases. A large minority of 37 percent used a reactive strategy. This means they did not plan and did not actively structure the environment, but simply reacted to demands they perceived. In total, a high amount of planning

Table 4.2
Descriptive Results of Psychological Factors, South Africa
(Percentages)

	Low	Middle	High
Psychological strategy			
Goal specificity	49	7	44
Goal difficulty	30	24	46
Complete planning	-	-	18
Critical point strategy	-	-	18
Opportunistic strategy	-	-	28
Reactive strategy			37
Coping and initiative			
Coping active*	33	53	14
Coping emotional*	27	21	52
Personal initiative*	23	31	46
Perceived environment			
Environment complex	28	13	59
Environment friendly	40	7	53
Environment stable	24	25	51
Environment controllable	55	15	31
Success			
Income satisfaction	42	-	55
Success (interviewer judgment)	73	-	27

*Cut-off points were, for coping, low = 1.0–1.5; middle = 1.55–2.50; high = 2.5+; and, for personal initiative, 1.0–2.5, 2.5–3.0, and 3.0+, respectively.

was not often practiced. Most of the entrepreneurs lived a day-by-day life and did the same in their business. Unfortunately, most goals mentioned require a determined and sustained effort over a long period of time. If there is little planning and proactivity, this may mean that the goals can actually better be defined as dreams or wishes than true goals. As we see in a later part of this chapter, planning and proactive strategies result in more success.

Goals can lead to high performance when they are specific and difficult (Locke & Latham, 1990). By asking the firm owners in detail about their goals, we could rate specificity and difficulty of their goals. Table 4.2 shows that most entrepreneurs set difficult goals (46%). The picture was a bit more differentiated in goal specificity. Either the goals were highly specific (44%) or unspecific (49%). In some cases, we were presented with a high goal that was not clearly specified. An example is wanting to expand the business but not having an idea of what this means in detail (instead of saying that one wants to achieve an increase of sales by 50%).

Personal initiative is characterized by a proactive, self-starting approach which overcomes problems when they occur (Frese et al., 1997). Initiative should have a positive relationship with success (Frese & Fay, 1999; Morris & Hooper, 1996). Initiative was measured with the overcoming-barriers method by Frese and colleagues, which asks how many barriers in a problem area the firm owner was able to solve. The number of barriers overcome were counted (and we decided based on prior studies that an average of 2.5 was low, between 2.5 and 3.0 was middle, and 3.0 and above was a high value). Overall, these numbers show that the degree of initiative was high (the average of 2.8 in South Africa was higher than the average in a general nonentrepreneurial sample in East Germany, which was around 2.5; see Frese et al., 1997).

Coping means that one deals with problems. Therefore, we asked the entrepreneurs for a recent problem they encountered and asked them several questions about how they had dealt with it. After they described the problem, a short questionnaire on coping was presented (the ways of coping questionnaire by Folkman & Lazarus, 1988). The two coping factors—emotional coping and problem solving—were derived from this questionnaire. Problem-oriented coping was less frequently used than emotionally focussed coping. A high score for problem-solving coping appeared for only 14 percent, while a high score for emotional coping appeared for 52 percent. Thus, emotionally focussed coping is the preferred mode of coping by South African entrepreneurs. We shall see later that this is not irrational, because it may also be an effective coping strategy under the circumstances given.

Environmental conditions in South Africa were not perceived by the entrepreneurs to be as difficult as one would assume. The environment was perceived to be highly complex but relatively friendly by the majority of owners. Friendliness is the opposite of hostility. This implies that the owners perceive selling and retailing to be relatively easy in this environment. Moreover, the environment is perceived to be relatively stable but not controllable.

Finally, income satisfaction was relatively high, even though most entrepreneurs in Africa were not completely satisfied with the income that they derived from their business. Table 4.2 also presents that a minority of 27 percent were judged to be overall successful by the interviewers, while 73 percent were not rated to be overall successful.

RELATIONSHIP OF SOCIOECONOMIC INDICATORS WITH SUCCESS

Figure 4.1 describes the relationships of socioeconomic indicators with success. Success was measured by a dichotomous variable: low or high success as summarized by the interviewer on the basis of the

Figure 4.1
Socioeconomic Indicators and Success, South Africa

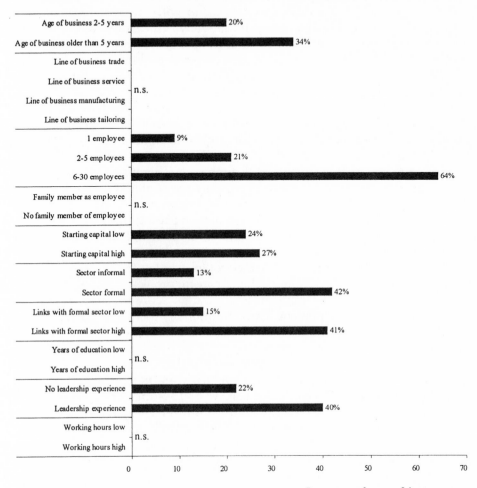

Percentage of successful entrepreneurs

interview (the other chapters in this book used a 5-point scale; in this study, a dichotomous variable was used). Thus, the first entry in Figure 4.1 can be interpreted as follows: Those firms that are two to five years old had a 20-percent rate of being successful. In contrast, firms that were older than five years had a significantly higher success rate of 34 percent (the black bars display the significant results, n.s. indicates results were statistically nonsignificant).

The line of business was not significantly related to success, although we found a slight difference between tailoring and trading on the one hand and manufacturing and service on the other (with the latter being a bit more successful). Such a difference may turn out to be significant in a much larger sample.

An obvious result is that the larger firms were more successful (of course, the interviewers used size and growth as criteria of success). Among the entrepreneurs with one employee, only 9 percent were successful, while among those with six to thirty employees, the success rate was 64 percent.

In contrast to many stereotypes by researchers in this field, employing family members does not imply nonsuccess. As a matter of fact, there was no significant relationship to success with employing family members versus not employing them.

Almost one-fifth of the sample started their business without any starting capital. The amount of starting capital had a relationship with success. Those with high starting capital were more successful than those with low starting capital. There was a relationship between being formal, company size, and success. The larger companies also tended to be formal and more successful. Therefore, it is not surprising that there was a large difference in success between the formal and informal entrepreneurs (42% versus 13%). However, the interesting fact remains that there was a minority in the informal sector that was successful (13%). Being linked to the formal sector was also related to size and success. Firms with a higher degree of links with the formal sector were more successful (41%) than those with a low degree of links (15%). We interpret this to mean that companies that have been successful and have grown tend to become formal.

Human capital is a traditional socioeconomic factor thought to be important. Not all human-capital factors measured in this study were significantly related to success. The number of years of schooling did not have a significant influence on success. In contrast, leadership experience was important. People with leadership experience were more successful (40%) than those without prior leadership roles (22%).

RELATIONSHIPS OF PSYCHOLOGICAL VARIABLES WITH SUCCESS

The results reported in Figure 4.2 on the relationship between psychological variables and success should be read in the same way as Figure 4.1; black bars signify a significant relationship and n.s. means that the relationship was not statistically significant.

Coping Strategies

Problems rated as difficult ("high threat") were more frequently dealt with by emotional coping. Problems rated as easy ("low threat") were

Figure 4.2
Psychological Factors and Success, South Africa

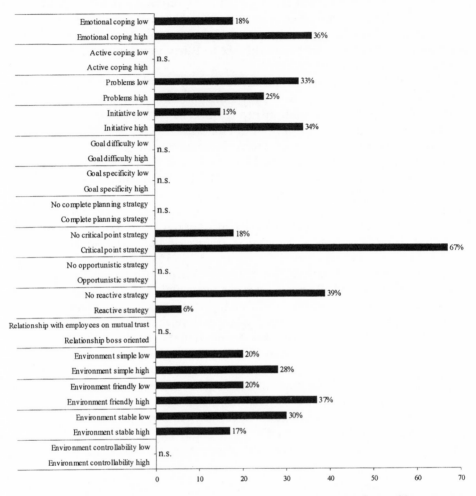

Percentage of successful entrepreneurs

dealt with by active coping strategies. Emotional coping was significantly related to success, but an active approach to coping was not
significantly related to success. This surprised us, as we had hypothesized that an active problem-oriented approach would be related to
success. Thus, it did not help the entrepreneurs to be eager to tackle
the problems at hand. In contrast, emotional coping had a positive
relationship with success. Nonconcern with the problem and even
wishful thinking may be quite successful in a harsh environment, or

successful entrepreneurs may show a higher degree of nonconcern and wishful thinking. We do not think that this result should be practically used at this point until the results are replicated in other studies in Africa, but it may point to an interesting interpretation: Distancing oneself from a problem may reduce the burden of those problems that one cannot solve anyhow. Emotional coping may be effective because it allows the entrepreneur to better concentrate on other aspects of the business that he or she can do something about. If one cannot change the situation, an effective strategy may be to change one's own emotions.

We asked the firm owners to describe problems that were important for them. Those who reported a high amount of problems were significantly less successful (25% success rate) than those with fewer problems (33% success rate). This is not surprising and exemplifies the importance of problems that appear for entrepreneurs in South Africa.

Initiative

Those entrepreneurs who were able to overcome barriers better were also significantly more successful (34% were successful) than their colleagues who were less able to overcome barriers (only 15% were successful). Thus, it is effective for entrepreneurs to take initiative and to continue to pursue goals even if barriers are in the way.

Goal Difficulty and Goal Specificity

Both goal difficulty and goal specificity were not significantly related to success. Apparently, a pure goal-setting approach (i.e., just increase your goals and you will be successful) would not work in South Africa. This is surprising, because there are data in the West that show that goal difficulty and specificity is related to success for entrepreneurs (see Chapter 1). On the other hand, we know that setting high goals does not work when one does not have control over the situation to reach the goal. This may be the case in South Africa.

Psychological Process Characteristics of Strategies: The Function of Complete Planning, Critical Point, Opportunistic, and Reactive Strategies

Complete planning was not significantly related to success. This means that it does not help in South Africa to be a meticulous planner. However, a critical point strategy was highly successful. Those who used this strategy showed a 67-percent success rate, while those who did not use this strategy displayed an 18-percent success rate. We interpret this to mean that the costs of planning may be high for South African entrepreneurs. On the other hand, no planning also does not help much. Therefore, the kind of localized planning that is typical of the critical point strategy is most useful. It means that one plans for that issue that is most important but does not bother to plan for other issues. The opportunistic strategy was also not related to entrepreneurial success. A nonplanning approach that just takes advantage of opportunities is not enough. Reactive planning was negatively related to success. Owners who were high on reactive planning showed a success rate of only 6 percent, while those who did not use a reactive strategy were successful much more frequently (success rate of 39%). This result is remarkably similar in many different cultures: Whenever an entrepreneur is neither proactive nor planning (the definition of a reactive strategy), failure is much more likely than when the person is either planning or proactive or both.

Boss–Employee Relationships

Figure 4.2 also presents some results on the strategy used toward employees. Surprisingly, it did not make a difference whether owners emphasized that they were the boss or whether they aimed for a relationship based on mutual trust. Cultural factors and individual factors probably codetermine success in this case. Since South Africa is a culture with high power distance, emphasis being boss is consistent with cultural expectations, and thus does not lead to negative effects. On the other hand, mutual-trust relationships help to reach success, even in a high power distance culture.

Business Environment

We have referred to the harshness of the situation in South Africa several times. The perceived environmental factors were related to success. In an environment that was perceived to be simple (high on simplicity), there was a higher success rate than in a complex (low on simplicity) environment. In an environment that was friendly (munificent), both in terms of ease of sale and ease of access of capital, the success rate was higher than in a hostile (nonfriendly) environment. Stability, on the other hand, was not a condition conducive to success. Stable, nondynamic environments were related to nonsuccess, while dynamic (nonstable) environments showed a higher success rate. Only controllability was not related to success.

CASE STUDIES

Case 1: An Unsuccessful Entrepreneur

The following case describes Mr. A and his business. He is fifty-nine years old and owns a business in manufacturing in a SBDC. He manufactures metal boxes made from empty lemonade cans. The boxes are mostly used for decoration and storage. The business has been in existence for ten years. Mr. A had worked in the timber industry for thirty-five years. He had five years of education and did not finish secondary school. Like all his brothers and sisters, he had to start work at an early age. He started as a cleaner in a furniture factory and acquired knowledge about manufacturing furniture during that time. Because of this experience, he then worked as a "real employee" in furniture manufacturing. Ten years ago, he began making little things out of empty lemonade cans at home. He did this in his spare time and he noticed that people in the neighborhood were interested in his products. People came to his home and wanted to buy his products, such as toys and kitchen tools. After a while, he thought of the possibility of starting a business. There were two reasons for this. First, he was tired of the hard work in the factory. Second, he wanted to be more independent. There was no particular product Mr. A wanted to make, and there was no clear-cut plan except his will to start his own business. His first problem was that he had no money. If people wanted him to make something, they had to pay in advance so that he was able to buy the material.

After a while he got the idea to make little boxes out of metal which he could get from a friend who worked in a factory which produced lemonade cans. To produce boxes, he needed a machine to cut metal. At that time, the SBDC offered him a workplace where he could make use of the machine he needed. It was a coincidence that he heard of the SBDC and he had not taken any steps himself to rent his shop there: A friend came up with the idea.

After starting to work in the SBDC, he met a person who was interested in the boxes he made. Until that time, he was still producing for the small number of customers already known to him. This person owned a gift shop in the center of Cape Town and wanted to buy a lot of boxes at one time. Mr. A then realized that his boxes were popular with Western tourists. His friend who helped him get the workshop in the SBDC became his employee and they wanted to sell more boxes in town. His friend was only paid when there was money, but he agreed to that because of their friendship. The next problem was how to get the products into town. They did not have enough money to buy a car and the only solution the owner could think of was that customers had to collect the boxes themselves. Another problem arose: They now knew that the boxes were popular but the number of customers did not increase. How could they manage to get more customers and orders? The owner's explanation was that they did not have a car and that they had no alternative to this mode of transportation.

He did not plan production and produced many boxes that could not be sold. His workshop was completely covered with metal boxes. Then there was the problem of renting his workshop. The SBDC wanted him to pay his rent regularly, which was not possible for him because he did not have sufficient income each month. He had heard that the SBDC was planning to privatize their workshops. This would mean the end of his business. He could not think of other premises where he could make use of the equipment he needed.

In spite of these problems, Mr. A was happy that he and his wife were able to live on what he was earning, although it was not much. In the years he had worked in the factory, he had a regular income which was higher than what he was earning now, but that was no reason to go back to another job in a factory. If there was an order he made more money than a month's salary in the factory and that gave him a good feeling.

In Mr. A's case, there was no indication of any planning. He clearly reacted to things that happened to him; thus, he used a reactive strategy. He had some goals, but when he was asked how he wanted to achieve the goals he was not able to elaborate. He did not show any initiative. Mr. A made a passive impression; he seemed to wonder how he could improve his business but was not taking any steps to do so. The solutions he thought of were rather simple and did not go further than the very first moment. He regarded himself as not being successful, he accepted the way things were, and he told us that he did not see any way of improving his business. For reasons of survival he continued and hoped that one day a miracle would happen.

Case 2: A Successful Entrepreneur

Mrs. V, thirty-three years old, owns a business in the township of Khayelitsha. She makes school uniforms that are sold locally to a school in Khayelitsha. She started her business in 1995 because she was unemployed. After her secondary school she had worked in a supermarket. Although she had twelve years of education, she had not been able to find a better job and had also not been able to study at the university (which she had wanted to do). Because she did not find her job in the supermarket inspiring, she wanted to do something else. She wanted to learn something, not just to do simple work.

At this point, Mrs. V already showed some level of initiative and active behavior, because she developed independent goals. Next, she got a job in a tailor workshop. This business was run by a White owner and the employees had to work many hours for little money. She had learned a great deal in this job, not only the skills to produce clothes but also knowledge about machinery and fabrics. She also got to know what was needed to run a business. Many clothing businesses face serious difficulties because of competition from Asia, where production is cheaper. For this reason, Mrs. V lost her job in the workshop and became unemployed. During this period, it was very difficult to find a new job; unemployment rates were and still are high in South Africa.

After a year of unemployment and growing poverty, she decided that she wanted to start her own business. From money she had saved, about 2,000 rand, she bought a secondhand sewing machine and fabrics to start with. She started to work from home to save money. Because of the competition from Asia in the clothing industry, she decided to make school uniforms, which were not imported from other countries. Thus, she thought she had found a niche in the market. She went to her children's primary school in Khayelitsha and tried to get a contract from the school so that it would at least buy some of her products. This was unsuccessful, and she found that she certainly had not been the only person to have the idea of producing school uniforms.

She then chose the personal approach and asked parents herself if they needed uniforms for their children. This proved to be a better strategy, and provided her with at least some customers. She mentioned word-of-mouth advertising as her best marketing strategy. After a year, she was able to buy another machine and she moved to a place where a friend worked as well. She only had to pay low rent and was very happy to have a real workplace where the customers could make personal calls. She then employed one person, a girl, eighteen years old. Mrs. V wanted her to start studying again, but in the meantime she wanted to keep her off the streets. She has a good relationship with her employee.

Mrs. V works five or six days a week, eight hours a day. In the afternoon, her children sometimes come to the shop because there is no one to look after them. Each year at the end of the summer holidays she makes a lot of money, as this is the time that children need new uniforms. She earns approximately 2,000 rand a month. The number of customers and sales increased during the last year. However, she does not regard herself as successful, since she still faces major problems, such as finances and finding new customers. She is thinking a lot about her business and about the problems but she tries to forget them. This way she can continue more easily with her work. Thus, she attempts to use a coping strategy of denial and distancing, although she still knows her problems. Other problems such as machine breakdowns or buying fabrics she deals with more actively. She repairs the machines herself and asks friends and family for help. She shows initiative and is quite ambitious and achievement oriented. She perceives her environment to be uncontrollable, unstable, unfriendly, and simple.

Although she impressed the interviewer as well organized and active, she did not plan much. Her plans for the future were surprising. Because there were too many producers of school uniforms, she was skeptical that is was possible to get a good market position. For this reason, she now wants to start a take-out restaurant. This plan is not well developed and specified, but it is a sign of Mrs. V's entrepreneurial spirit. She tends to use an opportunistic strategy, as she was always actively on the look out to improve her business or for other business opportunities.

Case 3: An Unsuccessful Entrepreneur

Mr. B is not doing well. He is trapped in a vicious circle and there does not seem to be a way out. He produces and sells leather products; for example, children's sandals, belts, and key-ring holders. He buys leather wherever he can get it cheaply. Usually, he can do this at factories which produce couches, shoes, or other leather products. The factories sell the leftovers at cheap prices. At the time of the interview, Mr. B had a huge pile of about one-hundred plastic bags filled with small and medium-size leather pieces in his workplace.

He lives in one of the biggest townships in Cape Town. He had only three years of schooling (actually, he is not quite sure how many years he went to school). He needed to work to make his living and to help his mother to support the youngest children. Mr. B used to have all sorts of unskilled jobs on a daily or sometimes weekly basis. Life was hard for Mr. B. At a young age, he was jailed for working for one of the local drug dealers in his township.

In jail, Mr. B learned the skills of a leather worker. One of the other prisoners taught him how to work with leather. He learned how to make belts, sandals, and other simple items. This was very exciting for him; he now saw an opportunity to start his own business once he got out of jail. When Mr. B was released, he started making leather products from his shack in the township. He soon found out that key-ring holders were most lucrative. Companies ordered a number of leather key-ring holders with the company name imprinted to hand them out as advertising material.

After two of these orders, Mr. B got too enthusiastic. He was so pleased with the success of his business that he began to look for a bigger workplace. He rented one at a business unit that was partly supported by government money. He also wanted more and more professional equipment, and borrowed money from his wife's family to buy secondhand equipment. He thought he had now made it; he had his own workplace, his own machines, and even his own employee.

However, a number of questions came up: Where do you find new customers? How do you get your customers to actually pay? Do you have to pay your employee if there is no work or money? How do you pay rent if there is no income? Moreover, how do you get into contact with new customers without means of transportation? How do you deliver your goods without transportation? Mr. B got highly preoccupied with his transportation problem. He essentially thought that all his business problems would be solved once he had his own pickup truck or "bakkie." He sought ways and means to get his own bakkie, but nobody was prepared to lend him more money. Actually, he had split up with his wife, and her family wanted him to pay back his debt to them. In other words, Mr. B desperately needed money. First, to buy himself a bakkie and second, to repay his wife's family.

At this point, Mr. B saw only one solution. He sold the machines he had bought to produce the leather key-ring holders, sandals, and belts. He now had the money to pay back his ex-wife's family and to buy the bakkie he wanted so badly. This brought him into the situation where he did not have the machinery needed. It was at this point that we interviewed him. He was just thinking of selling the bakkie again to be able to buy the machines to make key rings. This would mean losing the possibility to deliver products and visit potential customers again. Thus, he was torn between several alternatives and even oscillated behaviorally between them. This is an example of both lack of planning and lack of proactivity; thus, an example of a reactive strategy.

Case 4: A Successful Entrepreneur

This entrepreneur, Mr. E, started his career as a thirteen-year-old boy with no more than three years of education from one of the main townships in Cape Town. He was hired by a large company based in a well-to-do White suburb. The company provided equipment for people, schools, and other institutions: tents and related supplies like tables, chairs, and cutlery for their social gatherings. Mr. E was to help the driver unpack and put up the tents. This way, Mr. E learned about the practical side of the business. He learned about the differences in quality of the tents, their capacity, and the time and experience needed to put up different types of tents, and he got into contact with a different world outside the township.

Mr. E worked at this company for over twenty-five years and managed to save some of his wages. He did so because over the years he realized that renting tents and supplies could be a lucrative business in his own township community. In general, people in the townships do not have the space or accommodation to invite family, friends, and neighbors to their house. Traditionally, Blacks have a strong sense of family. It is not unusual at funerals to have hundreds of guests who stay for a long period to mourn and share meals. The same applies for weddings; a large number of guests is the rule rather than an exception. Heat in summer and low temperatures in winter make tents attractive in comparison to having the functions out in the streets. Thus, Mr. E had found a gap in the market.

From the little money Mr. E had saved, he bought a small second-hand tent. He started his business from his house. Through word-of-mouth advertising he rented his tent to people in his township for an amount that was a lot lower than what his former boss asked for so it would be affordable for the people in the township. As he expected, his tent was mostly used for funerals. Soon he was able to buy more and bigger tents. He hired people to help him set up the tents. Sixteen months later, business was going so well that Mr. E needed more space than his squatter home could provide. It was time to expand.

In order to make sure his customers could still easily reach him, Mr. E sought and found a location within his township. He rented a unit in an abandoned factory where a SBDC supported small-scale entrepreneurs. This made it possible to increase the number of tents and other supplies like tables and chairs. He used pamphlets to advertise in other townships as well. Up to this point, he had rented trucks to bring the tents to their locations. He bought a secondhand truck and hired a permanent driver. At this point in time, he started to work only from the office to organize the orders, give information, and close contracts with customers.

Mr. E not only had customers from the townships, but through his former job he also had contact with people in other areas of Cape Town. Mr. E tended to charge them a little more, but still less than his former boss and present competitor. The extra money he made with these jobs enabled him to be flexible when people could not afford a tent but needed one for a funeral. In those cases, he charged whatever people could afford. Nevertheless, he did not allow them to abuse this "rule." And since he was well-known and very respected in the township society, he claimed not to have any problems with nonpayment.

Mr. E was not only strict when it came to nonpayment, he was also very strict to his employees. Over the years, he had hired three drivers, two people who assisted him at the office (one of them his daughter), and several people for setting up, collecting, and cleaning the tents and supplies. The absenteeism problem many business owners complained about was easily solved by strictly deducting absent time from salary. Furthermore, Mr. E was permanently present to make sure his workers were doing their jobs the way he wanted them to be done. In his relationships with the staff, Mr. E was clearly the boss. He did not believe in a mutual-trust relationship.

At the time of the interview, Mr. E made 15,000 rand a month. He was over sixty years old but still had no plans to hand over his company to one of his children. As he said himself, his business is his life. He is very proud to have built up a successful business in spite of the political and economic problems in his country. Mr. E supports his ten children and grandchildren. He is very happy to be able to pay for his grandchildren's schooling.

SUMMARY AND CONCLUSION

In this study in South Africa, we found clear relationships between the psychological concepts of emotional coping, initiative, opportunism, and reactive strategies and entrepreneurial success.

Using emotional strategies vis-à-vis business problems turned out to have a positive relationship with success. This was surprising, particularly because an active approach to coping was not related to success, as we had originally assumed. We think that this finding needs to be replicated in another study before we can be sure of it. Obviously, one interpretation is that successful entrepreneurs are more relaxed and are, therefore, able to use an emotional form of coping (e.g., distancing). Another interpretation is that emotional coping is effective as long as the entrepreneur cannot change the situation (the situation is noncontrollable). Distancing oneself from a problem may reduce the burden, and emotional coping allows the entrepreneur to concentrate better on those aspects of the business that he or she can do something about.

There was a positive relationship between personal initiative and success. We think that personal initiative leads to a higher degree of success because entrepreneurs who are self-starting, innovative, and keep on fighting for an idea even if they are confronted with barriers will have more success (see Chapters 3 and 5). A reactive strategy (which is the opposite of planning and being proactive) is related to failure. In contrast, a critical point strategy is the most effective strategy. Thus, a certain amount of planning that is localized and does not invest too much into the planning process is related to success. Too much planning (as in complete planning strategy) and too little planning (that is still proactive, as in opportunistic strategy) are not significantly related to success but are also not detrimental. This picture is different in other parts of Africa. It should be kept in mind that South Africa is a relatively developed country and that it has a high degree of well-functioning state planning (unlike other countries in Africa). It is, therefore, much more similar to the developed European countries than other countries in Africa (even though many of the Black townships have the same "feel" as other parts of Africa and may often be less developed than other parts of Africa). Thus, there is a certain degree of stability which makes it possible to develop limited plans for important issues only.

In this study, we tried to ascertain which problems existed for small business owners. In total, those entrepreneurs who had many problems had a lower degree of success. Some of these problems were finance, giving credit, marketing, production, transport, and how to deal with employees and the competition. Selling goods or services on credit was a common marketing approach. Entrepreneurs complained about it, but they felt forced to do it because their competitors gave credit as well. Refusing credit would mean that customers would go to others where they received credit. However, giving credit turned out not to have a negative impact on the success of enterprises. Marketing tools were rarely used by the microbusinesses studied. The owners generally did not have enough knowledge of marketing issues. Those entrepreneurs who used marketing tools to promote their business (e.g., advertising, special offers), were more successful than entrepreneurs who did not use them. Most firms were located in the townships, which are far away from the city, which makes it difficult for customers from outside the townships to access these firms. This implies that they have to go to customers themselves, which produces transportation problems. To own vehicles is too expensive and public transport to and from the city is not well-developed. The best solution was to share ownership of a pickup truck or to borrow one when needed. Problems with employees (e.g., absenteeism and theft) occurred more frequently in the somewhat larger firms (more than four employees). Financial punishment turned out to be most effective in dealing with these problems.

We also asked the microbusiness owners to describe their business environment and were surprised that they perceived their environment to be relatively benign (except that it was not controllable). A simple and friendly (munificient) as well as dynamic environment was conducive to success.

Overall, this study shows that psychological factors are important when it comes to describing the situation and success of microbusiness in South Africa.

REFERENCES

Berthon, P., Morris, M., & Pitt, L. (Eds.). (1994). *Informal entrepreneurship and marketing: The Khayelitsha Perspective*. Oxon: Henley Management College.

Buckley, R. (Ed.). (1995). *Understanding global issues: South Africa after apartheid*. Cheltenham: European Schoolbooks.

Canesso, C. (1989). *South Africa: Places and people of the world*. New York: Chelsea House.

Erasmus, G. J. (1989). The informal sector in selected settlement areas in South Africa. *Journal of the Studies of Econometrics, 13* (1), 55–64.

Folkman, S., & Lazarus, R. S. (1988). *Manual for the ways of coping questionnaire*. Palo Alto: Consulting Psychologists Press.

Frese, M., Fay, D., Hilburger, T., Leng, K., & Tag, A. (1997). The concept of personal initiative: Operationalization, reliability and validity in two German samples. *Journal of Occupational and Organisational Psychology, 70*, 139–161.

Frese, M., van Gelderen, M., & Ombach, M. (in press). How to plan as a small-scale business owner: Psychological process characteristics of action strategies and success. *Journal of Small Business Management*.

Frese, M., & Fay, D. (1999). *Personal initiative (PI): A concept for work in the 21st century*. University of Giessen. Manuscript.

Lazarus, R. S., & Folkman, S. (1984). *Stress, appraisal, and coping*. New York: Springer.

Locke, E. A., & Latham, G. P. (1990). *A theory of goal setting and task performance*. Englewood Cliffs, NJ: Prentice Hall.

Mazwai, T. (1994). The black entrepreneur: Dynamo to grow the country. *Business Update*, 4.

Morris, M. H., & Hooper, V. A. (1996). Contemporary issues in entrepreneurship: Research perspectives from within South Africa. *South African Journal of Entrepreneurship and Small Business*.

Motsuenyane, A. (1989). *The development of black entrepreneurship in South Africa*. Lagos: Nigerian Institute of International Affairs.

Paton, J. (1990). *The land and people of South Africa*. New York: J. B. Lippincott.

South African Central Statistical Services. (1995). *October Household Survey*. Pretoria: Author.

United Nations Development Program. (1998). *Human development report 1998*. New York: Oxford University Press.

Van Dijk, M. P. (1992). Women in the informal sector in industrialising Zimbabwe. In H. H. Bess (Ed.), *African development and perspective yearbook 1991/ 1992*. Hamburg.

5

Microenterprises in Zimbabwe: The Function of Sociodemographic Factors, Psychological Strategies, Personal Initiative, and Goal Setting for Entrepreneurial Success

Michael Frese, Stefanie I. Krauss,
and Christian Friedrich

OVERVIEW

This chapter looks at a number of psychological characteristics and their relationship to success. The most important psychological characteristics are the following:

- Goal setting, particularly goal difficulty and specificity.
- Self-efficacy, that is, the belief that one is able to act effectively.
- Psychological characteristics of business strategies, particularly planning and proactivity.

In addition, this chapter looks at issues of human capital and sociodemographic characteristics which are important for development policies. We shall study the relationships with success for the following variables: prior unemployment, amount of starting capital, whether the business operates in the formal or informal sector, linkages to the formal sector, the line of business, years of education, highest employment position of the business owner, and some environmental conditions.

Goal Setting

Goal-setting theory has shown that high and specific goals are powerful motivators and lead to higher performance than most other motivational techniques (Locke & Latham, 1990; Guzzo, Jette, & Katzell, 1985). This suggests the hypothesis that owners who have high goals for their business and who are able to describe these goals in detail (level of specificity) have more success than owners who have low and unspecific goals. For example, if a business owner has the goal to produce twice as many products as before (e.g., twice as many window frames), he or she will show a higher degree of success than an owner who just wants to make enough money to live well. Most of these studies have been carried out with employees or have been experimental studies in Western countries. Most likely, one can generalize the findings of these studies to small-scale business owners (Baum, 1994) and to African countries, although this has not been previously shown. Therefore, it is of obvious importance to test this basic hypothesis on specific and high goals in our context.

Personal Initiative, Proactivity, and Self-Efficacy

Personal initiative (PI) has been defined as self-starting and overcoming barriers on the way to a goal (Frese, Fay, Hilburger, Leng, & Tag, 1997). PI also changes environmental conditions and is proactive. Thus, business owners who show a high degree of PI will be more likely to change bothersome situations, they will actively go out and search for opportunities to sell their products, they will actively enter those business areas which they perceive as being profitable, they will innovate more, and they will not give up when problems appear. In Chapter 3, we showed that PI was related to entrepreneurial orientation and that it was an important factor underlying the relationship between entrepreneurial orientation and success. In this chapter, we shall look once more at the relationship of PI with success.

Proactivity is conceptually related to PI. To be proactive means to take active measures toward the market, toward changing the product, toward improving the production (or service) process, and so on. For example, if an owner scans the market for opportunities, this is proactive. A shoemaker told us that he observed how much the shoes of guards were worn out (the shoes are part of their uniforms). When the shoes were worn out, he contacted their head office to make an offer to produce shoes for this company. A proactive approach also implies that one takes preventive actions. For example, it would be a good example of proactivity that an owner takes precautionary steps so that he or she can cope with a slump in business.

Self-efficacy "refers to beliefs in one's capabilities to organize and execute the courses of action required to produce given attainments" (Bandura, 1997, p. 3). Thus, it should be related to PI (it has been shown to be a factor contributing to PI in a large-scale longitudinal study in East Germany; see Frese, Garst, & Fay, 1998), and it should also be related to entrepreneurial success.

Strategies and Planning

In Chapter 1, we discussed our concept of psychological process characteristics of strategy development. We differentiated four characteristics of strategies which differ in the amount of proactivity and planning (Frese, van Gelderen, & Ombach, in press): complete planning, which is a top-down plan and is high on planning and proactivity; critical point planning, which plans only the most important issues and is, therefore, high in proactivity and moderate to low in planning; opportunistic strategy, which implies that one looks actively for opportunities to do business, and is high in proactivity but low in planning; and reactive strategy, which implies that the owner does what other people or the situation say to do, and is, therefore, very low in planning and a passive (nonactive) strategy. A reactive strategy has been found to be negatively related to success in several chapters in this book (as well as in research on The Netherlands; see Frese et al., in press). This means that the more one uses a reactive strategy as a business owner, the less successful the business is. We expect that these results will also appear in Zimbabwe.

Innovativeness and Competitive Aggressiveness

Innovativeness and competitive aggressiveness are the backbone of the concept of entrepreneurial orientation (Lumpkin & Dess, 1996; Covin & Slevin, 1989; see Chapter 3 of this book). These two orientations have several functions. The most important function is to keep the participating entrepreneurs alert and to make them fit for the market. If there is little innovation, there is little one can gain in participating in the market. If there is little pressure to compete locally, readiness and ability to compete with others in wider markets are reduced. A society gains from innovative and highly competitive entrepreneurs, because they will produce more innovative and competitively priced products. In addition, members within the society learn how to deal with a tough environment and therefore tough environments produce successful entrepreneurs (Shane & Kolvereid, 1995). Unfortunately, there is evidence that suggests that African entrepreneurs show little process and product innovativeness (Gray, Cooley, Lutabingwa, Mutai-

Kaimenyi, & Oyugi, 1996). For this reason, innovativeness is an issue of major concern. In this chapter, we shall examine how innovative Zimbabwean business owners are and how strongly innovativeness is related to success.

Lack of competitive aggressiveness may be another problem that is specific for African entrepreneurs. Since there is high pressure to conform to the standard practices in Africa, deviation from the traditional way of doing things is seen as negative, and there is a high degree of collectivism in Africa, there is pressure not to compete against other entrepreneurs. Again, we are interested to find out how high competitive aggressiveness is in Zimbabwe and whether it is related to success.

Human Capital and Sociodemographic Characteristics

It is often argued that the informal sector in Africa is essentially subsistence oriented and is, therefore, not really of any importance for the development of the country, and is even counterproductive at times (see Neshamba, 1997). Sometimes the analogy is used of four people selling tomatoes. If a fifth person joins them and sells tomatoes as well, little is gained for anybody because the fifth person probably does not add new customers and only reduces the meager existence of those who have occupied the corner before. None of these five businesses will grow and the owners would gladly give up their business if they could find a job in the formal economy. Indeed, this position is supported by evidence that in economically difficult times, informal businesses are established that are given up again when the economy booms and more formal sector jobs are created (McPherson, 1998). The question is how far one can generalize this observation and whether all participants in the informal sector have these problems. Many formal firms originally started as informal businesses (Neshamba, 1997). Moreover, many informal firms may actually show a similar trajectory of growth as formal firms. We also assume that our population of business owners with at least one employee is by and large not of the type discussed in the tomato example. It makes sense, however, that those firms that develop some connections to the formal sector are doing better than those operating only within the informal sector. These firms have wider options.

The reasons for becoming an entrepreneur can be related to the pushes of survival or the pulls of a better situation as a business owner. Many people started their business because they feared they might become unemployed or because they were unemployed. On the other hand, there is also a large group who started their independence from a formal employed job. We assume that this variable does not have any bearing on success, because it does not affect daily behavior once the business is established. Motives that were operative a long time ago do not necessarily have an effect on the actions of the entrepreneur today.

Large-scale research has shown that there is a liability of smallness (Bruederl, Preisendoerfer, & Ziegler, 1992) which we assume is also present in Africa. This means that those who start out with a high amount of capital are more likely to succeed than those who start out with little capital, because they have a headstart right at the beginning. Good equipment makes it possible to grow more quickly than when one has poor tools.

Finally, we are interested in whether human-capital factors (years of education, having prepared oneself for the work in this particular industry, and having management experience) are related to success (Bruederl et al., 1992).

THE SITUATION IN ZIMBABWE

Zimbabwe was one of the latecomers on the African continent to introduce deregulation and to encourage the informal sector. Originally, laws introduced by the White apartheid Smith government made it essentially impossible for Black Africans to develop small enterprises. These laws were not changed by the socialist Mugabe government when they came to power in 1980. The socialist government was never completely socialist, but it favored the formal sector and large corporations (except in the agricultural area). In contrast to many other African countries, Zimbabwe had a well-developed industrial base, which was partly a result of the isolation due to economic sanctions against the Smith government. This industrial base was able to function and to absorb at least a certain number of graduates from school (see, however, Chapter 7). Many of the large businesses are still owned by Whites. Zimbabwe has a well-functioning school system and a literacy rate of 69 percent (Dallas, 1995). In 1990, an Economic Structural Adjustment Program (ESAP) was introduced which attempted to reduce government interference in the market, to sell state monopolies, and to reduce government deficit. One of its goals was to encourage private-enterprise development, including development of microenterprises.

Zimbabwe has been characterized by a variable growth rate and medium to high inflation since 1990. The real Gross Domestic Product growth rate varied from 5.5 percent in 1996 to minus 5.3 percent in 1992 (a year with a strong drought), with an average of 3.2 percent across the ten years from 1988 to 1997 (McPherson, 1998, p. 1). The average inflation rate was roughly 21 percent per year during this period. At the time of our second study, there was a crash of the economy at the end of 1998 (partly motivated by a sharp decrease of the value of the Zimbabwe dollar), which led to a reduction in buying power and an increase in inflation.

There is an excellent database on microenterprises available in the form of three GEMINI studies (McPherson, 1991, 1998; Daniels, 1994). They established that in 1997 there were 860,000 microenterprises which employed 1,647,664 persons, roughly one-quarter of Zimbabwe's working population (McPherson, 1998, p. 9) (in addition, they studied microenterprises in agriculture and mining, which we are not concerned with here). The most important findings were the following (McPherson, 1998):

- On average, the microenterprises consist of the owner and one employee.
- In absolute numbers, there are more microenterprises in the rural areas, but the number of urban microenterprises increased much more quickly. In 1998, 41 percent of all urban households were involved in microenterprise activities. The urban enterprises also grew more quickly in size.
- Females are usually involved in the less profitable sectors; therefore, the growth rate of their enterprises is lower than for those owned by males.
- The firms in less profitable areas also show a higher closure rate.
- Overall, most people start a firm because they see a "profitable opportunity." The second most important reason is that there were no wage-earning opportunities (thus, the classic distinction between push and pull factors for firm growth is taken up here). The low-profit economic sectors attract more founders with push factors (no job opportunity), while the high-profit sectors attract more founders with pull factors (profitable opportunity).
- The general motive for people to start a microenterprise is that there are no other jobs. Thus, much of enterprise development is done in order to survive. Therefore, it is not surprising that the founding rate for microenterprises is higher in periods of economic hardship with higher unemployment than in periods of economic growth; however, it should be kept in mind that a large proportion of microenterprise development exists because people want to be independent business owners (this is a topic we will discuss again later).
- Marginal firms are given up more frequently in good economic times (probably to take up jobs as employees).
- The most important problems and constraints reported by microbusiness owners were marketing issues (such as not enough customers or too many competitors—these issues are particularly important for the rural sector), lack of finance (particularly important for the urban firms), and difficulties with supplies.
- Other constraints were high costs and reduced buying power by the customers (Harrison & Friedrich, 1990). The small-scale business owners did not know much about ESAP (only 50% had some concrete knowledge about it) and in general owners were quite pessimistic after the introduction of ESAP (although it was supposed to help them).
- In a case-based study, Harrison & Friedrich (1994) found problems, particularly in the area of human capital of the business owners. They had low

education, most often no education in the area of their business, no education for running a business, and, in particular, little knowledge on bookkeeping and accounting.

SAMPLE AND SAMPLE DESCRIPTION

This chapter is based on two different samples of Black Zimbabweans, both drawn from the greater Harare area, the capital city of Zimbabwe. In the first study, thirty-three owners of microenterprises participated, in the second the number was sixty-five. They were recruited with a random-walk approach in the Harare areas of Mbare, Chitungwiza, Dzivaresekwa, and Highfields. A description of each sample is presented in Table 5.1. In both studies, nearly all of the interviewees were males. Most firms were between one and five years old, and about 10 percent were only one year old. Most of them operated in the manufacturing industry (often window frames, woodwork, and garment industries), but a sizeable proportion was also in the trade and service industries.

It is often argued that township firms only work within the informal sector and that these firms only deal with other informal firms and have little relation with the formal sector. In both studies, the majority of the participants were in the informal sector. However, in the second study, there was also a large group that was formal and paid tax (27% and 43% were formal in the two studies, respectively). The interviewers also judged the extent of the microenterprises' links to the formal sector. Actually, there are more links than most researchers and even practitioners of microenterprises assume to be true. More than half of the entrepreneurs had a substantial link to the formal sector (e.g., by buying from and selling to formal-sector companies). These results show that there actually was a sizeable proportion of registered firms that paid taxes and/or were well-integrated into the formal-sector economy.

We asked only business owners who had at least one employee to participate. In the first study, this employee had to come from outside the extended family, while for the second study, it did not matter whether the employee came from inside or outside the family. As one can see from Table 5.1, nearly all of the business owners had between one and five employees. However, there were a few business owners who had thirteen and even twenty employees. Most firms did not employ family members; a few had done so in the past and were not doing it any longer, and only roughly one-third of the employers currently employed members from the extended family.

Starting capital was low, as is usual in the microbusiness sector; we roughly converted the Zimbabwe dollar starting capital into U.S. dollars and nearly all had a starting capital that was lower than $1,000. In

Table 5.1
Sample Descriptions, Zimbabwe

Characteristics	Percentage		Characteristics	Percentage	
	Study 1	Study 2		Study 1	Study 2
Gender			**Family members as employees**		
- Male	97	88	- no	58	54
- Female	3	12	- yes in the past	6	17
Year of business establishment			- yes currently	36	29
- 1997 (1yr)	9	11	**Starting capital (U.S. $)**		
- 1993 - 1996 (2-5 yrs)	48	66	- $ 1,000	85	69
- 1988 - 1992 (6-10 yrs)	42	17	- $ 1,000 – 5,000	6	26
- before 1988 (11 yrs or more)	-	6	- $ 5,000	9	5
Line of business			**Applied for loan**		
- Manufacturing	46	48	- no	-	65
- Craft and Trade	21	37	- yes	-	35
- Service	33	28	**Got a loan (total sample)**		
- Other	0	2	- no	88	86
Sector			- yes	13	14
- informal	73	57	**If loan, loan by**		
- formal	27	43	- bank	-	56
Linkage to formal sector			- family or friends	-	11
- low	46	45	- government or NGO	-	56
- high	55	55	**Unemployment as reason for**		
Number of employees			**entrepreneurship**		
- 1	9	5	- no	47	55
- 2-5	78	74	- yes	53	45
- 6-10	6	14	**Education of owner**		
- 11-50	6	8	- 1-6 yrs	16	3
			- 7-10 yrs	16	20
			- 11-13 yrs	29	57
			- 13 yrs	39	20
			Number of hours worked		
			- less than 44	12	3
			- more than 44	88	97

the second study, we also asked whether they had applied for a loan. A substantial group of roughly a third had applied for a loan. Yet, only a few obtained credit facilities (Study 1, 13%; Study 2, 14% of the total sample and 39% of those who applied for a loan). The loans were mostly given by banks, the government, or nongovernmental organizations (since some entrepreneurs received multiple loans, the numbers add up to higher than 100%).

About half of the business owners started their business because they were either unemployed or feared that they would become unemployed. The other half started a business from a job (usually a blue-collar job). Thus, there are many entrepreneurs who made a conscious choice to become self-employed in their career.

In terms of education, the firm owners could be divided into three groups. One group (roughly one-quarter) had up to ten years of education, the majority had between eleven and thirteen years, and a third group (roughly one-quarter) had more than thirteen years of education. The education of the microenterprise owners is higher than the average education in Zimbabwe.

We also asked the participants how many hours they worked in their enterprise. The work hours ranged from twelve to seventy-four hours, with a median of fifty-four hours per week. This is a little lower than the median work time for business owners in Germany. In comparison to the workers (who work mostly forty-eight hours per week) microenterprise owners did not work many more hours.

DESCRIPTIVE RESULTS OF THE
PSYCHOLOGICAL FACTORS

The descriptive results on the psychological factors in the two studies are presented in Table 5.2. All the ratings of the answers were done on a 5-point scale; this scale was transformed into three categories to make reading of the table easier—low is 1 and 2 on the answer scale, middle is 3, and high is 4 and 5. The first line of Table 5.2 should be read as follows: 13 percent of the respondents in the two studies had goals with a low degree of specificity, 33 percent had a mid-level specificity, and 54 percent of the respondents had a very specific goal.

Psychological Characteristics of Strategies

According to goal-setting theory (Locke & Latham, 1990), high degrees of goal specificity and goal difficulty are important motivators for success. Therefore, we rated how specific and how difficult goals were. The interviewers asked in great detail what their goals implied, what they meant, and what they really wanted to achieve with their goals. This was done to enable the interviewers to code how specific and difficult their goals were. Although this is obviously a difficult judgment to make, the interviewers were trained in great detail on how to make their judgments. Table 5.2 shows that the majority of the participants had specified their goals in great detail, while 13 percent had nonspecific goals. This is a very high percentage of people who have specific goals. Goal difficulty was also high.

Planning and proactivity of strategies were also measured. Planning implies that the owners have a set of rules to achieve their goals. Proactivity implies that the owners actively search for opportunities and are not just reacting to environmental pressures. Proactivity means that the entrepreneurs are involved and able to influence changes in

Table 5.2
Descriptive Results of Psychological Factors in Both Studies

	Percentages		
	Low	Middle	High
Psychological Strategy			
- Goal specificity	13	33	54
- Goal difficulty	2	40	58
- Planning in strategy	38	26	37
- Proactivity in strategy	24	29	47
- Reactive strategy	56	19	25
- Self-efficacy	14	37	49
Market and Product			
- Innovativeness	50	41	9
- Gap (niche) orientation	58	18	24
- Competitive aggressiveness	38	10	52
- Advice, not to employ family members	28	40	32
Success			
- Satisfied with own income	12	27	61
- Interviewer's estimate of entrepreneurial success	10	44	46
- Links to formal sector	52	4	44

Number of Employees	0	1	2-4	5+
- in 1993	20	17	40	23
- in 1997	2	16	58	24

their environment conditions. We ascertained strategies by asking very specifically how people went about reaching their goals. Thus, when a microbusiness owner said that he or she wanted to buy a new machine, we asked how he or she would go about it; for example, whether he or she had already laid aside money for the machine, whether he or she had explored cheaper alternatives, whether he or she had thought of producing the machine him- or herself, and so on. Thus, we used a detailed, behaviorally oriented approach to measure planning and proactivity. Our research aim was to measure the actual behavior of people as far as that is possible to ascertain within the constraints of a structured interview.

According to Table 5.2, 37 percent of the owners were planning a lot, and 38 percent were planning very little. Since planning is usually related to success, these results mean that 64 percent of the participants (those low or in the middle) were not doing enough to actually achieve their goals. The picture for proactivity is somewhat similar. Nearly one-half of the entrepreneurs were highly proactive and roughly one-quarter were either not at all active or held a middle position. Since proactivity and planning are two important factors to achieve success as a small-scale entrepreneur, our results suggest that there is room for improvement for about one-half to two-thirds of the participants.

Another way to look at this issue is to look at the number of owners who used a reactive strategy. A reactive strategy means that one does little planning and is at the same time not proactive. Twenty-five percent of the participants used a reactive strategy to a large extent and another 19 percent were in the middle. Both groups are more likely to have difficulties achieving success, on both a short-term and a long-term basis. On the other hand, more than half did not use a reactive strategy and are, therefore, probably successful.

Another area that is important for success is how microenterprise owners deal with common business problems. The problem perceived by the participants to be most important was to get and to be able to finance good equipment (50% of the participants saw this to be their most important problem; these figures are not shown in Table 5.2). The second most important category was getting enough customers, which was identified by one-third of the participants to be their most important problem. Much less frequently mentioned were issues of marketing and pricing. Very few experienced pressing problems with regard to suppliers, competitors, products, and personnel. This picture is clearly different from what one would find in small-scale enterprises in developed countries. The pressing problems of the micro-enterprises attest to the serious undercapitalization that is typical in Africa and to their difficulties attracting enough customers to their business.

People may believe they are more or less the master of their problems. Being able to cope with these problems is related to self-efficacy beliefs. Self-efficacy implies that one thinks that one is able to deal with a problem adequately. High self-efficacy implies that one expects to be a master of problems and does not have to yield or to seek assistance. Self-efficacy was high in the two samples. The majority (49%) had a high expectation, between 75 and 100 percent, that they would be able to solve the problems themselves. Of course, it is not just in the hands of the microenterprise owners to overcome the problems of getting good equipment and attracting enough customers. High self-efficacy does not solve a problem per se. For example, the problem of undercapitalization is not just done away by being self-efficacious. But having a mastery orientation helps because the person will attempt more stubbornly to save enough money to manage many of the problems associated with undercapitalization.

Market and Products

How do Zimbabwean entrepreneurs position themselves in the market and do they use innovative and niche strategies vis-à-vis their market? Do they have innovative ideas? We asked whether they were offering something special (e.g., a product, a special design, use of some special material, service, machine, or anything that their competitors would not have or do). We discussed in detail what they thought to be their innovative idea. The innovativeness of the business was then rated by the interviewers. This is obviously a difficult task, and one has to regard the interviewer judgments with a certain "grain of salt." On the other hand, the two raters agreed well in their judgment. Table 5.2 shows that only 9 percent of the business owners had a highly innovative idea, while another 41 percent were in the middle. Unfortunately, half of the entrepreneurs were low on innovativeness. Table 5.2 also shows that only a small minority (24%) filled a market gap or niche with their products or services. This means that the vast majority of the business owners were not using innovative strategies and did not have innovative product, production, and service ideas. Other research confirms the finding that African business owners lack innovativeness and niche orientation (Gray, Cooley, & Lutabingwa, 1997).

Lumpkin and Dess (1996) have argued that competitive aggressiveness is an important predictor of entrepreneurial success. Our hypothesis was that competitive aggressiveness is low in Africa because of the strongly collectivistic culture. However, this hypothesis turned out to be wrong, as shown by the results displayed in Table 5.2. The majority had a high competitive-aggressiveness orientation ("undo the competitor"). However, there was a large minority (38%) who did not take a highly competitive attitude toward the other microenterprise owners. The results suggest, however, that there may be more competitive aggressiveness in African microenterprises than was thought up to now.

An issue frequently discussed in the literature is the fact that African entrepreneurs are often forced by tradition and their families to employ members of their extended families who are not necessarily well-qualified (Wild, 1994). We had the impression that most entrepreneurs had thought long and hard about this issue. Apparently, it is an issue that comes up in discussions within families, and small-business owners are forced to develop explicit rules with regard to employment of family members. The majority do not want to employ any family members in their business. We asked them whether they would advise a friend to employ family members. One-third of them say that one should not employ a family member and another third is actively for it.

Success

Success was measured by overall success rating by the interviewer and by asking the participants whether they were satisfied with their business. It is much more difficult to be satisfied with one's current income than to be satisfied with the performance of one's firm. Therefore, we also asked how much the owners were satisfied with their current income. There were 61 percent who were highly satisfied with their income. It is often good to get a second opinion on how successful an owner is. We obtained this second opinion by asking the interviewers to give a general estimate of the enterprises' success. As one can see from Table 5.2, the interviewers perceived a high level of success in 46 percent of the firms, a large group ranging in the middle, and only a few owners with little success. (Obviously, the interviewers had to base their judgment on the interview, but in contrast to the interview partners, they were able to use a general framework of success, comparing each individual case with other participants and taking into consideration not only what the person said but also how the shop looked. Thus, their judgment is influenced by the interview, but is not completely dependent upon interviewees.)

By and large, there was a high degree of success in our sample, as the results in Table 5.2 show. This is also shown by the growth in employees. Most of the microenterprise owners started out by themselves and then slowly grew and increased the number of employees. While in 1993 a substantial minority of 20 percent had zero employees, in 1997 the vast majority had two to four employees (note, however, that this is partly due to our selection, because we only took employers who had a minimum of one employee at the time of our study. Note also that many of the employees had not started in 1993, but at a later time, so that the percentages are not completely comparable in each case). In general, the number of employees increased in our sample. This shows on a micro level the truth of the macroeconomic statement that microenterprises contribute to an increase of employment in a country.

Links to the formal sector were evenly split in the sample. About half had a low degree of links to the formal sector and 44 percent showed a high degree.

SOCIODEMOGRAPHIC FACTORS AND SUCCESS

Figure 5.1 presents the results on the relationships between sociodemographic factors and entrepreneurial success separately for the two studies. It is best to explain the figure using the example of whether the business operated in the formal or informal sector (the third entry

Figure 5.1
Sociodemographic Factors and Success, Zimbabwe

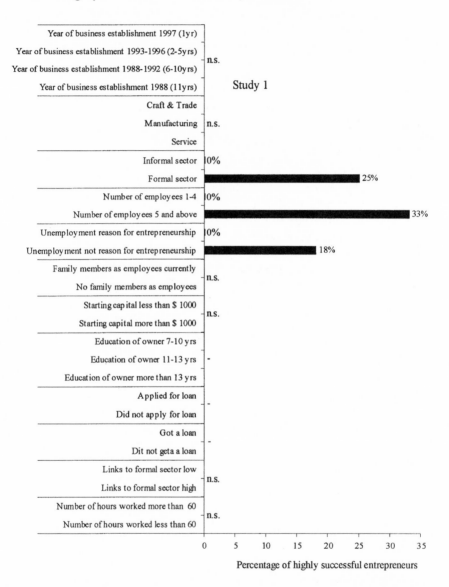

in Figure 5.1). Those owners who were in the informal sector were less successful than those who operated in the formal sector. In Study 1, the informal business people showed a 0 percent rate of being highly successful. This means that, of the informal sector participants, none were highly successful, while the equivalent percentage was 25 percent in the formal sector. The results in Study 2 were similar: Of those

Figure 5.1 (*continued*)

Study 2

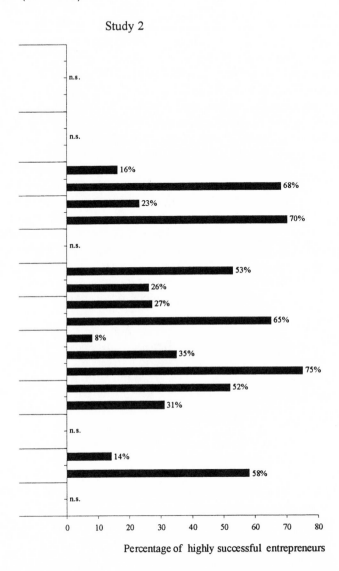

Percentage of highly successful entrepreneurs

in the informal sector, only 16 percent were highly successful, while among the formal sector participants, 68 percent were highly successful. The relationships between formality of the sector and success were significant in both studies. As one can see, there are fewer significant results in Study 1. This is due to the fact that there are fewer participants in Study 1: Therefore, statistical significance is less easily achieved (n.s. signifies that a result is not significant). It is important to note that it is not legitimate to compare the percentages across the two different studies. Thus, it is not possible to infer from Figure 5.1 that informal businesspeople were less successful in Study 1 than informal-sector participants in Study 2. The reason is that we used different success measures in the two studies (namely, economic success—a summary of items on the increase of customers, sales, and profits across the last five years—in Study 1, while Study 2 used the customary summary success variable provided by the interviewer; see Chapter 8). Moreover, in each study we used a separate cutoff point for being a highly successful entrepreneur (as cutoff points we used the mean plus one standard deviation of the success variable for that particular study; see Chapter 8 for the calculation of this cutoff point).

The first entry in Figure 5.1 is the age of business (year of business establishment), which did not matter much. In both studies, the effects were not significant, thus contradicting the concept of "liability of newness," which implies that newer companies should be less likely to be successful. The effect of the line of business on success was not significant in both studies. In contrast, the number of employees was strongly related to success. This is not surprising, because growth in the number of employees is an important indicator of success and those firms with a high number of employees have grown more strongly than the smaller firms.

With regard to unemployment before starting one's firm and success, the two studies were contradictory. Study 1 showed a relationship with success, as entrepreneurs who started their firms because of unemployment had a lower success rate than those who started their firm from a steady job. Study 2 did not show this relationship. The results of Study 2 confirm our suspicion that this relationship may not really be that important.

Another popular concept that is contradicted by the results of these studies is whether it is positive or negative to have extended family members in one's business. In Study 2, there is a clear relationship with success (the nonsignificant relationship in Study 1 goes in the same direction as the one of Study 2). Those who employ a family member in their business are more successful (53% highly successful) than those who do not (only 26% highly successful in Study 2).

In Study 2, those who had a higher starting capital were more successful than those who started with less than $1,000. In this case, there is a "long arm" from the start-up time to later success.

Education plays a positive role for success. Those who went to college or university (more than thirteen years of education) showed a higher degree of success (75% of them were highly successful in contrast to the other groups which had much lower degrees of success). Thus, human capital is important for being successful in Zimbabwe.

There is also a relationship of success with applying for a loan in Study 2. Note that most people who applied actually did not get the loan; more interesting, getting a loan was not related to success. There are three possible interpretations: First, those who are already successful apply more frequently to get a loan. Second, those who dare more and are more active apply for a loan more frequently and are also more successful. Third, the preparation involved with producing a formal business plan and rethinking what one is doing has a positive effect in the long run. In any case, applying for a loan is more predictive of success than getting a loan.

The results on the links to the formal sector show a clear relationship in Study 2 (58% are successful in the high link group in comparison to 14% in those with a low number of links to the formal sector). There is some overlap between being formal and having links to the formal sector.

The number of hours worked was originally thought to be an indicator of thrift. However, it may also mean that the business is not well organized. Possibly both factors play a role. In any case, the relationship with success is not significant in both studies.

PSYCHOLOGICAL SUCCESS FACTORS

Figure 5.2 describes the relationships of the psychological factors with success. Again, it is important to remember that the percentages of the two studies cannot be compared directly. Moreover, many of the results are significant only in Study 2, because of its higher number of participants. Surprisingly, in both studies, neither goal specificity nor goal difficulty were significantly related to success. This means that simply having specific and high goals is not enough for business owners to be successful. These results contradict findings from the United States (most notably Baum, 1995). They do not imply, however, that goals do not have any function at all. We also assume that firm owners should have a vision for their firm (Baum, Locke, & Kirkpatrick, 1998); however, we did not study vision.

Planning and proactiveness were of high importance for success in both studies. In the low planning group of Study 1, there is not one entrepreneur who is highly successful, while in the high planning group, the respective percentage is 15 percent. Similarly, in Study 2, there are many more highly successful firm owners in the high planning than in the low planning group. For proactiveness, there are three times more highly successful people in the high than in the low proactiveness group in Study 1; in Study 2, there are nearly twice as many highly successful entrepreneurs in the high proactiveness than in the low proactiveness group.

These results are replicated when we look at the results for the process characteristics of strategies in detail. If planning exists, as in complete planning and critical point planning, and if proactiveness is

Figure 5.2
Psychological Factors and Success, Zimbabwe

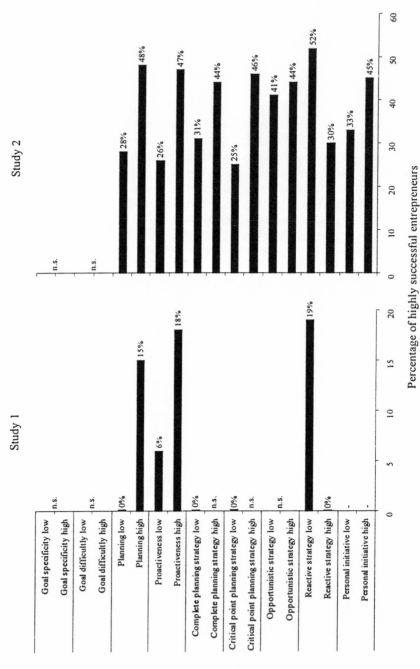

Figure 5.2 (*continued*)

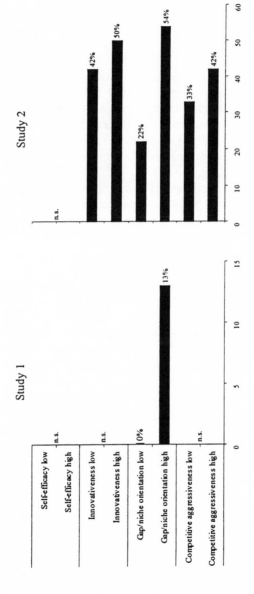

Study 1

Study 2

Percentage of highly successful entrepreneurs

strong, as in complete planning, critical point planning, and opportunistic strategy, there are positive relationships of the strategies with success in Study 2. While these results are not significant in Study 1 (because of the small number of participants), they point in the same direction as in Study 2.

The opposite is true of a reactive strategy. A reactive strategy is characterized by a low degree of planning and a low degree of proactiveness. This proves to be bad for business success. If one is high on a reactive strategy, there is a 0-percent chance of being highly successful, compared with a 19-percent chance to be highly successful in the low reactive strategy group in Study 1; similar percentages exist in Study 2, with 52 percent being highly successful among the low reactive entrepreneurs versus a 30-percent chance to be highly successful among the highly reactive owners.

Personal initiative has been discussed as being related to success as well; this is shown to be true in Study 2. If entrepreneurs are in the high initiative group, their chance to be highly successful is 45 percent. This percentage is lower (33%) if they are in the low initiative group.

The results for self-efficacy were surprising. The relationship of self-efficacy with success was nonsignificant in both studies. People who were high on self-efficacy did not have a higher success rate than those who were low. Possibly the problems that the business owners have to deal with are so complex that self-efficacy is not important.

Innovativeness is significantly related to success only in Study 2. This may be an indication that innovativeness is not always the most important factor for economic success in the microbusiness area. A gap or niche orientation is good in any case; both studies showed clear and strong relationships with success. Entrepreneurs who look for market niches and develop appropriate products or services for the niche are much more successful than those who do not.

Competitively aggressive owners were more successful in Study 2. Thus, this second factor of entrepreneurial orientation (innovativeness was the first) turned out to be a predictor of success.

CASE STUDIES

Case 1

Case 1 is a carpenter (thirty-six years old) who buys antique-style furniture and renovates it for resale; he also manufactures cottage furniture. He started his business, which is informal up to 1999, in 1980 with $250. In 1993, his staff consisted of eight employees and grew in 1996 to the current number of fourteen employees, thirteen of which are from his extended family. The owner went to school for seven years and his highest degree of formal education was grade seven. He was eighteen years old when he started his own company. He had acquired his business knowledge during his time as a delivery driver for one of the larger furniture manufacturers in Harare.

His workshop is located in one of the high-density home industries of Harare. This makes it difficult to get access to White customers. Since they are his main customers, access is one of his most pressing problems. White Zimbabweans hardly ever frequent his area, which forces him to sell his goods on the roadside in the White neighborhoods. To have a retail shop in one of the up-market areas in town is something he does not even dare think about when asked about his business goals.

His most important goals are to "improve the way to produce a product" and to "perform better than the competitors." Yet he is not very precise when asked to specify subgoals in these areas. He comes up with very general ideas of "making his business grow," "buy more things and resell them," and producing "nicely finished products." When he describes strategies to reach his goals, it becomes apparent that there is no real planning behind his business-related actions. His plans concerning "improving the way to produce a product" do not go beyond working hard, finishing the timber nicely, using the profit to buy more furniture, and building a better workshop when he gets the chance. The strategies for his second goal ("perform better than the competitors") only consist of replacing the hand tools with electric machinery should he be able to raise the money. All these strategies are based on a rudimentary level of planning and have not been seriously or actively worked out.

This owner does not have a written business plan, and he clearly does not plan ahead in any way. His goal descriptions are fuzzy and hard to bring to a point. They are more general hopes for growth than visions for the company. In addition, he shows no proactive behavior. For example, although he is currently selling his goods on the roadside, which is very common in Zimbabwe, he neither intends to change his situation nor is actively looking for a better approach to gain access to customers. This business owner can be described as using reactive business strategies. He is merely reacting to external events and does not attempt to change the business environment in an interactive way. The owner does not plan ahead. He has vague business goals, he does not come up with innovative or creative business ideas, and he does not show any efforts to actively seek change or find opportunities.

An example of his lack of initiative is that, although he has been in business for many years, he has never sought training or any other source for better ideas on antique furniture. As nobody ever taught him about antiques, he struggles to classify the pieces he is working with, which makes marketing and pricing more than difficult. He copes with his lack of knowledge by using a book (which he claims cannot be found in Zimbabwe) from one of his White colleagues in town for classifying his furniture. While this certainly is a clever way of improvising, after eighteen years in business he should have come up with a better solution.

On the other hand, the owner has been able to keep his business afloat and growing for eighteen years. However, he has now reached his zenith. There are no signs of improvement over the past few years in terms of modernization of the equipment (they are still using hand tools), the Third World standard of his workshop, or business growth (the number of employees has been the same over the last three years). The relatively high number of employees from the extended family (thirteen out of fourteen) might explain why this owner is still operating despite his poor management strategies. He considers his relatives as valuable to his business, especially because they all work well together as a team. This case also illustrates that sheer size of a firm is not always a good indicator of its success.

When describing the behavior of the employees from his extended family, the owner emphasizes their loyalty, their good teamwork, and the support they provide. In addition, since family members do not need to be paid in bad times, employing them helped him to keep his business afloat. Thus, skills or creative improvement of work methods were not issues he examined when employing people.

Case 2

Case 2 is also in the carpentry business and produces wardrobes, kitchen units, room dividers, and shop fittings. The owner and his two active partners started their business two years ago as a cooperative. It has since changed into a partnership and is in the process of becoming registered and enrolled for tax payments. The owners have two employees, neither of whom is from their extended families. When they started in 1996, they had capital of approximately $330 and no employees. In 1998, they employed two workers. The twenty-eight-year-old interviewee has O-level education and was formerly employed as a foreman in the assembling department of a big furniture manufacturing company. This experience gave him a decent background in carpentry and management practices.

When asked about his goals for the business, he ranks as most important to "perform better than his competitors," and, second, to "develop a new marketing strategy." Generally, he has high aspirations in these areas, but they are not very detailed. He mentions, for example, that he wants to produce beyond the needs of friends and family, as his comparable competitors do. He also wants to sell his goods abroad in Zambia and Mozambique, but cannot visualize how to actually go about this. His strategies to reach his goals can be mainly described as looking out for and seizing opportunities, as well as networking with other business owners. Thus, he uses an opportunistic strategy.

He actively approaches his competitors to discuss manufacturing problems and to exchange samples of designs. He has also sent a colleague to survey furniture in Zambia and has approached larger furniture sales companies to offer his products. The owners have managed to have a telephone line installed in their workshop, which can also be used for a small fee by their neighbors in the home industry. In addition, they sell some carpentry hardware to their competitors in the area. While the business owner is proactive, there is a lack of planning with regard to his business strategies. He notices and seizes opportunities when they cross his path, but neglects to plan beforehand. He has ill-defined and somewhat exchangeable goals. However, when the occasion arises, he is active even if there is little planning.

His most important business problems are "suppliers" and "equipment," which are both primarily caused by lack of capital. High-quality supplies, just like equipment, have to be paid for in advance. When asked about solutions to these problems, he refers to an "if-we-had-the-money" condition instead of focussing on the actual problem; for example, how to find ways to raise the funds. Nevertheless, being halfway through the registration process (to become formal) might help his enterprise to get access to loans and contracts with other formal businesses in the near future.

Case 3

This business owner is a formally registered consultant for taxation and accounting. He established his firm eight years ago in 1990. Now thirty-seven years old, the interviewee had been employed as a tax assessor in an authoritative position within the Zimbabwean tax department before he established his own business. Upon his retirement he received approximately $375, which he used to open his consultancy. In 1993, he had one employee and enlarged his staff in 1997 by one person to the present number of two clerks. The owner holds a Bachelor of Commerce degree, and he is a member of several professional associations, as well as a regular reader of professional journals.

The owner's goals for his business are very high and are all related to the higher-order goals of "improving the way to produce a product" and "developing a new marketing strategy." Specifically, he wants to add management consultancy to his services and work on an international scale, he wants to become the leading tax consultant in Zimbabwe, and he wants to establish a tax consultancy training institution with a structure like a business school. As accountancy ethics do not allow him to openly advertise his services, his subgoals are concerned with a new marketing strategy. The new strategy is not yet worked out completely, but it is realistic, as he is trying to enhance customer care and to get customers to recommend him to new clients. The owner has numerous strategies for reaching his goals. His main emphasis lies in improving personal customer care, which he intends to realize by delegating more clerical work to his employees and by spending more time with the customers himself. In order to be able to do so, he plans to recruit employees, who come straight from high school, and to train them personally. In addition, he wants to employ someone with a diploma in accountancy to supervise them. He also started to get computerized and is looking for possibilities to make himself and his staff more computer literate.

Other strategies to reach his goals are far less detailed and planned out. He is looking for an opportunity to get an MBA (which is a prerequisite for managing a training institution) on a part-time basis, and would like to move his business into an up-market area. He attempts to raise his fees in order to be able to work for fewer but better-paying clients. He also tries to get a more diversified clientele. At present, the majority of his clients are from the health sector, which underwent a reform last year and, therefore, now has serious financial problems. In addition, he often networks with previous colleagues from the tax department. The business owner illustrated how he used the 1997 tax blitz and his contacts with the tax department to attract more clients. In terms of strategy, he is highly proactive, yet does not do much planning. He is concentrating on one critical point, which is the future organization of his staff, so that he can spend more time outside the office with his clients. The other goals seem to be of minor importance and will probably be dealt with as soon as the most important goal is tackled (critical point planner).

He considers his main advantage in the marketplace his firm's personalized customer care, which exceeds that of larger companies, and his more advanced professional and educational background, which exceeds that of other smaller firms. This positive customer-care attitude is reiterated by his description of his strategies, where customer care is considered before handling any other goals.

Case 4

Case 4 owns a garage in one of Harare's home industries at the outskirts of the city. He carries out panel beating, spray painting, and car repairs, and sells hardware. In 1996, he started his business with a partner who lives in Bulawayo and occasionally comes to Harare for consultation. The now thirty-year-old interviewee holds 55 percent of the shares in the business, which was established with a starting capital of approximately $2,500. His qualifications include a National Diploma in Business Studies from the Harare Institute of Technology (a local polytechnic). In addition, he is a member of the Automobile Association of Zimbabwe, which is not common, even in his line of business. The business owner developed some management expertise while working as a shift supervisor for a tobacco-processing firm. He started out with two workers and currently employs three full-time and two part-time workers, none of whom are from his extended family. Although the workshop is situated in a remote area, it is furnished with a telephone line, is registered, and is enrolled for tax payments.

His business goals are not exceptionally high, yet very realistic. Most important are to "improve the way to produce a product" and "developing a new marketing strategy." His subgoals are to improve panel beating and spray painting in such a way that one cannot tell that his clients' cars have been involved in accidents. He also aims to improve the overhauling of engines in such a way that they are acceptable by the manufacturers' standards, and to deliver the best performance possible to customers, who will in turn recommend him to their friends. To ensure that he reaches his goals, the business owner only employs specialists (e.g., one mechanic, one spray painter, one panel beater). His management philosophy is "planning, organizing, and controlling." Not only is he making sure that his employees are equipped with the right machinery and materials to do a good job in the time agreed upon with the customer, he is also confident about motivating his staff. The owner has introduced a system of production-centered management, whereby, depending on their performance, the workers receive a bonus check of Z$500 every three months. The employees are also registered for medical aid, a pension fund, and workers compensation in case they have an accident. In his own words, he feels that he "makes sure that the employees are satisfied, not only moneywise, but also concerning self-actualization, self-esteem, and belongingness." In addition, he started to provide new spark plugs (material and labor) for first-time customers and for former clients who introduced new customers to him. The business has expanded by selling hardware products as an extra service. The business owner also has a financial consultant who advised and assisted him in his application for a loan. The bank has not yet responded to his request.

Although he did not write a business plan, the owner's business strategies can best be described as complete planning. In addition to actively looking for and seizing opportunities, he plans step by step to improve his business. As a top-down planner, he focusses on more than one point. He considers personnel and operational concerns as well as financial and marketing issues, and he has a detailed plan for how to handle each of them. This is emphasized when he talks about business-related problems. As is true for most microbusiness owners in Africa, one of his constraints is lack of capital. This means that the equipment is too old. This owner, however, took the initiative and attempted to establish a joint venture with other business owners who are in the same situation, even before he approached a financial consultant and applied for a loan (which is also not typical for the rest of the sample). Several entrepreneurs in the same line of business whom he considered trustworthy were encouraged to join their facilities in order to be more efficient. Unfortunately, they declined and the plan was never carried out.

Although his goals are somewhat restricted with regard to expanding beyond his present location, this business owner aspires to high goals regarding quality and customer care. He does not feel threatened by his local competitors at all. Despite recognizing the need for improvement, he is still very confident with his plan of action and his personal motivation toward success.

SUMMARY

Two studies in Zimbabwe gave rather similar results. Unemployment prior to starting one's business did not consistently contribute to failure, as often suggested. Running against common hypotheses, it was positive for success to employ extended family members. It did not really matter whether owners received a loan. However, those who applied for a loan had a higher percentage of successful entrepreneurs in their ranks.

Surprisingly, there was no relationship of specificity and difficulties of goals with success, in contrast to a study in the West (Baum, 1994), and in contrast to the vast literature on the motivational effects of goal setting for employees (Locke & Latham, 1990). One possible interpretation is that entrepreneurial tasks are very complex, and the literature has shown that goal setting is less effective in complex-task environments (Wood, Mento, & Locke, 1987).

The most important findings are related to psychological process characteristics of strategy development. Those entrepreneurs who were planning and proactive were much more successful than nonplanners and more reactive ones. The specific form of an active or planning strategy did not matter much in Zimbabwe. Complete planning, critical point planning, and opportunistic strategies were more or less similarly positively related to success. The most dramatic and consistent results occurred for reactive strategies: Whoever utilized a reactive strategy (and in Zimbabwe this strategy is employed strongly by 25% of the owners), had a high probability of failure. In some way, the opposite of a reactive strategy is to show a high degree of personal initiative. This, indeed, was positively related to success.

Because these two studies were cross-sectional, we cannot make causal inferences. Thus, we do not know whether the strategies led to success or whether success leads to a specific use of strategy. From a study in The Netherlands (Van Gelderen & Frese, 1998), we know that both processes happen; for example, a high utilization of a reactive strategy leads to failure, and failure, in turn, leads to a higher use of a reactive strategy. We assume that similar vicious cycles are operative in Africa as well.

Other important findings are that self-efficacy was not significantly related to success. On the other hand, innovativeness was a predictor of success, as suggested in the literature. A gap or niche orientation was an important predictor of success in both studies. These two findings have consistently been detected in the Western world as well. Entrepreneurs are well-advised to search for innovative products and innovative forms of production and to apply them in a niche market.

In all, these findings suggest that psychological variables such as innovativeness, psychological process characteristics of behavioral strategies, planning, and proactiveness are of particular importance in Zimbabwe. Thus, training, selection, and support systems ought to make sure that entrepreneurs are high in these factors. Moreover, these factors are more important than the simple sociodemographic factors that are often used in entrepreneurship research and practice.

REFERENCES

Bandura, A. (1997). *Self-efficacy: The exercise of control.* New York: Freeman.

Baum, J. R. (1994). *The relation of traits, competencies, vision, motivation, and strategy to venture growth.* Unpublished doctoral dissertation, University of Maryland.

Baum, J. R. (1995). The relation of traits, competencies, motivation, strategy, and structure to venture growth. *Frontiers of entrepreneurship research.* Proceedings of the 15th annual Entrepreneurship Research Conference. Babson Park, MS: Arthur M. Blank Center for Entrepreneurship, 547–561.

Baum, J. R., Locke, E. A., & Kirkpatrick, S. A. (1998). A longitudinal study of vision and vision communication to venture growth in entrepreneurial firms. *Journal of Applied Psychology, 83* (1), 43–54.

Bruederl, J., Preisendoerfer, P., & Ziegler, R. (1992). Survival chances of newly founded business organizations. *American Sociological Review, 57,* 227–242.

Covin, J. G., & Slevin, D. P. (1989). Strategic management of small firms in hostile and benign environments. *Strategic Management Journal, 10,* 75–87.

Dallas, R. (1995). *The Economist: Pocket Africa.* London: Penguin Books.

Daniels, L. (1994). *Changes in the small-scale enterprise sector from 1991 to 1993: Results of a second nationwide survey in Zimbabwe* (GEMINI Technical Report No. 71). Bethesda, MD: Growth and Equity through Microenterprise Investments and Institutions.

Frese, M., Fay, D., Hilburger, T., Leng, K., & Tag, A. (1997). The concept of personal initiative: Operationalization, reliability and validity in two German samples. *Journal of Occupational and Organizational Psychology, 70,* 139–161.

Frese, M., Garst, H., & Fay, D. (1998). *Control and complexity in work and the development of personal initiative (PI): A 5-wave longitudinal structural equation model of occupational socialization.* Manuscript submitted for publication.

Frese, M., van Gelderen, M., & Ombach, M. (in press). How to plan as a small scale business owner: Psychological process characteristics of action strategies and success. *Journal of Small Business Management.*

Gray, K. R., Cooley, W., & Lutabingwa, J. (1997). Small-scale manufacturing in Kenya. *Journal of Small Business Management, 1,* 66–72.

Gray, K. R., Cooley, W., Lutabingwa, J., Mutai-Kaimenyi, B., & Oyugi, L. A. (1996). *Entrepreneurship in micro-enterprises: A strategic analysis of manufacturing industries in Kenya.* Lanham, MD: University Press of America.

Guzzo, R. A., Jette, R. D., & Katzell, R. A. (1985). The effects of psychologically based intervention programs on work productivity: A meta-analysis. *Personnel Psychology, 38,* 275–291.

Harrison, D., & Friedrich, C. (1990). *Small business needs survey.* Harare: Friedrich Naumann Stiftung.

Harrison, D., & Friedrich, C. (1994). *A combined method questionnaire/case study survey of 7 informal sector business types.* Harare: Friedrich Naumann Stiftung.

Locke, E. A., & Latham, G. P. (1990). *A theory of goal setting and task performance.* Englewood Cliffs, NJ: Prentice Hall.

Lumpkin, G. T., & Dess, G. G. (1996). Clarifying the entrepreneurial orientation construct and linking it to performance. *Academy of Management Review, 21,* 135–172.

McPherson, M. A. (1991, December). *Micro and small-scale enterprises in Zimbabwe: Results of a country-wide survey.* (GEMINI Technical Report No. 25). Bethesda, MD: Growth and Equity through Microenterprise Investments and Institutions.

McPherson, M. A. (1998). *Zimbabwe: A third nationwide survey of micro and small enterprises.* Final report prepared for USAID/Zimbabwe, Pricewaterhouse Coopers.

Neshamba, F. (1997). The transition of enterprises from informality to formality: Some evidence from Zimbabwe. *Small Enterprise Development, 8* (4), 48–53.

Shane, S., & Kolvereid, L. (1995). National environment, strategy, and new venture performance: A three country study. *Journal of Small Business Management, 33,* 37–50.

Van Gelderen, M., & Frese, M. (1998). Strategy process as a characteristic of small scale business owners: Relationships with success in a longitudinal study. *Frontiers of entrepreurship research.* Proceedings of the 18th annual Entrepreneurship Research Conference. Babson Park, MS: Arthur M. Blank Center for Entrepreneurship, pp. 234–248.

Wild, V. (1994). *Versorgungskapitalisten.* Muenchen: Weltforum.

Wood, R. E., Mento, A. J., & Locke, E. A. (1987). Task complexity as a moderator of goal effects: A meta-analysis. *Journal of Applied Psychology, 72,* 416–425.

6

Development and Growth of Small-Scale Business in Zimbabwe: A Practical View

Christian Friedrich

Despite the vast opportunities created by the technological revolution of the twentieth century, more than 1.3 billion people live on less than $1 a day, a standard of living that Western Europe and the United States attained 200 years ago (Frankfurter Allgemeine Zeitung, 1999). Since 1981, when the World Bank published its first warning on the deteriorating African economies, almost every report published has sounded more desperate. At first, the world was told of the grave situation. By 1989, it was from "crisis to sustainable growth" (World Bank, 1989). It is not an exaggeration to say that the continent lags behind all continents in terms of development. Africa's share of the world Gross Domestic Product (GDP) during the last twenty years is less than 2 percent against population growth of approximately 3 percent. As long as population growth exceeds economic growth, there will be less jobs and the people will become poorer and poorer. Of the 160 countries on the U.N. Development Index, thirty-two of the poorest are in Africa. Food production in the middle of the 1990s was 20 percent less than it was in 1970, although the population has doubled in the meantime.

ZIMBABWE

Zimbabwe, a landlocked country in the southern African region, only became independent in 1980. The average growth of GDP from independence to 1997 was 3 percent a year (Afrika-Verein, 1998). The growth of GDP lagged behind the growth of population, which was 3.2 percent since independence. For a long time, Zimbabwe has had a relatively well-developed physical infrastructure, sound agricultural and mining industries that are the principle production and export sectors, and a broad and fairly strong manufacturing industry base that supply most of the domestic consumer good and needs. After having experienced fifteen years of sanctions between 1965 and 1979 during the period following Rhodesia's unilateral Declaration of Independence, the Zimbabwean government, after independence in 1980, embarked on a more or less socialistic economic policy. It was a dull business environment in which business organizations such as the banks could do little to promote business development. The banks could not change their interest rates and their access equity because of strict investment controls. In 1991, the Zimbabwean government decided to embark on an Economic Structural Adjustment Program, together with the World Bank and the International Monetary Fund (IMF).

With the adoption of the economic reform program, the government has made a remarkable U-turn in its policies, recognizing above all else that employment creation is urgent. Zimbabwe was and is still having a problem of severe unemployment. From figures provided by the Statistical Year Book, it is estimated that, in 1996, 28 percent of the economically active people were without jobs. Some NGOs estimate unemployment to be up to 50 percent of the adult population. One of the reasons is that the formal sector is unable to offer adequate employment opportunities, especially in the present unfavorable economic climate. The formal sector is unable to create more than 20,000 to 25,000 jobs a year. A little more than 300,000 young well-educated people are leaving schools every year in Zimbabwe. That means that less than 10 percent find a job in the formal sector.

SMALL BUSINESS ADVISORY GROUP (SBAG)

After 1980, many different initiatives were started to create employment, especially for the Black population. One focus in the late 1980s was the promotion of small businesses. Many nongovernmental organizations and bilateral organizations were running programs, and the Zimbabwean government, through different organizations like SEDCO (Small Enterprise Development Corporation), was trying to help. But there was a lack of coordination. Both government and NGOs did not know what the other ones were doing. In 1991, there was an initiative of the German Naumann Foundation to coordinate the efforts in the small-scale business sector. Government, ministries, and donor agencies were brought together in several meetings. The core problems were identified and the group developed an action plan which different organizations were free to implement. At approximately quarterly meetings, members reported on progress in their field of action. To make the whole process more vibrant, a newsletter was published in which members could report about their activities. Another approach of the SBAG was to host experts from foreign countries and to run conferences to inform the government about successful strategies from other countries in such areas as deregulation and privatization.

The major achievements of the SBAG were effective communication of experiences and ideas in the small-scale sector between government and the donor community, and the support of research and conferences in this field. Through a system of action plans, SBAG effectively pressed for change. SBAG can be a model for other countries to improve cooperation, coordination, and communication for the micro- and small-scale business sector.

BUSINESS LINKAGES AND SUBCONTRACTING FOR SMALL-SCALE ENTERPRISES

The relationship between informal and formal established enterprises is a complex one. As large- and medium-scale enterprises become more specialized, they subcontract work, but they cannot compete with small-scale enterprises. The reasons why large companies would want to subcontract are to achieve greater efficiency through functional specialization and greater flexibility, but also to reduce labor costs and transfer risks. Procurement lists are published to give the small-scale sector the opportunity to tender for large supply contracts. However, the procurements are too complex for most micro- and small-scale enterprises to consider making serious bids. In addition, small enterprises often find the ironical situation that as cash customers they have to pay more for their raw materials than established enterprises that purchase their raw materials on credit. In the clothing business, for example, items involving low-value textile inputs and small differentials in procurement costs can have a significant impact on competitiveness. At its best, subcontracting can provide an important initial market base, allowing the small enterprise to develop production and management skills and improve quality to a point where it can compete openly in any market. There are some examples of successful subcontracting in Zimbabwe. For example, a Bulawayo clothing company has eleven subcontractors, with a full-time supervisor for each to ensure quality and delivery dates.

Without the transfer of skills on a continuous basis, every subcontracting program will fail. There should be an emphasis on the transfer of technical skills, human resources, and training skills. It is not enough just to transfer money from the big company to the small entrepreneur to make him or her successful.

TRAINING AND CONSULTANCY FOR EMERGING BUSINESSES

At the beginning of the 1990s, there was not much knowledge about the needs of small-scale business in Zimbabwe. Therefore, we conducted a survey to find out what the major problems of small enterprises in Zimbabwe were (Harrison & Friedrich, 1990). This survey dealt with four questions:

1. What are the major difficulties that Zimbabwean small-business owners or managers think they have?
2. What forms of consultancy and training support were perceived to be necessary by Zimbabwean small-business owners?
3. What are the preferences of Zimbabwean small-business owners when they are presented with an appropriately explained range of consultancy and training possibilities?
4. What are the preferences of Zimbabwean small-business owners with regard to the various methods of providing consultancy and training support?

Altogether, 168 small entrepreneurs were interviewed. Sixty-five came from big cities, sixty-eight from rural areas, and thirty-five from so-called "growth points" (centralized areas for rural entrepreneurs). The results showed a strong need for management training, training in the latest technology, sourcing materials, and marketing. An unexpected and important outcome was the high level of need expressed by firm owners in the growth points. They experienced very high levels of stress, and strong needs for many forms of advice in general management, bookkeeping, security, finding business premises, marketing, advertising, and selling. Very little intention to enter the formal sector was expressed by the informal-sector respondents, because of bureaucracy and tax levies.

It was surprisingly difficult to find rural communal manufacturing businesses. The majority of small businesses in this section of the sample were informal, small-scale, casual producers who evidenced significantly lower levels of both needs and apparent stress than their growth-points counterparts.

Major findings have been the low level of general awareness of existing forms of support for small businesses. Shortages of raw materials and equipment and lack of knowledge of international markets, styles, and fashions were major concerns of the manufactural sector.

What were the preferences of Zimbabwean small-business owners with regard to the various methods of providing consultancy and training support? Small-course formats were not popular. They preferred individual advice, especially for the purpose of increasing sales.

Training and consultancy schemes based on the results of this survey were developed. The starting point was a one-day workshop on how to start and run a small business, which was mostly disseminated in English. Very soon it became obvious that this first training course should be translated in the two major local languages, Shona and Ndebele, because, especially in the rural areas, many of the participants could not fluently speak English. In this first one-day training course, business basics were taught; for example, every business is selling something, whether it is a trading business such as a shop selling groceries or sweets or other things, a production business such as a dressmaker selling clothes, a business selling a service such as a haircare salon, a childcare center, or a repair business. Besides this, business basics were taught, such as what is profit, what is income, what are costs, how to do pricing and calculate costs and cash-flow, and how to work out a business plan.

Very soon it became obvious that a one-day training course for somebody who would like to start his or her own business was not enough. So two more training courses were developed: one on cash management and another on marketing. For the one-day marketing course, objectives were for the participants to be able to describe the market for their business and list some strategies to increase this market. Participants should be able to apply marketing principles concerning price and products to goods and services. They should be able to choose the advertising medium to use for their businesses and to select an appropriate message to improve their market share and the selling techniques used in their businesses. Last, participants should be able to develop a marketing plan to suit their own business plans.

Objectives in the one-day cash management course were for participants to learn why capital is essential in business and the importance of capital if they want their businesses to grow. Another objective was to enable them to make budgets for their businesses, use the necessary data, and work out the break-even point for products. Furthermore, they should be able to keep a cash book to record and control income and expenses. Participants should also be able to keep up their cash book and make cash-flow projections.

A training and consultancy unit was founded together with the Zimbabwean National Chamber of Commerce (Small Business Support Unit [SBSU]), where trainers and consultants were employed. The trainers of this unit were responsible for the nationwide program, especially in growth points in rural areas. Approximately 2,500 upcoming entrepreneurs took part every year. The program was subsidized by the German government. Nevertheless, every participant had to pay a nominal fee for every training and for every consultancy. Approximately 10 percent of the participants finally opened a business.

The survival of small business in developing countries strongly depends on the growth of the economy. Micro- and small-scale enterprises in their start-up phase normally do not export; they are depending on the local market and local buying power. In 1992, Zimbabwe was facing a devastating drought and GDP dropped by approximately 6 percent in one year. This negatively influenced almost every business, because local buying power decreased. Large and medium-size businesses often had some savings to survive for a period of twelve months or longer. Upcoming businesses did not. According to our experience, more than one-third of the businesses which started in 1991 had to close down in 1992 or 1993. In 1994, the figures were more stable, because of an increase in GDP and a better overall business environment. Unfortunately, most service providers do not follow up the success of the participants in the training courses. This was also true of this project. Future projects should do an in-depth evaluation.

Another approach to training in Zimbabwe is, for example, the Informal Sector Training and Resource Network (ISTARN) by the GTZ (Gesellschaft für Technische Zusammenarbeit), based in Masvingo province (Nell, Kohlheyer, Muza, & Masaka, 1998). The project aims to address the issue of unemployment by strengthening the informal sector. ISTARN is seen as a regional training and resources network which is training-needs driven and is making use of existing training capacities in situations, such as local nongovernmental organizations (NGOs). The program has four main areas:

1. Traditional Apprenticeship Program.
2. Informal Sector Associations Support Program.
3. Small Business Advisory Program.
4. Marketing Intermediary Support Program.

SUMMARY

It could be shown that in Zimbabwe there is a great need for training and consultancy, especially outside the big cities. But even with the best training programs, small enterprises will not contribute to a high degree of employment if there is no conducive business environment and no access to credit for small-scale enterprises. Last but not least, a good coordination of donor aid through a monitoring body can help to make the whole sector more prosperous.

REFERENCES

Afrika-Verein. (1998). *Jahresbericht*. Hamburg: Author.

Frankfurter Allgemeine Zeitung. (1999, April 27). *Immer mehr Menschen gleiten in die Armut ab*, p. 17.

Harrison, D., & Friedrich, C. (1990). *Small business needs survey*. Harare: Friedrich Naumann Stiftung.

Nell, M., Kohlheyer, G., Muza, A., & Masaka, M. (1998). *Informal sector training and resources network (ISTARN)* (project progress review). Frankfurt: Gesellschaft fuer Technische Zusammenarbeit (GTZ).

Statistical year book. (1997). Harare: Government Printer.

World Bank. (1981). *World development report*. New York: Oxford University Press.

World Bank. (1989). *From crisis to sustainable growth*. New York: Oxford University Press.

7

Formalization: The Major Criterion of Success in Developing Countries

David Harrison

BACKGROUND

Studies of entrepreneurs in Africa have sampled businesses ranging from single-proprietor operations with no other employees to businesses with up to fifty employees. However, approximately 95 percent of the proprietors interviewed have run businesses in the informal sector with five or less employees. Although the distinction between formal and informal can be disputed, the businesses have been unregistered and unlisted for tax purposes, and, in many cases, have infringed relatively unpoliced regulations of one form or another. With few exceptions (e.g., Harrison & Friedrich, 1994) the patently illegal informal sector has been ignored by the literature. Most authors have mentioned economic growth, employment creation, and so on as the meta-objectives of such research. Unfortunately, there is strong evidence that a very high percentage of the businesses studied have produced only bare subsistence levels of earnings. The Gemini 1993 study, for example, showed minimal growth into the formal sector: "Three percent of all MSEs added paid workers during their life and 1 of 250 MSEs increased the number of workers from below 10 to more than 10 workers" (Daniels, 1994, p. 54). Daniels stated in the follow-up seminar, shortly after publication of the survey results, that these data showed a negligible net gain in the number of formal-sector businesses. Research writers have, understandably but very misleadingly, alluded to the economic importance of small businesses. In concluding his report of the first Gemini study, McPherson (1991) stated that the survey, "made it clear that micro and small enterprises are an important part of the Zimbabwean economy, and a major generator of income for the country's citizens." However, this importance can only be based on the well-established finding that, in Zimbabwe, the 95 percent of those working in the small-scale sector endure a barely subsistence level of living.

Zimbabwean-based international financial consultant Eric Bloch and Zimbabwean economist John Robertson in their book, *Zimbabwe: Facing the Facts*, have this to say:

Zimbabwe currently has an estimated 2.6 million people potentially employable but not employed, out of a total employable population estimated to approximate a little more than 4 million. In other words, about 24 percent of the total population, irrespective of age or gender, and about 60 to 65 percent of the employable population is unemployed. As it is estimated that the current cost of creating a single job within the formal sector of the economy averages $130,000, Zimbabwe would need almost $340 billion to cater to the present unemployed, or almost twenty times its GDP. And the situation progressively worsens, for each year about another 300,000 school leavers enter the job market, while only about 40,000 leave the workplace and, in recent years, only approximately 10,000 new jobs are created each year. Thus, Zimbabwean unemployment annually increases by a further quarter of a million people. As unemployment escalates and growth in GDP is minimal, per capita income declines and ever-greater numbers struggle for survival on incomes well below the Poverty Datum Line. (1997, p. 62)

The second Zimbabwean GEMINI study (Daniels, 1994) illustrates the poverty level of microbusinesses in Zimbabwe. The average "profit" over all businesses surveyed was Z$30,678 or US$4,579 per year (US$12.54 per day). This is a very low figure, as profit was calculated as income less normal sales and costs of hired labor. Thus, the US$12.54 was distributed, as the only income, between the proprietor and all family employees not receiving any formal wage. For the lowest three quintiles, the average annual profit, as defined, was only Z$10,516 or US$1,600 (US$4.30 per day). The highest profit quintile comprised mostly formal businesses: printing, retail, autoworks, general trade, and so on (i.e., easily identifiable, registered, formal-sector businesses). The high average profit for this quintile of Z$132,140 should be noted as a source of positive bias in estimating the overall average, and as an illustration of the massively higher formal-sector profits.

In a situation of massive and urgent need, as illustrated, only businesses that become genuinely profitable, grow, and create employment will be considered economically and socially beneficial. Accordingly, from an economic perspective the objective of African research on small businesses should be to understand the factors that lead to growth rather than analyze in detail samples from a reference population of highly probable failures. In 1991, the Friedrich Naumann Foundation commissioned a Small Business Needs Survey to be carried out by Human Resources (Pvt) Ltd., which involved focussed interviews with sixty-five respondents from major towns, sixty-eight from rural/communal areas, and thirty-five from growth points/business centers (Harrison & Friedrich, 1991, 1992). Among the findings of that research was evidence that growth points were experiencing very high levels of stress, with strong needs for many forms of advice in general management, accountancy/bookkeeping, security, finding business premises, marketing, advertising, and selling, for example. The study also found that businesspersons of the informal sector were not motivated to expand into the formal sector, as they regard the taxation levels and regulatory restrictions of the formal sector as prohibitive.

An important but perhaps disheartening outcome of the GEMINI studies and other investigations which have not focussed upon success, as here discussed, should be the conclusion that little growth can be expected from undereducated and socially disadvantaged entrepreneurs. Acceptance of the validity of this conclusion may stimulate business-orientated educational programs and systems of taxation and regulation which are enabling and motivating, in place of the almost insurmountable barriers to formalization which currently exist. Zimbabwe's small-scale sector (and probably many others in Africa) is a sociopolitical opiate. It is misleading to infer that "importance" as attributed by research writers is equivalent to "motivating or producing economic growth."

We must distinguish between the significant growth that has been sustained by the entrepreneurial sector in the developed technologies and the stagnant, depressed helplessness of a small-scale sector, such as Zimbabwe's, which has produced minimal employment growth into the formal sector since 1975. Unless research is able to demonstrate otherwise, it would appear that Zimbabwe is representative, rather than unique, in the African context.

In this chapter, I assume that formal-sector growth is the "way out" of trouble for many African economies, such as Zimbabwe, with population growth exceeding 3 percent, in which 2.5 percent of the population enters an employment market with minimal job opportunities each year. The increasing contrast, in lifestyles and wealth, between the middle and upper classes and the small-scale business and agricultural sectors cannot be sustained. Mass starvation and sociopolitical upheavals would appear to be inevitable. In this context, psychology's most significant role would be that of analyzing the formalization barrier, establishing what aspects can be reduced as impediments, and assessing the backgrounds, educational levels, motives, attitudes, occupational interests, competence, and psychometric and mental abilities that are required in those who might have a chance of crossing the barrier with whatever support might be available. In this chapter, I illustrate the impenetrability of the psychological barrier to entrepreneurial progress into the formal sector in the hope that research might be stimulated into the investigation of the socially and economically important entrepreneur, the rare individual who enters the formal sector and succeeds in creating employment.

PRODUCTION AND OPERATIONAL
SKILL REQUIREMENTS

In this section, I attempt to illustrate the enormity of the formalization barrier for disadvantaged and unskilled small-scale-sector proprietors. The continuum of progress in entrepreneurial businesses in Zimbabwe is represented schematically in Figure 7.1. The informal sector growth curve is a hypothetical representation of progress to the stage when the need to formalize is perceived and the attempt is made. Future research will show the proportions that fail at the barrier, and at what stages success or failure occurs after the barrier has been passed.

Let us first examine the possible impact of the formalization barrier by considering the nature of the small businesses that the first GEMINI study identified. The largest category—textile, wearing apparel, and leather production—involves basic crocheting, knitting, and shoe-making (30%); wood and wood processing (18%) refers to hand carvings and the products of carpenters with no formal training; and retail trade (26%) is primarily the selling of goods, often purchased at retail prices by the entrepreneur, who provides the transport and is essentially paid a heavy premium for making the goods available for purchase. The illegal sector is probably underestimated at 20 percent. In a pilot study preparing for a larger survey, it was found that, despite their illegalities, some types of businesses are clustered in high densities in urban areas and are therefore a challenging problem for sampling.

Elementary forms of manufacture compose a high proportion of manufacturing businesses. Few of the proprietors or employees are qualified for the formal sector, although remarkable skills are often identified by interviewers. The vast majority of products are sold for marginal levels of profitability to a relatively impoverished population. The middle class tends not to buy such products. Accordingly, the labors of perhaps 80 percent of the small-scale sector provide little in the way or preparation or training for production of goods at what might be termed the "registered business" level or for selling in the

Figure 7.1
The Formalization Barrier

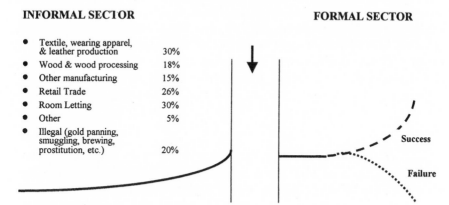

Direct costs of registration etc.
Employment costs for new skills
Need for knowledge & understanding of regulations &
penalties, basic business practices, etc.

INFORMAL SECTOR

FORMAL SECTOR

- Textile, wearing apparel,
  & leather production   30%
- Wood & wood processing   18%
- Other manufacturing   15%
- Retail Trade   26%
- Room Letting   30%
- Other   5%
- Illegal (gold panning,
  smuggling, brewing,
  prostitution, etc.)   20%

Success

Failure

Data estimated from available research. Categories not mutually exclusive.

retail sector. This aspect of the barrier might be termed the "step to modernization."

COGNITIVE SKILLS AND SOCIOEMOTIONAL ATTRIBUTES NECESSARY FOR CROSSING THE FORMALIZATION BARRIER

The following is an outline of some of the minimal skills required for progress through the formalization barrier:

Literacy in English

English is the language of the formal sector. Laws and regulations are published in English. With few exceptions, they are not translated into the major vernaculars, Shona and Ndebele. A rough estimate of the literary level required would be school examination success in English after three years of secondary education. At this stage, the average Zimbabwean student would be sixteen years of age.

Computations

The entrepreneur must be able to prepare quotations, add up the day's takings, and assess profitability by subtracting all forms of expenditure from earnings. The nature of these computations will be apparent from the case study described later in this chapter. More complex, but important for success, are computations necessary for maximizing the tax advantages of a new business. Only a small proportion of entrepreneurs take tax advice, although such advice can be crucial for the survival of the business in the important first two years. For example, one of the many opportunities available to those informed about the tax legalities is that the business may claim a special initial allowance of 25 percent per annum (until write-off) on capital equipment which is brought into the business at the start. Few entrepreneurs understand and make use of this advantage (including, in the past, myself). As noted, there are many other exploitable possibilities from which only a very small percentage of entrepreneurs are properly equipped to benefit. The requirements are essentially "reading, writing, and arithmetic," and intelligence is an obvious correlate of these skills. It seems reasonable to infer that at least average general intelligence is necessary for any entrepreneur to have a reasonable chance of coping with the intellectual requirements of the barrier.

Socioemotional Attributes

The list might also include such psychometrically accessible factors as persistence in the face of obstacles, tolerance of bureaucracy, ability to visualize and sustain medium- and long-term goals, and independence from collective and family pressures.

Ability to Delay Gratification

It can be inferred that a person able to save has been proactive. However, the key requirement of being able to save would appear to be the capacity to delay the gratification that can be achieved with cash. The 1991 GEMINI survey employed fifteen enumerators. They were highly selected from persons with four years of secondary education, most of whom had not previously been employed. Despite advice at the outset that some earnings should be saved, only one enumerator had been able to save any cash at all by the end of the survey, although meals, accommodation, and transport expenses had been provided throughout. This illustrates the difficulty which is probably experienced by persons in most cultures who are suddenly provided with relatively large amounts of cash after having experienced many years of poverty. The entrepreneur who makes his or her first few dollars is similarly tempted, and the person who has the self-control to save is a rare individual.

THE "PULL" OF THE ILLEGAL SECTOR: A FURTHER
ASPECT OF THE FORMALIZATION BARRIER

Becoming "even less legal" can be an alternative to crossing the barrier into formality. In 1993, it was apparent that Zimbabwe's crime rate was rapidly increasing and interviews from several surveys conducted by the author had reported informally that there were several types of business which either did not operate in the daytime or operated "undercover" and therefore were not being sampled. These were what might be termed the "more illegal" type of informal business. (It is almost impossible to find an informal business that does not substantially infringe on one kind of regulation or another. Strictly speaking, therefore, all are illegal.) The Friedrich Naumann Foundation concurred that this might well be an important new area of research which could add to the understanding of a significant economic variable in Zimbabwe. Accordingly, the foundation commissioned Dr. Christian Friedrich and me to conduct a combined-method questionnaire and case study survey of seven informal business-sector types (Harrison & Friedrich, 1994). The businesses covered were gold panning, *shebeen* operators, *kachasu* brewers, *kachasu* sellers, cross-border traders, within-border traders, and unlicensed/uncertified technicians and manufacturers. The case-study method enabled the interviewer to establish a rapport with interviewees and gain information otherwise inaccessible through normal enumeration methods. A surprising finding was that all cross-border traders, within-border traders, and uncertified technicians and manufacturers expressed intentions to formalize their businesses. All thirty proprietors expressed the desire to become "less illegal." Only two of the proprietors claimed to pay direct tax. None of the other proprietors were keeping formal financial records. The authors concluded, "The case study technique, employed as part of this research has, we believe, yielded valid information about attitudes towards taxation and has shown that the prospect of being taxed at current levels is a major disincentive in the MSE sector" (p. 1). The more sensitive method of interviewing led to open comments about the inconvenience of bureaucratic regulations and restrictions and appeared to provide a further refutation of Daniels's (1994, p. 54) conclusion from the second GEMINI study: "Based on these results, the expectation that the entire MSE sector will flourish once regulations are revised is questionable." While it would be inappropriate to infer that the informal sector would "flourish," there is accumulating evidence that excessive regulations and bureaucracy are significant disincentives in the formalization barrier, at which the joint "illegal" appeals of minimal regulations with "easier" profits are a powerful pull, perhaps especially for the very risk takers and idea generators which might be needed in the formal sector.

CASE STUDY: SOLOMON'S GATE BUSINESS

Solomon (name changed by author) is a twenty-five-year-old Zimbabwean male. He has had four years of secondary education and has obtained ordinary level passes in English, mathematics, and geography (for progress to advanced level and university entrance, approximately six subjects must be passed at O level). He left school at seventeen. After two years of unemployment, he was taken on as a general hand in a ten-employee business engaged in installing and repairing electrical gates. Having acquired six years of experience, Solomon decided to start his own business. He has, through advertising in the newspaper and following up various contacts, installed six gates. By saving and from his recent entrepreneurial work, he has accumulated capital of Z$70,000 and approximately Z$20,000 worth of tools and equipment. He now wants to employ one person and to formalize his business. Although the difficulties of the process of formalization are often tacitly admitted by writers, I have not been able to find any studies which provide sufficient detail for a clear insight to be achieved about the competencies involved. Accordingly, the following requirements are listed to illustrate the range and complexity of the problems faced by Solomon in his quest for formalization:

1. Maintenance of books of accounts
   - Payment of accounts
   - Checking of invoices to statements
   - Invoices
   - Credit control
2. Monthly Procedures
   - Wages
   - Deductions
   - Pay As You Earn (PAYE)
   - National Social Security Authority (NSSA)
   - Government levies (manpower and development, standards, etc.)
3. Monthly Returns
   - PAYE to the Commissioner of Taxes
   - Workers' Compensation and NSSA to the relevant authority
   - Medical Aid payment
   - Levies to relevant departments
   - Sales tax returns to Collector of Taxes

4. Quarterly Employment Returns
   - To Central Statistics Office
5. Annual Reconciliations
   - PAYE (tax reconciliation, each employee)
   - NSSA payment summaries
   - P6 forms (employer responsible by law to provide P6 to each employee)
   - Tax returns:
     End of year accounts
     Profit and loss statement
     Lists of assets
     Lists of outstanding debtors and creditors
6. Rental of Premises
   - Payment of rates
   - Rental deposit
   - Electricity installation fee and deposit
   - Telephone installation fee and deposit
7. Labor Regulations

Zimbabwe has a relatively modern labor relations act, with comprehensive protective legislation for employees and substantial penalties for transgressing employers. Solomon will be required to pay sales tax, but may elect to apply for a sales tax number allowing nonpayment of sales tax in certain conditions so difficult to interpret that reference must frequently be made to tax consultants specializing in sales tax. The government plans to introduce a value-added tax in 2000. This will require considerable training and is much more complex for the business owner than sales tax collection. These requirements include obvious business risk, and there are also risks of heavy fines should statutory payments be ignored.

Solomon faces a further problem, which is typical of his form of business growth. He has identified further customers. However, he is not able to fulfil the orders that he has received, as the gate manufacturing company from which he must purchase does not meet its production promises. Should Solomon succeed, he will have deployed much effort and skill in solving a large number of problems, many of which face him contemporaneously.

CONCLUSION

Currently, 300,000 school leavers are entering the Zimbabwean employment market annually. No more than 20,000 of these are being employed. This expanding unemployed group is a sociopolitical powder keg. The only feasible solution lies in business formalization and growth, and vague exultations to "support the small-scale sector" will have little impact unless those capable of crossing the formalization barrier are identified and helped over it, quickly.

REFERENCES

Bloch, E., & Robertson, J. (1997). *Zimbabwe: Facing the facts*. Harare: Thomson.

Daniels, L. (1994). *Changes in the small-scale enterprise sector from 1991 to 1993: Results of a second nationwide survey in Zimbabwe* (GEMINI Technical Report No. 71). Bethesda, MD: Growth and Equity through Microenterprise Investments and Institutions.

Harrison, D., & Friedrich, C. (1991). *The ZNCC membership needs survey*. Harare: Friedrich Naumann Stiftung.

Harrison, D., & Friedrich, C. (1992). *The economic structural adjustment program (ESAP) and Zimbabwean small businesses*. Harare: Friedrich Naumann Stiftung.

Harrison, D., & Friedrich, C. (1994). *A combined method questionnaire/case study survey of 7 informal sector business types*. Harare: Friedrich Naumann Stiftung.

McPherson, M. A. (1991, December). *Micro and small-scale enterprises in Zimbabwe: Results of a country-wide survey* (GEMINI Working Paper No. 25). Bethesda, MD: Growth and Equity through Microenterprise Investments and Institutions.

8

For the Specialist: Methodological Issues of the Studies in Zambia, Uganda, South Africa, and Zimbabwe

Michael Frese

This chapter presents some methodological details on the studies presented in Chapters 2, 3, 4, and 5. We have attempted to write this book for the nonspecialist who is not used to psychological methodology. Therefore, study designs, details on reliability, interrater reliability, measurement, interviewer ratings, and so on were not presented. We have also not dwelt on potential biases, our approaches to minimize them, methodological pitfalls, and methodological limitations of our studies. These will, therefore, be shortly discussed in this chapter. Moreover, we have not produced correlational or regression analysis results as would be customary in psychology. The steps we went through in the analyses will be discussed in this chapter as well. We do not want to be too technical in this chapter's presentation, but we want to clarify the general strategy of study design and analysis.

STUDY DESIGN

In each case, our studies were based on interviews, sometimes with a short questionnaire presented and filled out by the participants in the middle or at the end of the interview with the interviewer present. In most cases (except in the Zimbabwe studies, which relied on paid local and German interviewers), the interviewers were psychology students from The Netherlands in their last year of training for their Master's degrees, who worked under the editor's supervision and were trained by the editor of this book. Training was usually done in a one- or two-day course that was prepared by reading scientific literature (the local nonpsychologist interviewers were trained for at least ten days). Interviewers were trained by means of a role-play procedure in which the general way of asking questions, theoretical backgrounds of the questions, coding of the answers, and taking notes for the protocols were taught. In many cases, real-life interviews were done under the supervision of the editor. In addition, the teams of trained interviewers did ten to twenty interviews together. In these common interviews they trained themselves to use the same questions, the same type of protocol, and the same ratings.

The interviews were written down and then coded by the interviewer. We did not use a verbatim transcription of the interviews because they are expensive and did not add any new insights that we needed. However, the protocols of the interviews were extensive. They were used as the basis of calculating interrater reliabilities (thus, in these cases, the second interviewer coded the interviews of the first and vice versa). At the beginning of our studies, we had experimented with various forms of documentation of the interviews (among others, with tape recordings). We found, however, that the noise level was so high that it was nearly impossible to use recorders (remember, the interviews were often done next to noisy streets, in yards with several hundred other manufacturing groups, in noisy metal factories, etc.).

All the interviews were based on a structured interview script with additional prompts that were applied, depending upon the situation. Here is an example of such a procedure: After presenting a few cards that were rank ordered by the participants and that were the basis of discussing the goals of the owner/managers, the structured interview asked for the following:

You have said: . . . (**repeat the goals and subgoals that participants have developed**). How do you go about to achieve this goals/these goals? or How do you reach this goal? or How do you do it?

What have you already done to achieve this goal? (possibly ask this question twice; ask for examples). How have you done this in the past?

As for concreteness, realism, planning, and proactiveness. **Prompts:** What do you mean by . . . ? Can you give me an example? Can you give me an example for . . . ? Do you want to do it differently in the future, how? **General prompt:** Repeat what the participants just said. **Don't say** e.g. "Are you planning this in detail?" **Don't stop until you know, which strategy is used here** (opportunistic, critical point, complete planning, reactive).

In this way, it was possible to obtain very detailed information from the participant. For example, these questions took approximately fifteen minutes to answer. The answers were then coded (i.e., a number was assigned to each of the strategy characteristics) by the interviewers. The coding scheme used for this part is presented in Figure 8.1 (goal 1 refers to the first goal; the same questions were asked for a second goal).

Figure 8.1
Coding Scheme Example

		1	2	3	4	5	
	amount of planning	1	2	3	4	5	
plan1	(strategies goal1)	low				high	
	proactiveness	1	2	3	4	5	
proac1	(strategies goal1)	low				high	
	action in the past	1	2	3	4	5	
actpa1	(strategies goal1)	low				high	
	complete planning	1	2	3	4	5	high: everything is planned out
compl1	(strategies goal1)	low				high	in detail: e.g., all necessary steps including some substeps are described.
	critical point planning	1	2	3	4	5	high: one important crucial
critp1	(strategies goal1)	low				high	point is described in detail, everything else is left vague; however, high goal orientation keeps goal in mind.
	opportunistic	1	2	3	4	5	high: does not plan in advance,
oppor1	(strategies goal1)	low				high	but actively looks for business chances and exploits them; easily deviates from a goal.
	Reactive	1	2	3	4	5	high: goes from one issue
react1	(strategies goal1)	low				high	/problem to the other; does not produce changes, but waits for them to happen and reacts then; no goal orientation.

While information from the participants went into the coding, it was not biased by the participants but was determined by the interviewers. Other literature shows that structured interviews of the type used here produce good validity (Wiesner & Cronshaw, 1988), and we think that this procedure has several advantages: It eliminates the problem that the interview participants cannot compare their own situation with those of others; it reduces the anchor problem (each person takes a different anchor in a questionnaire response); and it mixes the advantages of a qualitative approach (really getting to know the situation of the respondents) with the advantages of a quantitative approach (getting precise numbers that can be used to do statistical calculations and to test hypotheses).

In addition, the interviewers gave an overall rating at the end of the interviews of the success of the participants. While these ratings were subjective, as the interviewers were not relating their ratings to any specific answers in the interviews, they give a summary impression based on a careful interview. The interviews took between one-and-a-half and two-and-a-half hours, depending upon country and study design.

We checked the interrater reliabilities of the codings. Sometimes all and sometimes half of the interview protocols were coded by two raters and then the correlation between these two raters was calculated. Whenever the interrater reliability was lower than 0.60, we either recoded this variable or we were particularly careful in analyzing this variable. Whenever it was lower than 0.50, we did not use this variable in the analyses (the overall interviewer estimate of success was not treated in this way; more on this later). Whenever possible, we developed scales and indices. Scales were developed when we had more than three items that measured the same construct. Scales had to have a minimum reliability (Cronbach's alpha) of at least 0.60 to be used in the calculations. However, we generally achieved 0.70 and above. In all, we think that our data collection and the care that we took in getting the data is one of the strong points of the studies done and that our data-collection process rivals the best studies that have been done in developing countries.

MEASUREMENT OF SUCCESS

We measured entrepreneurial success in four different ways. First, personal or "subjective" success was indicated by the entrepreneurs themselves. They estimated their success on 5-point scales. We asked whether the owner thought that he or she was successful in the opinion of others, whether he or she had a financially sound business, and whether he or she was satisfied with the current income from the business. Second, we asked for financial information; for example, the increase or decrease in the number of customers, profits, and sales in the last one or two years. This we called the "economic" success scale. Third, we took from Bruederl, Preisendoerfer, and Ziegler (1992) a graphic presentation of the success of a firm (displayed in Chapter 9), which was filled out by the participants. Fourth, the interviewers were also asked to rate the overall success of the participant on a 5-point rating scale (in South Africa, this was collapsed to a 2-point scale). We regard this to be a good summary measure of success. It is rather independent of the subjective ideas of the owner/managers. An overall measure is useful, because the observations of the interviewers of the shop could be incorporated as well. For example, if an owner said that he or she was exceptionally successful and that there was a lot of work to do but the interviewer saw most of the employees idly playing a cardboard game, this information was included in the interviewer measure of success. This measure was a summary measure. Therefore, an increase in the number of employees during the last years affected it as well as the fact that the owner was able to do certain things with his or her money (e.g., owned a car or a house, sent children to an expensive secondary school, etc.).

The economic success measure actually appears to be more objective than the scales used by the interviewer. However, there are a few problems with this scale. For example, in some studies we asked the participants to talk about the development of sales or numbers of employees for the last two, three, or five years. However, some firms only existed for one or two years. In these cases, we had missing data and could not include those firms in our analyses. This would have been a problem, for example, for the question of whether age of the firm had an influence on success. The interviewers were able to take this issue into account and provided ratings for younger firms.

During our first pilot study in Africa, we had the impression that the answers of some owners/managers were influenced by social desirability. Social desirability implies that the participants attempted to make themselves (and, therefore, their success) look good so that the interviewers would be impressed. Therefore, the level of social desirability was measured in some studies by interviewer ratings. Results showed in the Zambia study that social desirability influenced those success measures that were based on the answers by the owners/managers. Empirically, we found that social desirability was a moderator of the relationship of the interviewer overall success measure and economic and subjective success measures. In other words, the correlations between interviewer success and the other two success measures were high when the interviewers rated the social desirability of the partici-

Table 8.1
Intercorrelations of Success Variables

Success Variables	Subjective							
	Za	U	SA	Zi 1	Zi 2	r̄	Za	U
Interviewer	0.41**	0.41**	0.55**	0.49**	0.15	0.41	0.26*	0.40**
Subjective	————————————————————————						0.23*	0.31**
Economic							———	

pants' answers as low, and the correlations were low when the social desirability of the participants' answers were high. This means that the influence of the interviewees' answering tendencies had a lawful negative effect on subjective and economic success. Based on these results, we decided to use the interviewer estimate of success as our dependent variable because the interviewers were able to abstract from the tendencies of owner/managers to make things look good. Thus, we feel that the interviewer measure is a good overall measure of success. (There was only one exception to this rule: In the Zimbabwe 1 study, we used the economic success scale.)

Table 8.1 shows the empirical correlations among the success scales and suggests that there were appreciable intercorrelations between the interviewer estimate and the subjective and economic success scales. The interviewer estimate of success correlated well with both subjective and economic success, and this correlation was higher than the one between subjective and economic success. This is in line with our expectations that the interviewer rating of success is a good over-all indicator of success.

We did not use profit rate or other quantitative indicators. The major reason is that we do not trust these indicators. Whoever has done research among the informal and microbusiness sector in Africa knows that bookkeeping is not one of the strengths of these owners. Moreover, one of the reasons why many people stay in the informal sector is that they are not required to keep books because they cannot do it

Table 8.1 (*continued*)

Economic				Graphics					
SA	Zi 1	Zi 2	r̄	Za	U	SA	Zi 1	Zi 2	r̄
0.44**	0.58**	0.28*	0.38	-	0.19	0.29**	0.48**	0.10	0.24
0.41**	0.30	0.25	0.29	-	0.17	0.11	0.37**	0.21	0.18
				-	0.36**	0.30**	0.34*	0.05	0.27

Key: Za = Zambia, U = Uganda, SA = South Africa, Zi 1 = Zimbabwe 1, Zi 2 = Zimbabwe 2, r̄ = Average r with success; * = $p < 0.05$; ** = $p < 0.01$.

and professional help would be much too costly (they often charge high fees). Thus, only a small part of our sample could have provided accurate figures. Moreover, the participants were often reluctant to report such figures, even if they knew them. They feared leaks to the tax office. We gave clear assurances of our professional background and the fact that we treat all data confidentially. In general, the owners trusted us, as far as we could tell. However, whenever we wanted to know detailed figures on businesses, suspicion prevailed. For these reasons, we refrained from asking for such figures. (However, in the meantime we have been impressed by the procedure to give an approximate estimate of profit rates used by McPherson [1998], and are using it in further studies.)

STATISTICAL PROCEDURES AND ANALYSES

As mentioned, we did not want to overload this book with statistical procedures and correlation-based analyses. Therefore, we showed significant relationships as percentages. This was done in the following way: Whenever a correlation was significant (significance criteria were 0.05 one-sided in those cases where we had a clear and directed hypothesis and two-sided when we did not have a directed hypothesis or when the relationship was controversial), we transformed it as follows: For the dependent variable (usually success), we calculated the mean plus one standard deviation for this particular study and called them "highly successful owners or entrepreneurs" (in South Africa, we used a dichotomous dependent variable and called the people who were successful "successful entrepreneurs"). The independent variable was split at the median to produce a high and a low group. The percentage of highly successful entrepreneurs for each of these subgroups was then reported graphically (e.g. Figures 2.1, 2.2, 3.1, 3.2, etc.).

This procedure has pros and cons. The most important reason for using it was that it produces results that are easy to understand for people who are not used to correlation analyses (as a matter of fact, the size of differences with this presentation is often even surprising for professionals). Moreover, some people have argued forcefully that such methods should be used to show the real influence of psychological variables (Rosenthal & Rubin, 1982). However, there are also disadvantages. The most important is that one cannot compare the percentages across the studies, because the percentage of highly successful entrepreneurs is specific for each sample. For this reason, we had to revert to presenting correlations in Chapter 9. We have warned the readers of this book in various chapters that this cross-study comparison is not permissible. Another problem with this procedure is that a median split and presentation of percentages works well in normal bell-shaped curves. When they are skewed (and this, of course, happens frequently), a median split may distort the relationships to a certain extent. A strong distortion occurred only in rare cases. However, in general, the best form to present a linear relationship is, of course, the correlation. A final problem common to both correlation and our mode of presenting results is the issue of linearity. While most hypotheses assume a linear relationship and, therefore, our procedure is useful, there are exceptions. For example, risk taking has been hypothesized to have a curvilinear relationship with success (too much and too little does not lead to success). This hypothesis has not been tested as yet in our studies.

In most cases, we took additional care when analyzing the psychological variables. Since it is plausible that the relationships of the psychological variables with success can be influenced by parameters that we were not per se interested in, we used hierarchical regression analyses. The first step in these analyses partialled out potential control variables. In most studies, the following controls were added: age of business, gender, and line of business; in some studies we also added starting capital. The effect of these controls on the resulting standardized regression weights was very small in nearly every case and we may, therefore, conclude that these variables did not affect the correlations between our psychological constructs (e.g., strategy) and success.

LIMITATIONS AND STRENGTHS OF THE STUDIES

The studies reported in this book are based on a cross-sectional design which does not allow any causal ordering of the variables. For this reason, we cannot be sure whether variables deemed to be independent are really contributing to changes in the dependent variable. As a matter of fact, in one of our longitudinal studies on entrepreneurial success in a Western country (van Gelderen & Frese, 1998), we found circular processes in operation: A reactive strategy led to nonsuccess, which in turn led to a higher use of a reactive strategy.

Our studies were based on interviews with the owners themselves. Thus, strictly speaking, we do not have another source of information except the microbusiness owners. Getting information from the same source is a particular problem in questionnaire research. It is much less of a problem with our type of study design. The interviewers made the final judgment of how to code the answers of the participants. Potential misunderstandings by the interviewees, widely fluctuating anchor points for the answers, and so on were detected by the trained interviewers, who could repeat the questions, interpret the answers, and the like. Thus, this study design takes care of many problems that beset questionnaire research or interview studies which only record the answers of the interviewees (but do not code them). One prerequisite is, of course, that the interviewers are trained well on how to do the interviews and the coding. This we have done and we are, therefore, confident of the quality of the data collected in our studies.

Another potential problem is the fact that the interviewers knew the hypotheses of the studies and, therefore, might have had a tendency to code the answers to be consistent with the hypotheses. Unfortunately, we are not able to reject this potential criticism. However, we have attempted in the training process to inoculate the interviewers against this problem by discussing it openly (which has been shown to work successfully in other studies). As a matter of fact, the interviewers often voiced their worries with regard to this problem and attempted to work against it. Moreover, the correlations of the interviewer judgments with the other success scales that were strongly influenced by the participants (see Table 8.1) also speak against this potential criticism.

Finally, there is the problem of power. Our studies recruited between sixty and one-hundred participants (except Zimbabwe 1). This is typical of in-depth psychological studies. However, a small number of participants always leads to a lower degree of power to detect statistically significant results. Therefore, some of the findings that apparently contradict other studies with a larger sample (e.g., between our study and McPherson [1998] or Bruederl et al. [1992]) may be due to this lack of power (we have discussed this at several points in the chapters). However, we are not worried about this. First, statistical significance should not to be confused with practical significance. When a study is based on 1,000 participants, all of the relationships—even if they are very small—will turn out to be significant. We were more interested in practically significant findings, which are large enough to become significant in sample sizes of around one-hundred participants. Second, to overcome some of the problems, we calculated the average correlations, which are presented in Chapter 9. They are based on data from several hundred participants. Moreover, these correlations allow us to look at the factors that operate in different African countries and cultures. A particular advantage of the design is that many of the results could be replicated in different countries and cultures and may, therefore, be taken much more seriously than studies based on only one country (see Mead & Liedholm [1998] for a similar approach).

Obviously, there are methodological and theoretical problems in our studies. One might want, for example, to look at subgroups in more detail. One might want to examine the processes by which entrepreneurs stay informal or become formal, the ways strategy characteristics have an effect on success need to be investigated in more detail, and so forth. All these and more limitations apply to the set of studies presented in this book. However, we believe with some confidence that we have presented a unique set of studies with a surprisingly clear picture of the results. We hope that they contribute to putting psychological research squarely in the center of studying entrepreneurship in developing countries. In the last analysis, success is dependent upon the concrete actions of owner/managers of microbusinesses, and this needs to be studied in collaboration with psychologists who have examined, in detail, actions since the beginning of the twentieth century.

REFERENCES

Bruederl, J., Preisendoerfer, P., & Ziegler, R. (1992). Survival chances of newly founded business organizations. *American Sociological Review, 57,* 227–242.

McPherson, M. A. (1998). *Zimbabwe: A third nationwide survey of micro and small enterprises.* Bethesda, MD: Growth and Equity through Microenterprise Investments and Institutions.

Mead, D. C., & Liedholm, C. (1998). The dynamics of micro and small enterprises in developing countries. *World Development, 26,* 61–74.

Rosenthal, R., & Rubin, D. B. (1982). A simple, general purpose display of magnitude of experimental effect. *Journal of Educational Psychology, 74,* 166–169.

Van Gelderen, M., & Frese, M. (1998). Strategy process as characteristics of small scale business owners: Relationships with success in a longitudinal study. In P. D. Reynolds, W. D. Bygrave, N. M. Carter, S. Manigart, C. M. Mason, G. D. Meyer, & K. G. Shaver (Eds.), *Frontiers of entrepreneurship research* (pp. 234–248). Babson Park, MS: Babson College.

Wiesner, W. H., & Cronshaw, S. F. (1988). A meta-analytic investigation of the impact of interview format and degree of structure on the validity of the employment interview. *Journal of Occupational and Organizational Psychology, 61,* 275–290.

9

Executive Summary, Conclusions, and Policy Implications

Michael Frese

EXECUTIVE SUMMARY

To our knowledge, this is one of the first in-depth psychological studies on microenterprises in Africa. Two broad issues stand in the foreground of our five studies in four countries (Zambia, Uganda, South Africa, and Zimbabwe). The first area covers psychological topics: goal setting, planning and proactivity, psychological process characteristics of strategies, personal initiative, innovativeness, entrepreneurial orientation, and coping with problems. The second area is concerned with the strength of the relationship between sociodemographic factors and entrepreneurial success. Examples of such factors are human capital of owner, starting capital, loans, firm age, type of industry, family members as employees, formal/informal, linkage to formal sector, and start-up because of unemployment or other reasons. The motive to work in this second area was to replicate and extend findings from other researchers within an in-depth study of a psychological nature.

The theoretical basis is displayed in Chapter 1. Its main assumption is that the actions by the entrepreneurs are central for success. Thus, only when a business owner takes a certain action—for example, buys cheap supplies—can this be translated into success (or failure). The environment is also influenced by these actions; for example, if the owner finds a niche in the market. Therefore, personality, human capital, and environmental forces, all work through the actions by the entrepreneur. There is only one pathway to success and that is through actions. A psychological study is uniquely equipped to study issues of actions, because effective actions (performance) have long been studied within work and organizational psychology (Frese & Zapf, 1994).

We did not conceptually distinguish between entrepreneurs and nonentrepreneurs among the owners/managers/founders of our studies. We looked at those who were all three, founders, managers, and owners of their microbusinesses. We sampled one particular group of micro- and small-business owners; that is, those who had at least one employee. We argue that this group is relevant because it has assumed responsibility for others, it has started to become entrepreneurial, and it is a group from which potential high-growth firms develop. Most of the entrepreneurs studied had two to five employees. Most of the owners worked within the informal sector, although there were large differences between the different countries (e.g., there were no informal-sector participants in our Uganda study; in the other studies, the percentage of participants from the informal sector was about 70%). As we used a one-employee cutoff point for participation in the study, there were more males than females in our samples, because male-owned firms tend to grow faster than female-owned firms (Mead & Liedholm, 1998). However, the percentage of females ranged from quite high—43 percent in Zambia—to low—only 3 percent in Zimbabwe.

Psychological Factors for Entrepreneurial Success

The five studies show that psychological variables are important predictors of success of microbusiness firms. The results are summarized in Table 9.1. This table is to be read as follows: For example, entrepreneurial orientation was measured and analyzed in two studies. In each case, there was a statistically significant finding. In the group which had a low entrepreneurial orientation, there was a 10-percent chance to be among the highly successful owners in the Zambian sample. However, in those with a high degree of entrepreneurial orientation, this percentage was much higher (21% of this group of highly entrepreneurially oriented Zambian entrepreneurs were highly successful). Unfortunately, one cannot compare the percentages across the countries. This can only be done by means of correlations. Therefore, we have presented the average correlation as the last entry in Table 9.1. For this we computed all the correlations in all countries and averaged them across these countries (weighted by the number of participants in the studies; see Chapter 8). For entrepreneurial orientation the average correlation is 0.49 (which is quite high).

Table 9.1
Overview of Psychological Factors and Success

Percentage of Highly Successful Owners

		Zambia	Uganda	South Africa	Zimbabwe 1	Zimbabwe 2	Average $\bar{r}$ with success
Entrepreneurial orientation	low	10	10	-	-	-	
	high	21	33	-	-	-	0.49
Innovativeness	low	16	9	-	n.s.	42	
	high	20	40	-	-	50	0.34
Competive aggressiveness	low	14	12	-	n.s.	33	
	high	17	36	-	-	42	0.27
Personal initiative	low	-	13	15	-	33	
	high	-	35	34	-	45	0.38
Market niche strategy	low	14	-	-	0	22	
	high	38	-	-	13	54	0.37
Reactive strategy	low	20	-	39	19	52	
	high	12	-	6	0	30	-0.43
Complete planning	low	8	-	n.s.	n.s.	31	
	high	18	-	-	-	44	0.24
Critical point strategy	low	n.s.	-	18	n.s.	25	
	high	-	-	67	-	46	0.22
Opportunistic strategy	low	4	-	n.s.	n.s.	41	
	high	27	-	-	-	44	0.19
Goal difficulty	low	-	-	n.s.	n.s.	n.s.	
	high	-	-	-	-	-	-0.02
Goal specificity	low	-	-	n.s.	n.s.	n.s.	
	high	-	-	-	-	-	0.00

Entrepreneurial Orientation

Entrepreneurial orientation is a specific attitude to strategies. The orientation helps to focus entrepreneurs on certain themes. Eight such themes were differentiated (all eight were researched in the Uganda study, which concentrated on entrepreneurial orientation): risk taking, autonomy, competitive aggressiveness, innovativeness, emotional stability, learning orientation, achievement orientation, and personal integrity. For general entrepreneurial orientation, all eight themes were combined into one scale of entrepreneurial orientation. Table 9.1 shows that general entrepreneurial orientation is highly related to success. This is true for both countries in which we studied entrepreneurial orientation. However, in the Uganda study, which operationalized this variable in the most detail, entrepreneurial orientation is most highly related to success. When the eight themes were analyzed separately, two turned out to be particularly important for success in Africa: innovativeness and competitive aggressiveness. African entrepreneurs often experience difficulties in being innovative. One contributing factor is probably related to the high degree of traditionalism in Africa (Gebert, 1992).

We also hypothesized that most African microbusiness owners would have difficulties competing aggressively because African cultures are characterized by a strong collective orientation (see Chapter 1). However, this hypothesis turned out to be only partially right. There was a large group of people who were able to compete aggressively, as indicated by our descriptive results in the individual chapters. However, those who did not compete aggressively were generally less successful than those who did (although, this factor was less important than innovativeness). Other factors of entrepreneurial orientation clearly related to success were learning orientation (attempting to learn from problems and mistakes), achievement orientation, personal integrity, and, to a lesser extent, risk taking. Emotional stability and autonomy were not related to success. It may be surprising for researchers of entrepreneurial orientation that our results suggest a unifying theme for all of the entrepreneurial orientation factors and that this unifying theme is related to being highly active and initiating in one's approach.

Personal Initiative and Reactive Strategy

The second area is personal initiative and its opposite, the reactive strategy. Personal initiative implies that an owner is self-starting (starts something without being forced, told, or shown by example) and proactive, and changes the environment. The reactive strategy responds to environmental demands, is not proactive, and does not imply any self-starting. Owners who fall into the category of reactive strategy show the following behaviors: They wait for orders instead of actively finding them "out there," they have other people tell them what they should do rather than going ahead themselves, they react to situational demands but do not attempt to change the situation itself, they do not actively scan for business opportunities, and they do not attempt to plan for events that may be bothersome in the future (e.g., for changes in fashion, for a change in the economy, for new competitors entering the area). Therefore, they have difficulties dealing with problems, with preparing solutions for future events, and with being active in the market. They do not try things out and keep those that work, but instead wait until it is clear what has to be done.

Both personal initiative and reactive strategy were highly and consistently related to success (as shown in Table 9.1). This means that whenever a business owner uses a reactive strategy, he or she will more likely fail. In contrast, business owners with high personal initiative (the opposite of a reactive strategy), were more likely to be successful (a similar result also appeared in an East German sample; see Zempel, 1999). These results were replicated in several studies in different countries. Moreover, personal initiative functions as a background variable that works on both entrepreneurial orientation and success (as shown in Chapter 3). It follows that the most important steps that can be taken to maximize success prospects in a country are to increase the level of initiative taken by microbusiness owners and to reduce the frequency of their use of reactive strategies.

By and large, there are too many microbusiness owners who use a reactive strategy. It is used most frequently in South Africa and Zimbabwe, and least often in Zambia. In South Africa and Zimbabwe, 25 percent or more of owners used this strategy. On the other hand, personal initiative was relatively high in entrepreneurs in all countries sampled.

Niche Strategy

A specific example of an active strategy is to develop niche products or to provide a niche service. It is active because it changes the environment. Once an entrepreneur services a niche market, he or she does not have to worry as much about competition as if he or she supplies a mass market. Niche markets in Africa are different than niche markets in Europe. Thus, the entrepreneur described in Case 1 in Chapter 3, who searched and found a niche by producing business cards, had set up a specially advantageous area of production in Kampala. This would not necessarily be a niche in other cities or countries. The profit rate is usually higher in a niche. A clear result in our studies was that those who developed a niche strategy were more successful than those who did not (see Table 9.1).

Active and Planning Strategies

Complete planning, critical point planning, and opportunistic strategies are differentially related to success, depending upon the countries in which they are used (see Table 9.1). Complete planning implies that a person thinks about the relevant issues and makes an overall plan of action. He or she takes into consideration potential problems in such a planning process and deals with issues of the future. This strategy is always active to a certain extent. A critical point strategy minimizes planning costs but still plans for the most important critical point. Thus, this strategy involves a certain amount of planning, but it minimizes the time and effort that goes into the planning process. An opportunistic strategy implies that there is very little to no planning. However, in contrast to the reactive strategy (which is also a nonplanning strategy), an opportunistic strategy is active. Thus, entrepreneurs actively scan the environment for business opportunities and then use opportunities once they occur.

We have data on these strategies in Zambia, South Africa, and Zimbabwe. In terms of success, a complete planning strategy was mostly positive; however, the exception was South Africa, where it did not show a significant relationship with success. A critical point strategy was also related to success in most countries. It showed the strongest relationship with success in South Africa. Zambia is the exception, where no significant relationship of critical point strategy and success existed. Finally, opportunistic strategy had generally positive effects. However, South Africa was the exception again. Zimbabwe was in the middle, as there were significant positive relationships of all of these strategies to success in the second and more important study.

It may be premature to speculate on why there are country differences in these relationships. We tend to think that they are due to environmental differences (and possibly also to cultural differences). Some of the countries, such as South Africa, have a well-organized and regulated market and give a lot of support to small-scale entrepreneurs. Zambia is clearly the country with the lowest degree of structure and the smallest amount of control of industry. Accordingly, it can be regarded as the country with the highest degree of chaos. Zimbabwe is in an intermediate position, between these two countries. Survival in a chaotic situation may require really detailed planning, which would involve a detailed plan for all things that could go wrong, or no planning at all, but a proactive orientation. This would explain why, in Zambia, either complete planning or an active, nonplanning approach—the opportunistic strategy—was successful. In contrast, in South Africa, with its more regulated market, the moderate planning approach—the critical point strategy—was most successful.

It is important to keep in mind that in some countries there was a positive relationship between these three strategies and success, while in others there was no relationship. However, in no case was there a negative relationship. Thus, at worst, complete planning, critical point planning, and opportunistic strategies do not lead to success, but they do not hurt. Therefore, it pays to increase the use of these strategies, and it would particularly pay to make business owners aware that they can use different strategies and train them in the use of such strategies.

Goal Difficulty and Specificity

Surprisingly, there was no relationship between goal difficulty and specificity and success in any of the countries, as illustrated by the average correlation being near zero (Table 9.1). This is surprising, because we know from motivational experiments and other studies that people are more motivated if they have high and specific goals. However, it is possible that in a complex situation—and entrepreneurs have to deal with a multifaceted situation of high complexity—there is little relationship with success (Wood, Mento, & Locke, 1987). This may be so because having a high goal is not enough as long as many other factors have an influence on success, such as choosing a right strategy with regard to a complex environment.

Other Factors

A number of important results are not shown in Table 9.1 because they have only been ascertained in one of the participating countries. The procedures of systematically motivating employees, training them, and checking employees and products were studied in Zambia. All of these factors turned out to be clearly and strongly related to success. Successful entrepreneurs seemed to use a strategy of motivating employees, but at the same time they checked performance and other factors in the business so that they were able to provide feedback if necessary (see also Gebert [1992] for a similar finding).

Stress and coping have been studied in South Africa. Coping can either involve problem-oriented coping, which entails the attempt to deal with the stressor itself or to get help, or emotionally focussed coping, which is dealing with one's emotions by wishful thinking or distancing oneself from the problem. The most surprising result was that active problem-oriented coping was not significantly correlated with success. In contrast, emotional coping was positively related to success. This may point to the fact that a fatalistic attitude sometimes helps to deal with stressors, particularly in a situation that is noncontrollable, as is true of many South African microenterprises.

Sociodemographic Factors and Entrepreneurial Success

Sociodemographic factors have proven to be by and large of less predictive importance for success than psychological variables. If one compares the average correlations of Table 9.2 with Table 9.1, there are obviously more and larger average correlations with success in Table 9.1 than in Table 9.2. Most of the time, n.s. signifies that no statistically significant finding was found for sociodemographic factors. Note again that the average correlations can be compared across studies and across domains; however, one is not able to compare the percentages of highly successful entrepreneurs directly across the studies. Thus, the main conclusion to be derived from the comparison of the two tables is that it is much more important to pay attention to psychological factors than to the typical sociodemographic factors, which have received more attention in the past and have been focussed on by donor countries, state policies, training concepts of development professionals, and specialists for entrepreneurship. The prediction of success is much higher for psychological factors; therefore, these factors need to be considered in a systematic approach to maximize success in small-scale entrepreneurs. However, there are three substantial relationships with success in Table 9.2: the function of starting capital, whether one works in the formal or informal sector, and the number of links to the formal sector.

Age of Business

The age of a business has a significant relationship with success only in South Africa. In all other countries, the relationship is nonsignificant. The average correlation is nearly 0. This leads us to the conclusion that the liability of newness, a well-established fact in Western countries (Rauch & Frese, 2000; see also Chapter 1), does not exist in Africa in a significant way. Thus, one should not be concerned about this factor at this point in time. There are a number of potential interpretations. First, most enterprises are quite new in the African countries studied. The political climate made it hard or nearly impossible for indigenous would-be entrepreneurs to establish firms prior to 1990. Therefore, our studies have a restricted range of age. This may have contributed to a nonsignificant relationship between age of business and success. Second, it is commonly assumed that the mechanism for the liability of newness is that the stronger companies get selected

Table 9.2
Overview of Sociodemographic Factors and Success

		Percentage of Highly Successful Owners					
		Zambia	Uganda	South Africa	Zimbabwe 1	Zimbabwe 2	Average $\bar{r}$ with success
Age of business	low	n.s.	n.s.	20	n.s.	n.s.	0.02
	high			34			
Line of business	manufacturing	n.s.	n.s.	n.s.	n.s.	n.s.	n.s.
	trade						
	service						
Unemployment as reason for start-up	no	n.s.	-	-	18	n.s.	-0.05
	yes		-	-	0		
Starting capital	low	-	10	24	n.s.	27	0.30
	high	-	45	27		65	
Received loan	low	n.s.	n.s.	-	-	n.s.	0.00
	high			-	-		
Education	no	-	n.s.	n.s.	n.s.	43	0.16
	yes	-				66	
Sector	non-formal	13	-	13	0	16	0.38
	formal	18	-	42	25	68	
Links to formal sector	low	-	-	15	n.s.	14	0.42
	high	-	-	41		58	
Family members as employees	no	-	n.s.	n.s.	n.s.	26	0.05
	yes	-				53	
Perceived environment hostile	low	-	n.s.	37	-	-	-0.10
	high	-	n.s.	20	-	-	
Perceived environment dynamic	low	-	n.s.	17	-	-	0.10
	high	-	n.s.	30	-	-	

and the weaker ones go bankrupt. Maybe this mechanism is not at work in Africa because the subsistence orientation of many entrepreneurs lets them continue even when they are not optimally producing. Third, another potential mechanism is that the entrepreneurs learn from experience and, therefore, the longer they have worked in their business, the better (and more resilient) they become. Maybe there is a higher degree of individual learning from experience in Western firm owners than in Africa. Fourth, older firms are usually also bigger, and bigger companies survive better. Maybe this relationship of size and age does not appear in Africa. Maybe older firms do not grow as quickly because of the survival orientation of many entrepreneurs in the microbusiness sector. Finally, the studies on the liability of newness focussed on mortality data, and we have used success data, which may have produced different results. Although we cannot rule out any of these interpretations at the moment, we tend to think the most plausible interpretation is that the practical importance of the liability of newness has been overrated and it is really a small effect that only appears in very large data sets but that it is not of high practical importance.

While there is no evidence for the liability of newness in our data, there is evidence for the twin concept of liability of smallness. Larger firms are much more successful than smaller ones. However, this is completely due to our use of success as the dependent variable. Obviously, success is highly related to size—bigger firms are, by definition, more successful because they have grown more—and, therefore, this is not an interesting finding per se (therefore, it is not reported in Table 9.2).

Line of Business

Line of business has been suggested to be an important predictor of whether microbusiness firms are successful (Mead & Liedholm, 1998). We did not find any significant differences across the different industries (no average correlation was calculated, because categorical constructs cannot be translated into a correlation and the lack of significance of the relationships made it unnecessary to focus on it). Note, however, the difference between our studies and the ones upon which Mead and Liedholm have based their observations. We only took enterprises with one or more employees into our sample, while the vast majority of Mead and Liedholm's samples were single-person microenterprises. Therefore, we have no single hawkers or tailors in our sample who make up the low end of participants in Mead and Liedholm's studies. We assume that line of business plays a much larger role in those owners who do not have any employees. This is a very optimistic and positive finding. It shows that with ingenuity, initiative, innovativenesss, entrepreneurial orientation, and good strategy, microenterprise owners can grow and be successful in any line of business.

Unemployment as Reason for Start-Up

Many development-aid specialists and others (including Harrison, in Chapter 7) argue that subsistence orientation of microbusiness units is one of the reasons why they do not grow. This is one reason why they are skeptical about the contribution of microbusinesses to the growth of employment and their contribution to the national economies of developing countries. One objective indicator for such a subsistence motivation is unemployment or fear of unemployment as a reason for start-up. Those who are unemployed are desperate to do anything to earn enough to live, and as long as they do not find a job, they work as a business owner. Our hypothesis has been different from the one just outlined. We assume that the reason why one becomes self-employed is not important for eventual success. More important than the reasons for becoming self-employed are the actions of the entrepreneur. We, therefore, hypothesize that there should be no relationship between unemployment and success.

As Table 9.2 shows, there is only one significant relationship between this factor and success, but this relationship is exactly the opposite to the hypothesis advanced in relation to subsistence motivation: In Study 1 in Zimbabwe, those microbusiness owners who started their firm because of unemployment were more successful than those who had other motives (e.g., financial gain, reason in the family, or becoming independent). This is a fascinating finding. It tells us that there is by and large no relationship between start-up motivation and success, but, if anything, it is exactly the opposite of the popular stereotypes among developmental-aid professionals. Incidentally, a similar finding appeared in East Germany. Those who became small-scale business owners because of (fear of) unemployment were not less successful but showed an even higher increase of their personal income than those who had other motives (Galais, 1998). Keep in mind that there is a higher start-up rate in times of crisis (Mead & Liedholm, 1998). Once start-up entrepreneurs pass the threshold of employing one person, their growth is independent of the reasons why they started their firms.

Starting Capital

It is commonly assumed that starting capital is too low in the developing countries, particularly in Africa. This is certainly the case (Gray, Cooley, Lutabingwa, Mutai-Kaimenyi, & Oyugi, 1996). Moreover, starting capital is important to achieve one's goals with a firm. In three of the four studies, there are significant relationships of starting capital with success (in the fourth study, the tendency is the same, it just did not become significant due to the lower number of participants in this study). The overall mean correlation is sizeable (mean r = 0.30; see Table 9.2), and approaches the level of correlation that we saw for psychological factors. Thus, the problem of undercapitalization and its effects on reducing success reappears in our studies.

There are two contrasting interpretations of this finding. One argues economically that enough capitalization increases the choices; for example, adequate machines can be bought to produce good quality products. The other interpretation is more psychological and argues that there is an underlying psychological dimension. Those people who have saved a lot of money (or those whose family has been able to save money), are more likely to have high starting capital. Saving is a sign of a deferred gratification pattern (see Chapter 7), which has often been hypothesized to be a prerequisite of becoming a successful entrepreneur. We shall show in the following that getting credit does not help the entrepreneur to be more successful. This speaks for the psychological interpretation, rather than the purely economic one.

Received Loan

Given the fact that the amount of starting capital determines the success of microbusiness owners to a certain extent, it is surprising that receiving a loan does not help at all. There is no country in which there is a significant relationship between receiving a loan and success (see Table 9.2). The average correlation is simply 0; that is, there is truly no relationship between receiving a loan and being successful. The result is a bit less surprising if one knows that bank interest rates are often very high (e.g., about 80% in Zambia and 45% in Zimbabwe at the time of our research). Loans are, therefore, a mixed blessing, because it is difficult to pay the interest rate. Note, however, that the psychological factor of having applied for a loan (thus, having shown a high degree of goal-oriented activity) is an important contributing factor to success, as shown in Zimbabwe Study 2. Thus, if people are active and are showing that by applying for a loan, it helps to be successful. Getting the loan is not necessarily positive. As discussed, this result speaks against a purely economic concept of having enough capital available and points to a psychological interpretation.

Education

Education is often seen as the most important contributing factor to entrepreneurial success. This is not the case in our studies. Only in one study is there a significant relationship (although, Study 1 in Zimbabwe shows a similar pattern). Education does not play an important role for success in Uganda and South Africa. One should add that the education of the owners sampled was mostly high (as the individual chapters show). The entrepreneurs often had at least the equivalent of the British O level (roughly the American high school level), or even an A level and beyond. But again, our data show that it is possible to overcome handicaps due to lack of education. Some of our most successful entrepreneurs had relatively little education, as some of the case studies exhibit. Education may have a certain entry-barrier function (only people with a higher education or a high determination to become independent may become entrepreneurs), but once they are business owners, it does not play an important role for the development of success.

Formal versus Informal Sector

Whether a business owner works within the formal or the informal sector is highly related to success (this is so in every country in which we had participants from both the formal and the informal sectors). Note, however, that we have only determined a relationship between being formal and being successful and that various causal interpretations of this relationship are possible. One interpretation argues that being formal leads causally to success. We think that other causal relationships are much more plausible. First, a certain degree of success is necessary to be able to actually become formal. Thus, successful entrepreneurs eventually become formal. Second, entrepreneurs who have "the stuff" to become successful are more likely to be able to overcome the barriers that make it so difficult to become formal (as discussed by Harrison in Chapter 7). Thus, a certain degree of initiative, entrepreneurial orientation, and astute strategy make it possible to become successful and are prerequisites to overcoming the formality barriers. A third interpretation combines various interpretations. When we asked microenterprise owners whether they mainly saw advantages or disadvantages in being formal, the advantages dominated: They could more easily participate in official tenders, get orders from large firms and the government (African governments are not always optimal contractors, however, because they often delay payment considerably), use certain tax advantages (for example, not having to pay value-added tax for all their supplies), become more legitimate, and increase their prestige. Thus, being formal may be a prerequisite to continue growing beyond a certain size. Thus, the argument is that success leads to becoming formal. If they choose not to become formal, they have difficulties continuing on a growth path.

Being formal may contribute to success and success may be a prerequisite for becoming formal.

It is important to keep in mind that there is no dichotomy of formal versus informal, because there is a process from informal to formal (and probably, though investigated less, also a reverse process, in which some entrepreneurs who have failed in the formal market reappear in the informal sector). A large number of participants in the formal sector originally started in the informal sector some years ago (Neshamba, 1997). There is no doubt that policies that support the conversion of informal business into formal business need to be instituted in Africa, because formal companies are more useful participants in the economy and in society.

Links to the Formal Sector

It is useful to have many links to the formal sector. The average correlation with success was 0.42 and is the highest correlation in Table 9.2. However, we again cannot assume that it is the links with the formal sector that produced success. Rather, we would suggest success breeds more relations to the formal sector. Moreover, those already working in the formal sector also have more links with it. Thus, the two factors—links to the formal sector and working in the formal sector—are not independent of each other. Much of what we said about the formal sector also applies to links to the formal sector.

Employees from the Extended Family

It is often argued that there is pressure on microbusiness owners to employ family members who are ill-equipped for the jobs to be done (Wild, 1994). Yielding to such pressure leads to less success. This hypothesis is not only advanced by researchers and development-aid professionals, but also by the entrepreneurs themselves. Many have commented spontaneously that it is not good to employ family members because they assume "they are special and, therefore, produce ill-feelings among the other employees." Most business owners have thought long and hard about the issue of employing family members, and they came to very polarized conclusions. A large group has firmly decided not to employ any family members (except maybe sons or daughters). Another large group is equally firmly for family-member employment. Our results show that the hypothesis that employment of family members leads to failure is not supported by the facts. In contrast, there was a slight tendency in the second Zimbabwe study for those who employed family members to be even more successful than those who did not.

We assume that the hypotheses and the facts reported here are right, even though they seem to be contradictory. It is useful to employ family members up to a certain point in the lifecycle of a microbusiness. Smaller firms in their first stage of the lifecycle are better off to employ family members because of their loyalty to the firm and their greater acceptance of nonpayment if business is slow. However, at a later stage when the firm has grown and the firm owner is perceived to be successful, family members have a tendency to become demanding. Thus, in a later stage of the lifecycle success may actually be hampered by employing family members.

Perceived Environment

Perceived environmental hostility and perceived dynamism are not related to success. The only exception is South Africa. In this country, it is easier to be successful if the firm works in a nonhostile and friendly environment. We actually thought that a dynamic environment allowed entrepreneurs to use opportunities and, therefore, they should be more successful in a dynamic environment. However, with the exception of South Africa, this does not seem to be the case. Thus, the data suggest that perceived environment has little direct consequences on success. However, there may be indirect effects, because certain strategies work only in certain environments. For example, there is evidence for an interaction of uncertainty and detailed planning in Germany (Rauch & Frese, 1998): Planning a lot only leads to success in the group with high uncertainty. High uncertainty makes it useful to invest in planning so that one has back-up plans available if things turn out not to work well. However, this hypothesis has not been tested in this book and needs to be addressed in future analyses.

Other Results

Some results appeared only in country-specific analyses. One example is that organization of knowledge was found to be an important factor related to success in Zambia. This means that those entrepreneurs who were able to communicate their ideas about the business in an organized fashion (differentiating quickly between important and unimportant issues or developing a small theory on success factors) were more successful than those who did not have a good organization of knowledge.

An interesting finding on goals appeared in Uganda. If the entrepreneurs were mainly interested in making profits, they were less successful than when they had broader interests; for example, when they also wanted to improve the product or use creative marketing strategies.

None of the studies found a significant relationship between the number of hours the entrepreneurs worked and success. This shows that a simple mechanistic model of motivation (in the sense of putting in time) does not work. It is much more important to use clever and thought-out strategies than pure effort.

Overall Success

Figure 9.1 presents the overall success rate as seen by the participants themselves (the Zambia data are based on thirty-three participants who filled out a questionnaire that we were not concerned with in this book). This graphical method was taken from the study by Bruederl, Preisendoerfer, and Ziegler (1992), who have used this method successfully. It gives a good overall presentation of how the entrepreneurs see their business success evolving over time. The picture is overwhelmingly positive with few differences between the African countries and studies. A rapid positive development (Graphics 1, 5, and 6 in Figure 9.1) was perceived by 70 percent of the Zambian, 52 percent of the Ugandan, and 55 percent of the South African entrepreneurs, and by 48 percent in Zimbabwe Study 1 and 37 percent in Zimbabwe Study 2. A slow positive development (Graphic 2 in Figure 9.1) was dominant in Zimbabwe. The stagnant Graphics 3 and 7 were ticked by 21 percent of the Zambian, 13 percent of the Ugandan, 16 percent of the South African, 9 percent of the Zimbabwean Study 1, and 7 percent of the Zimbabwean Study 2 participants. A negative trend (Graphics 4 and 8) was perceived by 6 percent of the Zambian, 6 percent of the Ugandan, and 3 percent of the South African owners, and by 6 percent in Zimbabwe Study 1 and 2 percent in Zimbabwe Study 2. Thus, we can take away from Figure 9.1 that microbusiness owners see the development of their firms in a very positive light. While there are small differences between the countries, these differences should not be overinterpreted. The important conclusion suggested by the results presented in Figure 9.1 is the overall positive development in all African countries.

Both the results based on the judgments of the interviewers and the impression by the entrepreneurs themselves paint a positive and moderately optimistic picture of the situation and the success rate of African entrepreneurs. In general, we think that the entrepreneurs do a remarkable job in a difficult environment. While there are clearly areas in which there is room for improvement (e.g., innovativeness, proactive and planning orientation, niche orientation), microbusiness owners show, in general, a high degree of goal orientation and initiative.

When talking to microbusiness owners, we felt (in 5% to 20% of the cases) that some owners were remarkably modern. Issues that are dis-

Figure 9.1
Comparison of Success across Different Countries

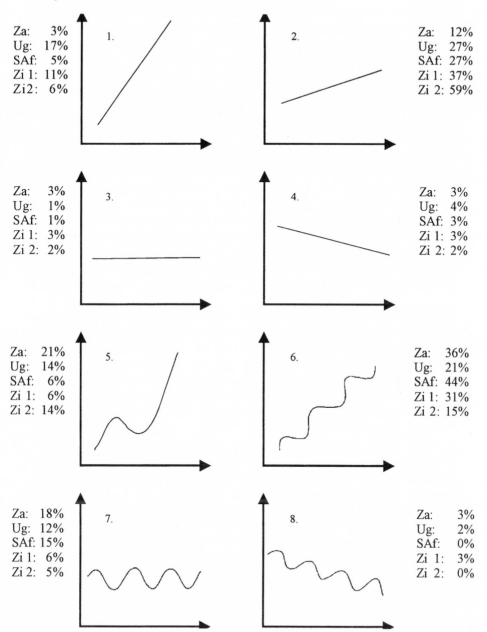

Za: 3%
Ug: 17%
SAf: 5%
Zi 1: 11%
Zi2:   6%

Za: 12%
Ug: 27%
SAf: 27%
Zi 1: 37%
Zi 2: 59%

Za: 3%
Ug: 1%
SAf: 1%
Zi 1: 3%
Zi 2: 2%

Za: 3%
Ug: 4%
SAf: 3%
Zi 1: 3%
Zi 2: 2%

Za: 21%
Ug: 14%
SAf: 6%
Zi 1: 6%
Zi 2: 14%

Za: 36%
Ug: 21%
SAf: 44%
Zi 1: 31%
Zi 2: 15%

Za: 18%
Ug: 12%
SAf: 15%
Zi 1: 6%
Zi 2: 5%

Za: 3%
Ug: 2%
SAf: 0%
Zi 1: 3%
Zi 2: 0%

Key: Za = Zambia; Ug = Uganda; SAf = South Africa; Zi 1 = Zimbabwe Study 1; Zi 2 = Zimbabwe Study 2.

cussed in modern management textbooks in the West were also discussed by these microbusiness owners; for example, increase of quality, customer orientation, and increasing process efficiency. While there is no doubt that the starting point is lower in Africa than in the West, we found it amazing how similar issues were seen and dealt with among the microbusiness owners in Africa and managers of large firms in the West. Thus, one gets the impression of a high degree of modernity among a sizeable minority of entrepreneurs in Africa.

ISSUES OF INTERPRETATION

The most important result is that psychological factors are very good predictors of success and failure in microbusinesses in Africa. These factors, therefore, need to be understood better and research and practice needs to focus more strongly on these factors. Factors such as entrepreneurial orientation (particularly innovativeness, competitive aggressiveness, learning and achievement orientation), personal initiative, active and planning strategies, and motivating employees are of utmost importance. Most practitioners interested in increasing the competence of entrepreneurs have been at least implicitly aware of the importance of psychological factors. For example, Harper (1976) has shown in case studies that the cry for additional capital is often not really warranted and can be overcome with ingenuity and initiative. However, little to none of these variables have been systematically studied in entrepreneurship research in developing countries, and as far as we can tell there is practically no recourse to psychological knowledge by practitioners in the field of entrepreneurship training and consulting. Manu (1998) has argued that support programs for microbusiness have not been successful enough and we concur with his analysis (albeit not with his conclusion). He suggests that one should only support those firms that have already shown a high degree of growth. We think that whether a firm grows is also a psychological question. The owner must want to grow, must be able to overcome psychological barriers that hinder growth (e.g., dealing with envy, dealing with one's family and demands from them, the difficulties of delay of gratification and reinvestment, innovation, initiative, etc.). Thus, only a psychological approach can actually predict whether a firm owner will be growth oriented or not. We do not agree with the idea that only high-growth firms should be supported; rather, one should support high potentials, that is, those would-be entrepreneurs who have the potential to become high-growth firm owners. A fresh approach is needed, and it ought to take psychological factors into consideration.

There are a number of fascinating new questions once one takes a psychological perspective. One is discussed by Harrison in Chapter 7:

The barriers that inhibit owners to register their firm as a formal company are often psychological ones and are not only in the area of taxation and knowledge. Similarly, there are psychological approaches to banks and funding agencies to get adequate funding. Again, a psychological approach helps to understand why some people get their funding while others with similar securities do not. (Some participants mentioned how helpful networking and personal connections—including family connections—were to get access to loans.) Only those entrepreneurs who learn from their mistakes and errors will be successful in the long run. Again, this is a psychological question of under which conditions one learns and under which conditions there is little learning from experience. What are the factors that stimulate personal initiative and innovation? Some situations are seen by some entrepreneurs as unsurmountable barriers while others lead to the feeling of challenge. How can networks be made profitable and which personality, orientation, strategy, and competence compositions lead to failures of networks?

The importance of psychological issues becomes obvious if one takes into consideration that entrepreneurs have to act in order to be successful (or to fail). Thus, all factors that are related to these actions need to be studied in more detail if one wants to improve entrepreneurship in the developing countries.

The Causal Path

Our studies were cross-sectional, which makes it difficult to establish a causal order. Do reactive strategies lead to failure or does failure lead to reactive strategies? Only a longitudinal study would allow us to draw a causal inference. On the other hand, it is plausible that psychological strategy use leads to success. An active orientation in which one flexibly tests what is good and what is bad leads to better results, even in a difficult environment. Moreover, there are some longitudinal data in The Netherlands which show that a reactive strategy leads to failure in the causal sense; however, the reverse is also true. Thus, there is a vicious cycle: A reactive strategy leads to failure and failure leads, in turn, to a reactive strategy (van Gelderen & Frese, 1998). This makes sense, because a crisis often lets people react rather than plan or proactively deal with the crisis.

However, the positive cycle was much more complicated in The Netherlands. Originally, critical point planning was the major determinant of success; however, success did not lead to a higher degree of critical point planning but made the owners become complete planners. And complete planning related to success at this later stage in the business-development process. One possible interpretation of this result is that when companies grow bigger, the owners need to develop more plans because their firms have now become more complex. In addition, when owners do business in a stable environment (such as The Netherlands), they get to know it better and are, therefore, able to plan things out in more detail. Therefore, at a later stage, complete planning is a better strategy. For the Africa studies, our current knowledge does not allow us to decide how the mechanisms work in detail (note that this problem exists for most of the other nonlongitudinal studies as well and, as far as we can see, longitudinal studies have been very infrequently performed and are nearly nonexistent in Africa).

However, our knowledge is good enough to suggest that owners should be taught the necessary skills and knowledge to develop more planning and proactive strategies. Of course, they have to decide in each instance whether the planning costs are too high in a certain area (this would then speak for decreasing the planning costs with a critical point strategy) and whether the environment makes it possible to follow through on plans. A certain amount of flexible use of these strategies should be a part of such a training concept.

Bias

Any research design has pros and cons. In the last analysis, our data are based on what the owners told us about themselves and their companies. Thus, one could argue that there is a bias in our data. Arguably, entrepreneurs are often highly optimistic and, therefore, they paint an optimistic picture of their own abilities and their firms' situations. This may sometimes lead to exaggerated accounts of relationships between owner characteristics and firm success. However, the interviewers acted as safeguards against such a one-sided bias. As discussed in Chapter 8, it was the interviewer who had to make the decision, for example, whether a person's strategy was called reactive or not. We think that they were in a better position to make such distinctions because they were trained to check and to question superficially optimistic statements. With this method, purely presentational exaggerations were probably detected and dealt with by our research design. Therefore, our results present a more valid and true picture of the situation of microbusiness owners and the processes that take place than the results of research projects that use a simpler design and where the data are collected by interviewers who are not specifically trained to be able to call the answers by the entrepreneurs into question. In these studies, the data are not filtered through a more objective lens (the trained interviewer in our case), but are taken directly from the interview participants and have to be believed at face value. Interestingly, many economic studies are based on such procedures.

Another potential bias may result from the interviewer judgments of success. Any success measures for microbusinesses are problematic because professional records are kept very rarely and microbusiness owners simply do not know whether they have made a profit or how high it was. We, therefore, developed an interviewer evaluation as the final judgment on how well an enterprise was doing. We consider this to be a good methodological choice, as this measure is related both to the more subjective and to the more objective economic success measures, without being redundant with them (see Chapter 8).

Our sampling procedure has substantial implications: When comparing our results with the results presented by other research groups, it should be remembered that we are talking about a group of entrepreneurs who have surpassed the first barrier to success: They already have hired their first employee. We think that it was a good choice to sample from this group of entrepreneurs, because they have a higher potential than the self-employed without employees, they probably have a higher commitment to their role as entrepreneur, and they contribute more to employment growth in the developing countries. This is a relevant and large group of microbusiness owners in Africa.

The sample size of each individual study was small. In order to interpret the results, it is necessary to keep in mind that sample size has an influence on whether a relationship becomes statistically significant. Large studies often produce significant findings where we do not; for example, for relationships of success with liability of newness, human capital, or line of business. We did not find such effects in our studies. One possible interpretation is that this is a result of the smaller sample size. When interpreting the results it is important to remember, however, that some relationships may be statistically significant but not necessarily practically relevant. Thus, just being statistically significant is not a good criterion for the importance of a variable. The relationships of success with the psychological variables used in our study were large and should, therefore, be taken seriously. But more important, some of them could be replicated in several studies in several countries in Africa. This is a meaningful sign that they are not only statistically significant but also practically useful.

POLICY IMPLICATIONS

The essential implication of this research is that policy decisions have to consider psychological factors for entrepreneurial success much more strongly than has traditionally been the case. Psychological factors have been shown in this study to be more important than purely economic factors in predicting entrepreneurial success. We do not want to engage in a useless disciplinary confrontation between economic,

political, sociological, and psychological approaches. They are necessarily complementary and should be treated as such. However, psychological approaches have often been overlooked. Our studies show
that psychological approaches should be taken into account in the process of promoting entrepreneurial success.

It is often difficult to translate psychological issues into dollar terms.
Therefore, a hypothetical example is used to underline the importance
of psychological changes. Let us assume that we are able to reduce
people's use of a reactive strategy by one standard deviation by using
certain training. Let us further assume that the average yearly income
of the training participants at the moment is 43,000 Zimbabwe dollars
(which is roughly equivalent to the income of the metal manufacturing sector in Zimbabwe in 1997; see McPherson, 1998). We also assume a linear relationship between our measure of success and the
actual dollar rates that entrepreneurs earn. We can now calculate how
much these participants will earn after the training. The average income of those entrepreneurs who participated in such a workshop
would be Z$46,500 per year after the training. Thus, the profit margin
would increase by 8 percent per year because of this training (the calculation is based on a regression analysis approach using the data of
the second study in Zimbabwe). Note that a nonreactive strategy is
only one of the many psychological factors contributing to a higher profit
margin. In reality, a training workshop would not only reduce reactive
strategies of entrepreneurs; it would also increase innovativeness, niche
orientation, and personal initiative, and would improve business knowledge on how to calculate profit and prices and improve marketing. Therefore, each area would add additional profits, and the cumulative
increase in the yearly profit could be around 15 to 30 percent.

Of course, there are limits to a psychological approach. It is still
necessary to further reduce political barriers to the development of
microenterprises (e.g., bureaucracy surrounding the tax laws, costs of
registration; see Chapter 7), and it is necessary to stimulate small-scale
entrepreneurs economically (e.g., by providing sufficient funding for
growth). In addition, one has to increase innovation, personal initiative, entrepreneurial orientation, and proactive and planning strategies. We therefore suggest the following program elements.

Psychological Program Elements

Psychological programs are focussed on individuals. They should
not just be directed at acting entrepreneurs, but also at the following
groups: high potentials, that is, people who would do well as entrepreneurs; people who want to become entrepreneurs; and people forced
to become entrepreneurs because of unemployment and poverty. Es-

sentially, there are three approaches: First, detect and select the right people; second, train and counsel in the right way; and third, provide a psychologically supportive infrastructure.

Detection and Selection of the Right People

We do not assume that people are born to be good entrepreneurs or that there is only one best way to be an entrepreneur. As a matter of fact, we think that there is a high degree of plausibility in the approach by Miner (1997), who distinguished four types of successful entrepreneurs: the personal achiever, the real manager, the expert idea generator, and the empathic supersalesperson (much of this is still in the stage of idea generation and not yet tested rigorously enough, however). We also do not believe that a certain personality type makes entrepreneurs successful. Personality is obviously important (and often underrated), but it is not everything. It is more important that people know their strengths and weaknesses and manage their personality. For example, somebody who is not outgoing (high on the personality factor of extroversion) may employ somebody who is very extroverted and leave the customer relations with him or her. Thus, an entrepreneur can compensate for certain weaknesses and be successful.

Nevertheless, we think that it is in principle possible to select high potentials in their middle teenage years. Given our knowledge in this area, high potentials would be people with a high degree of action orientation, achievement orientation, initiative, innovativeness, flexibility, intelligence, good learning, and good people skills. Once they are selected, they can be taught the necessary skills and be expected to become entrepreneurs (of course, many will not and will instead go into other areas, but even here we assume they would probably do well and enhance intrapreneurship in their respective firms; that is, entrepreneurship within a company).

Obviously, selection should not be a government endeavor which determines who is and who is not allowed to become an entrepreneur. Such a program would definitely fail. However, there needs to be a selection whenever resources are scarce, such as when entrepreneurs want to receive extra training (e.g., at the university) or when special needs should be met (e.g., to receive a stall in a growth point at a cheap rent or to get capital from a nongovernmental organization or a bank or advice from expensive consultants). Banks usually select candidates for loans considering, among others, the following factors: How good and promising is the business idea and the business plan? Is the person able to provide collateral for the loan? Are the skills right? We suggest that additional factors to be considered should be the psychological ones mentioned, because they are more highly predictive of success than a good business plan (Rauch & Frese, 2000). (Obviously, there are additional problems and issues related to banking for the informal sector that we did not touch upon in this chapter or anywhere else in this book; see, e.g., Harper, 1998; Yunus, 1989.)

An additional reason why it is useful to select and further high potentials is because many would-be entrepreneurs may not actually even think of becoming an entrepreneur and should be encouraged to do so. We shall take up this point a little later in this chapter.

Training

There are excellent training concepts available that are especially suited for entrepreneurs in developing countries (see Chapter 6; Awasthi & Sebastian, 1996; Harper, 1976; Harper & Finnegan, 1998; Kolshorn & Tomecko, 1992; Nuebler, 1992; Yaffey, 1992). These programs often teach specific skills, such as writing a balance sheet, developing a marketing plan, stock taking, salesmanship, and so on. There is no doubt that training of skills and knowledge in these areas are useful. But again, these skills need to be complemented by general psychological skills, such as learning how to be proactive, planning, initiating, and innovating.

Adult training should be exploratory and give the trainee the "ownership" of the training process. He or she should be an active participant in the training process. At the same time, training should not fall into the other extreme and be "completely open." It should have a clear curriculum and should help the entrepreneur to learn those skills that allow him or her to deal with the environment on his or her terms, as World Bank advisor Ellerman (1999) pointed out. These skills are mainly psychological in character and include the strategies discussed in this book, such as learning from mistakes and increasing one's self-reliance and personal initiative. In this way, training has a sustainable effect, because it makes it possible for the entrepreneur to initiate his or her own changes as they are deemed necessary. Our data suggest that such psychological training should have the following components.

First is learning from mistakes. We have developed a methodology in another context in which one explicitly learns from mistakes (it was originally used for teaching computer skills; see Frese, 1995). This can be transferred to the issue of entrepreneurship; its most important facet is to emphasize that errors and mistakes should be used as learning devices. At least in the Western European context, small and mid-size enterprises with a high mastery orientation toward errors (talking about them, learning from them, and taking them seriously) showed a substantially higher profit rate than companies that did not have a mastery-oriented culture to deal with errors (Van Dyck, Frese, &

Sonnentag, 1998; this issue was never studied in the African context, as far as we know). Moreover, in East Germany, a learning orientation with regards to errors and mistakes was also related to success in small-scale entrepreneurs (Goebel, 1998).

Second is learning from others. We do not want to overemphasize this issue, because our impression has been that African entrepreneurs are often too eager to learn from the successes of others around them. This is then translated into imitating the successful ones in their immediate environment and, thus, producing competition for those who have detected a market niche; such a procedure just leads to destroying the niche. The alternative would be to develop one's own market niche rather than just imitating others. On the other hand, benchmarking— learning from the successes of other firms—is a good device if it does not lead to giving up one's strategy too quickly and as long as it looks at the process and deep-level characteristics of the competitors and not only at the superficial level. Thus, it is not very useful to mimic the move by a competitor who starts to offer not only paint for cars but also coke and food during lunch hours. Adding coke to the line of products will not help a lot. Rather, one should learn from this competitor that it may be useful to scan the market for niches that have not been satisfied and to attempt to service this niche in combination with the products that one sells (or produces) at the moment. Therefore, a good training course will attempt to teach how to analyze competitors' performance and draw the right lessons from benchmarking (not just superficial lessons).

Third is encouraging and teaching how to be innovative with regard to product and process. Several issues need to be taught to increase innovativeness: One must learn that one has to increase the pure quantity of ideas to select the best ones from them (the model that is behind brainstorming; see Diehl & Stroebe, 1991). One must also learn to "leave the field" and not to stick to just one framework for the solution of problems. Thus, one should attempt to break out of traditional contexts and traditional orientations to be creative and to attempt completely new solutions to old problems (King & Anderson, 1995). One prerequisite is a certain degree of modernity and, possibly, the rejection of traditions and old solutions (Gebert, 1992). Since African cultures are often quite traditional and do not encourage the search for "other" solutions, this skill is of particular usefulness. To be innovative, one also needs a clear vision or idea of what one wants to achieve, a safe group climate which allows one to even propose nonsense ideas, a climate for excellence in the group, and norms that support innovation (West, 1990). One problem is the high power distance that typically exists in African cultures. High power distance does not help subordinates to come up with new ideas.

Training for innovation is highly related to personal initiative, because innovation not only implies the need to have a creative idea; this idea has to be translated into action, as well. Thus, one has to be willing to push the idea through against barriers and problems and possibly also against resistance from colleagues, family, and employees. The latter is often particularly difficult for members of a collectivist society. (One of the Black entrepreneurs interviewed told us that her employees call her *murungu*, a White person, behind her back because of her Westernized leadership style which encourages employee participation and initiative.)

Fourth is increasing personal initiative. Our research group is currently developing modules to teach personal initiative to German unemployed and employees. We think that some of the skills developed here can also be taught to would-be and de facto informal-sector participants. The training program should include such aspects as development of self-efficacy to overcome problems, change orientation because every initiative changes one's situation, an interest and expectation to control one's situation, skills to produce many ideas of how to overcome barriers and knowledge of what constitutes self-starting, and a firm commitment to a self-starting orientation. Obviously, a training concept that works in the West needs to be adapted to the African context and then needs to be evaluated again.

Such training should be combined with training in marketing and finding a niche. Marketing is an area in which one has to try several approaches and keep what is useful. Proactive approaches work best; namely, an active scanning of the environment for business and marketing opportunities, an active approach to relevant business partners and customers, an active search for feedback from customers and other relevant people, and an active use of this information to formulate a program for the firm. The search for niches requires a high degree of overcoming barriers. For example, one of the participants in our study did not have enough money to buy a machine that would have opened up a niche for his business. He therefore constructed his own machine at a lower cost within a year, continuously experimenting and finally succeeding.

Fifth is planning. Planning does not only refer to developing a good business plan in the beginning stage of one's business. Rather, it means that one continuously develops good plans (either from the top-down or in the sense of critical point planning) throughout one's work for weeks, months, or years. We have sometimes observed entrepreneurs planning for their own sake; they developed nice plans that had little to do with reality and were not translated into action. Therefore, a tight coupling between planning and action has to be emphasized and needs to be a part of the training concept.

Psychologically Supportive Environment

The government, cooperatives, chambers of commerce, nongovernmental organizations, and community workers must develop the right psychological environment. There must be good role models in the community and it would help to give awards to innovative indigenous entrepreneurs to increase the chances to learn from such role models. It is possible to introduce networks that make it possible for the entrepreneurs to buy their supplies and sell their products better (such as ISTARN; see Nell, Kohlheyer, Muza, & Masaka, 1998). Entrepreneurs should also be encouraged to help each other with peer reviews to increase their productivity. Peers (who are not direct competitors and come from other lines of business) are particularly good for suggesting solutions that are appropriate within the culture and the environment. An interesting side effect of a peer review process is that not only the person who is the target of the consultation learns a lot, but the peers who are in the role of consultants learn even more. Consulting peers are forced to make their own ideas explicit and, therefore, the chances are increased they will come up with new solutions for their own problems, as well. Such a peer review strategy may work even better in Africa, since competitive aggressiveness is probably lower in Africa than in Europe or the United States.

A Holistic Regional Approach

We think that it is possible to produce a holistic regional approach from a psychological perspective. Many countries, particularly the early socialist ones (even poor ones), have used an early selection approach of high potentials in the areas of sports and music. Thus, often four- or five-year-old children were selected in competitions and offered unique training opportunities in special schools. We think that a similar model can also be used in the area of entrepreneurship. It is possible to select high potentials in entrepreneurship among the fourteen- or sixteen-year-old youngsters in a country. This program would select young people in schools who already show a high degree of entrepreneurial orientation and personal initiative.

This selected group would then get additional schooling in administration, management, and technical skills. They may get privileged access to funding and venture capital because of their early grooming for a start-up career. Most important is an early hands-on experience with entrepreneurship. We suggest lending these youngsters a few dollars while they are still in school to develop and test their ideas on how to make money. The amount of credit could then be raised continuously after they have shown their talents. These youngsters should be rewarded for their mistakes and encouraged to learn from them (many great entrepreneurs failed for a while before their business actually took off). Local talent can be promoted at relatively low cost in this way. Such a systematic approach could first be developed for a smaller region within a country and could be carefully evaluated (Harper & Finnegan, 1998). Our research suggests that such an approach might have a powerful positive effect on the economies of a region or country.

One might even go one step further and suggest that school curricula should be changed so that practical entrepreneurship can be taught in schools for students fifteen years and older (including all psychological and social-skill factors, business knowledge, and tax issues). It is hoped that the disadvantages that exist in developing countries can actually be transformed into advantages by these countries.

ISSUES FOR FURTHER RESEARCH

Obviously, a set of studies such as those reported in this book do not answer all questions and cannot deal with the full complexity of all issues. We think that the following issues are of particular relevance to be researched in the future.

First, there should be a serious attempt to look at different pathways to success. We are thinking here of using the taxonomy of Miner (1997) as a starting point. Second, we need to know more about the efficacy of psychological strategies for shrinking economies, because African economies often show wild fluctuation from shrinkage to high increases in their gross domestic products. It is possible that different skills are necessary in different economic cycles. Third, we think that there is need to look more into interactionistic models that hypothesize contingent relationships. For example, Rauch and Frese (1998) have shown that planning is useful in hostile environments but not in benign ones (and may even be detrimental because of high planning costs). Similarly, different strategies may be useful at one stage of the development of a firm but not at others. For example, transforming a firm from quick growth to being well-managed requires different goals, skills, and strategies than dealing with a more static firm. Similarly, environmental contingencies related to a high influx of foreign goods or to competing mainly in a domestic market and slowly expanding to neighboring countries need to be researched. All these factors need to be examined as they interact with psychological process characteristics of strategies, strategic orientations, or the content of strategies. Fourth, the more important of these studies should be done longitudinally so as to be able to tease apart cause and effect more clearly. Finally, more controlled interventions should be done that provide the ability to check whether these interventions actually achieve success and whether they are cost effective. Whatever the specific needs for additional research, it should be obvious from this book that psychological approaches need to be taken seriously in this area and have to be pursued alongside more traditional economic approaches.

REFERENCES

Awasthi, D. N., & Sebastian, J. (1996). *Evaluation of entrepreneurship development programmes.* New Delhi: Sage.

Bruederl, J., Preisendoerfer, P., & Ziegler, R. (1992). Survival chances of newly founded business organizations. *American Sociological Review, 57,* 222–242.

Diehl, M., & Stroebe, W. (1991). Productivity loss in idea generating groups: Tracking down the blocking effect. *Journal of Personality and Social Psychology, 61,* 392–403.

Ellerman, D. P. (1999). Global institutions: Transforming international development agencies into learning organizations. *Academy of Management Executive, 13,* 25–35.

Frese, M. (1995). Error management in training: Conceptual and empirical results. In C. Zucchermaglio, S. Bagnara, & S. U. Stucky (Eds.), *Organizational learning and technological change* (pp. 112–124). Berlin: Springer.

Frese, M., & Zapf, D. (1994). Action as the core of work psychology: A German approach. In H. C. Triandis, M. D. Dunnette, & L. Hough (Eds.), *Handbook of industrial and organizational psychology* (2d ed., Vol. 4, pp. 271–340). Palo Alto: Consulting Psychologists Press.

Galais, N. (1998). Motive und Beweggruende fuer die Selbstaendigkeit und ihre Bedeutung fuer den Erfolg. In M. Frese (Ed.), *Erfolgreiche Unternehmensgruender: Psychologische Analysen und praktische Anleitung fuer Unternehmer in Ost- und Westdeutschland* (pp. 83–98). Goettingen: Hogrefe.

Gebert, D. (Ed.). (1992). *Traditionsorientierung und unternehmerischer Erfolg.* Saarbruecken: Breitenbach.

Goebel, S. (1998). Persoenlichkeit, Handlungsstrategien und Erfolg. In M. Frese (Ed.), *Erfolgreiche Unternehmensgruender: Psychologische Analysen und praktische Anleitung fuer Unternehmer in Ost- und Westdeutschland* (pp. 99–122). Goettingen: Hogrefe.

Gray, K. R., Cooley, W., Lutabingwa, J., Mutai-Kaimenyi, B., & Oyugi, L. A. (1996). *Entrepreneurship in micro-enterprises: A strategic analysis of manufacturing industries in Kenya.* Lanham, MD: University Press of America.

Harper, M. (1976). *Consultancy for small businesses.* London: Intermediate Technology Publications.

Harper, M. (1998). *Profit for the poor.* London: Intermediate Technology Publications.

Harper, M., & Finnegan, G. (1998). *Value for money? Impact of small enterprise development.* London: Intermediate Technology Publications.

King, N., & Anderson, N. (1995). *Innovation and change in organizations.* London: Routledge.

Kolshorn, R., & Tomecko, J. (1992). Competency-based economies: GTZ and self-sustained small enterprise development. *Small Enterprise Development, 3* (2), 53–56.

Manu, G. (1998). Enterprise development in Africa: Strategies for impact and growth. *Small Enterprise Development, 9* (4), 4–14.

McPherson, M. A. (1998). *Zimbabwe: A third nationwide survey of micro and small enterprises.* Bethesda, MD: Growth and Equity through Microenterprise Investments and Institutions.

Mead, D. C., & Liedholm, C. (1998). The dynamics of micro and small enterprises in developing countries. *World Development, 26,* 61–74.

Miner, J. B. (1997). *A psychological typology of successful entrepreneurs.* Westport, CT: Quorum Books.

Nell, M., Kohlheyer, G., Muza, A., & Masaka, M. (1998). *Informal sector training and resources network (ISTARN)* (project progress review). Frankfurt: Gesellschaft fuer Technische Zusammenarbeit (GTZ).

Neshamba, F. (1997). The transition of enterprises from informality to formality: Some evidence from Zimbabwe. *Small Enterprise Development, 8* (4), 48–53.

Nuebler, I. (1992). Training microentrepreneurs: Does it pay? *Small Enterprise Development, 3* (4), 34–44.

Rauch, A., & Frese, M. (1998). A contingency approach to small scale business success: A longitudinal study on the effects of environmental hostility and uncertainty on the relationship of planning and success. In P. D. Reynolds, W. D. Bygrave, N. M. Carter, S. Manigart, C. M. Mason, G. D. Meyer, & K. G. Shaver (Eds.), *Frontiers of entrepreneurship research* (pp. 190–200). Babson Park, MS: Babson College.

Rauch, A., & Frese, M. (2000). Psychological approaches to entrepreneurial success: A general model and an overview of findings. *International Review of Industrial and Organizational Psychology, 15.*

Van Dyck, C., Frese, M., & Sonnentag, S. (1998). *Organizational error management climate: On enhanced error handling and organizational performance.* Manuscript submitted for publication.

Van Gelderen, M., & Frese, M. (1998). Strategy process as characteristics of small scale business owners: Relationships with success in a longitudinal study. In P. D. Reynolds, W. D. Bygrave, N. M. Carter, S. Manigart, C. M. Mason, G. D. Meyer, & K. G. Shaver (Eds.), *Frontiers of entrepreneurship research* (pp. 234–248). Babson Park, MS: Babson College.

West, M. A. (1990). The social psychology of innovation in groups. In M. A. West & J. L. Farr (Eds.), *Innovation and creativity at work* (pp. 309–334). Chichester, England: Wiley.

Wild, V. (1994). *Versorgungskapitalisten.* Muenchen: Weltforum.

Wood, R. E., Mento, A. J., & Locke, E. A. (1987). Task complexity as a moderator of goal effects: A meta-analysis. *Journal of Applied Psychology, 72,* 416–425.

Yaffey, M. (1992). Financial analysis for microenterprises. *Small Enterprise Development, 3* (3), 28–36.

Yunus, M. (1989). Grameen Bank: Organization and operation. In J. Levitsky (Ed.), *Microenterprises in developing countries.* London: Intermediate Technology Publications.

Zempel, J. (1999). Selbstaendigkeit in den neuen Bundeslaendern: Praediktoren, Erfolgsfaktoren und Folgen—Ergebnisse einer Laengsschnittuntersuchung. In K. Moser, B. Batinic, & J. Zempel (Eds.), *Unternehmerisch erfolgreiches Handeln* (pp. 69–92). Goettingen: Verlag Angewandte Psychologie.

Author Index

Subject Index

About the Editor and Contributors

Michael Frese studied psychology in Regensburg and Berlin and completed his Ph.D. in 1978 in Berlin. He currently holds a chair for Work and Organizational Psychology at the University of Giessen, is also a professor at the University of Amsterdam, and visiting professor at London Business School. Frese is an internationally well known organizational psychologist and is editor or coeditor of two scientific journals. Frese has written more than fifteen books and 200 journal articles and book chapters. He is an advisor and lecturer for the management of many companies and works as a consultant for banks and the automobile, electricity, telecommunication, and computer industries. Contact: University of Giessen, Dept. of Psychology, Otto Behaghel-Str. 10F, 35394 Giessen, Germany. E-mail: michael.frese@psychol.uni-giessen.de

Christian Friedrich studied psychology and education in Giessen, Bern, and Berlin, and works as a consultant in Germany and other countries. He is a professor for organizational psychology at the University of Applied Sciences in Giessen, Germany. From 1990 to 1994, he worked as a consultant in several countries of southern Africa, focussing on consultancy for industrial associations, like chambers of commerce, commercial and service industries, and small-scale entrepreneurs. Contact: Fachhochschule für Verwaltung, Talstr. 3, 35394 Giessen, Germany. E-mail: chris.friedrich@vfh-hessen.de

David Harrison holds degrees from University College, London, and the London School of Economics. He has lectured at Middlesex Polytechnic and University of Zimbabwe (industrial psychology, psychometrics, statistics and personnel psychology). He retired from academic teaching in 1983 to develop the psychological, industrial, and commercial consultancy, training, and research activities of Human Resources (Pvt.) Ltd. Contact: Human Resources (Pvt.) Ltd., P.O. Box 3426, Harare/ZIMBABWE. E-mail: hres@harare.iafrica.com

Madelief Keyser studied work and organizational psychology at the University of Amsterdam. During her studies she specialized in small-scale entrepreneurship in Africa, in particular, Zambia. She is an educational and training consultant for national and international organizations. Contact: Prinsengracht 818, 1017 JL Amsterdam, The Netherlands. E-mail: madeliefkeyser@hotmail.com

Sabine Koop studied work and organizational psychology at the University of Amsterdam. She is a human-resource manager for a multinational firm for electrical products and systems. Together with a partner she recently started a restaurant. She is responsible for the organizational aspects of this business. Contact: Marktstraat 1, 7622 CP Borne, The Netherlands.

Stefanie I. Krauss is a research associate and Ph.D. student at the Department of Work and Organizational Psychology, University of Giessen, Germany. Her research interests center around psychological success factors of small-scale business owners. She focusses on entrepreneurship in Zimbabwe, where she conducted extensive research. Contact: University of Giessen, Dept. of Work and Organizational Psychology, Otto Behaghel-Str. 10F, 35394 Giessen, Germany. E-mail: stefanie.krauss@psychol.uni-giessen.de

Mechlien de Kruif studied organizational psychology at the University of Amsterdam with a major in entrepreneurship in developmental countries. She is temporarily working and orienting more toward a marketing direction. Contact: Govert Flinckstraat 52 I, 1072 EJ Amsterdam, The Netherlands. E-mail: m.dekruif@worldonline.nl

Anne Maartje Lauw received her degree in work and organizational psychology from the University of Amsterdam in 1998. From there, she moved toward the commercial side of psychology and is currently working as a junior consultant for a branding consultancy firm. Contact: Kloveniersburgwal 61 D, 1011 JZ Amsterdam, The Netherlands.

Tamara de Reu studied work and organizational psychology at the University of Amsterdam. She is busy starting up a sales department for a distribution company as a sales manager. After her study of entrepreneurship in Uganda, she is using a great deal of entrepreneurial skills herself. Contact: Bankastr. 17, 1094 CC Amsterdam, The Netherlands. E-mail: tamara@media-online.nl

Gwenda van Steekelenburg studied English in London and psychology at the University of Amsterdam. She is currently working as recruiter at KLM Recruitent. Contact: Kuipersstraat 55 II, 1074 EG Amsterdam, The Netherlands. E-mail: G._van_Steekelenburg@ heineken.nl

Kobus Visser is a member of the Department of Management, University of the Western Cape, South Africa, and specializes in entrepreneurship and enterprise development. He is coauthor of two textbooks, has published a number of articles on small and medium-size enterprises, and has presented papers at international conferences. Contact: Department of Management, University of the Western Cape, Bellville 7535, South Africa. E-mail: kvisser@uwc.ac.za

ISBN 1-56720-296-9

EAN

9 781567 202960

90000>

HARDCOVER BAR CODE